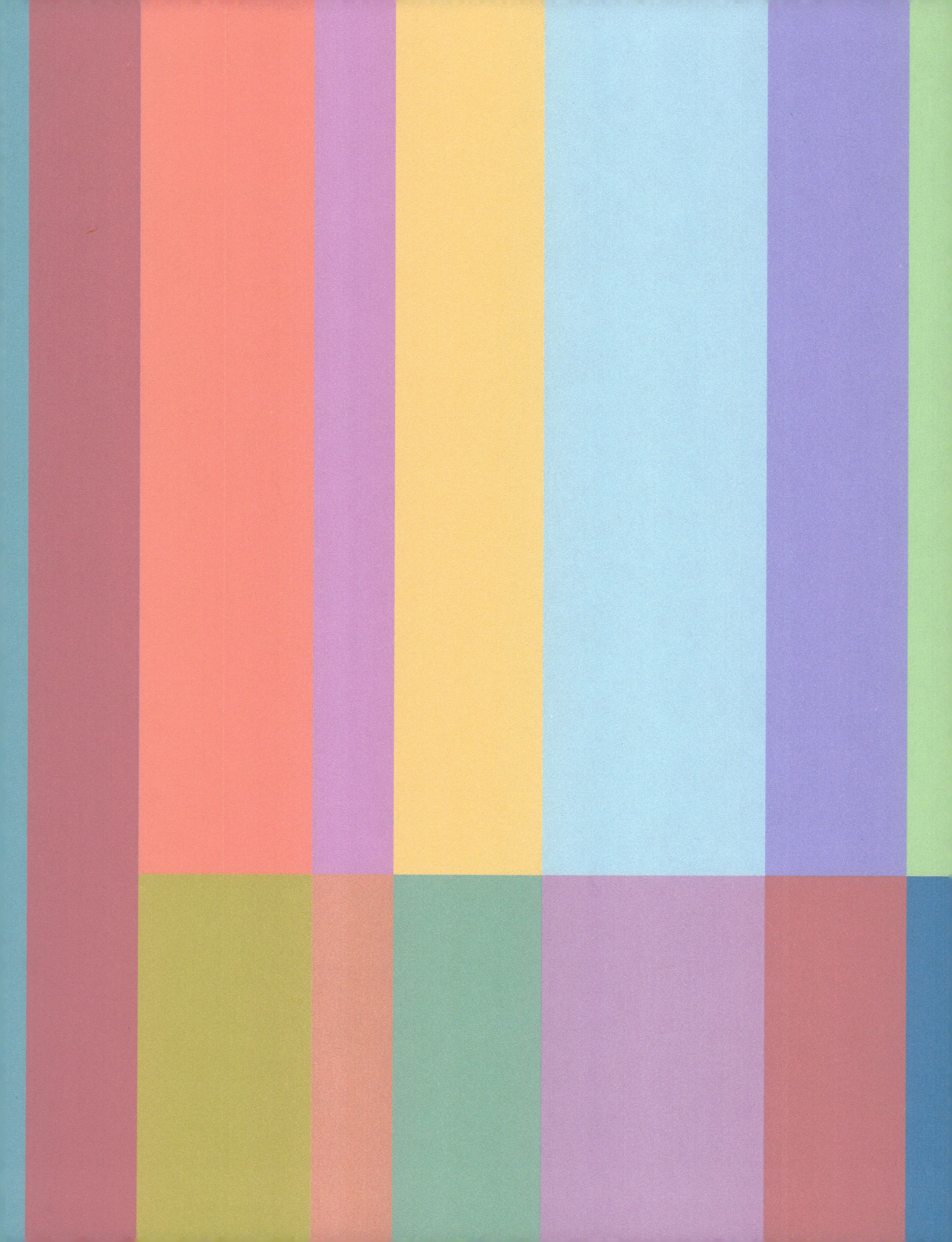

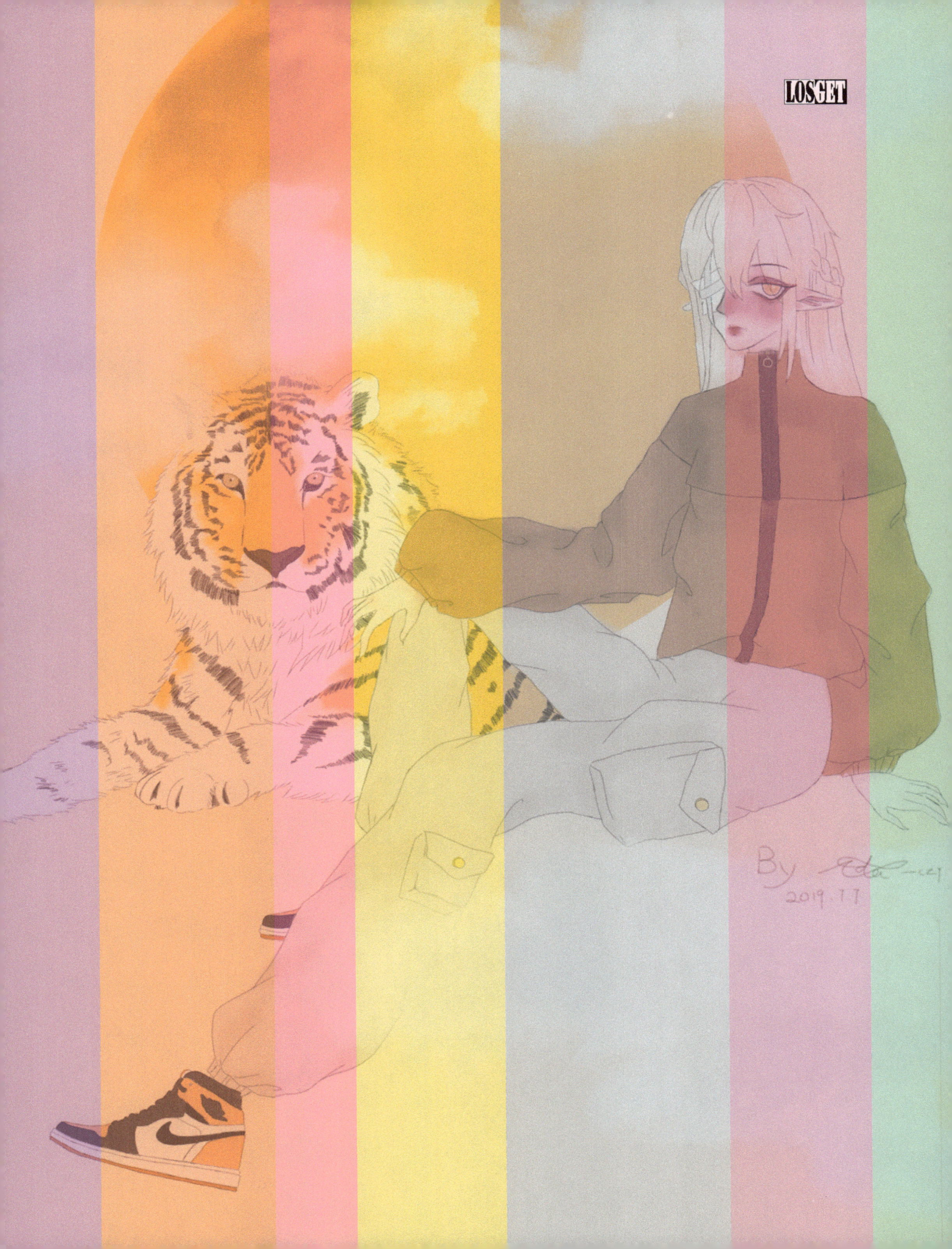

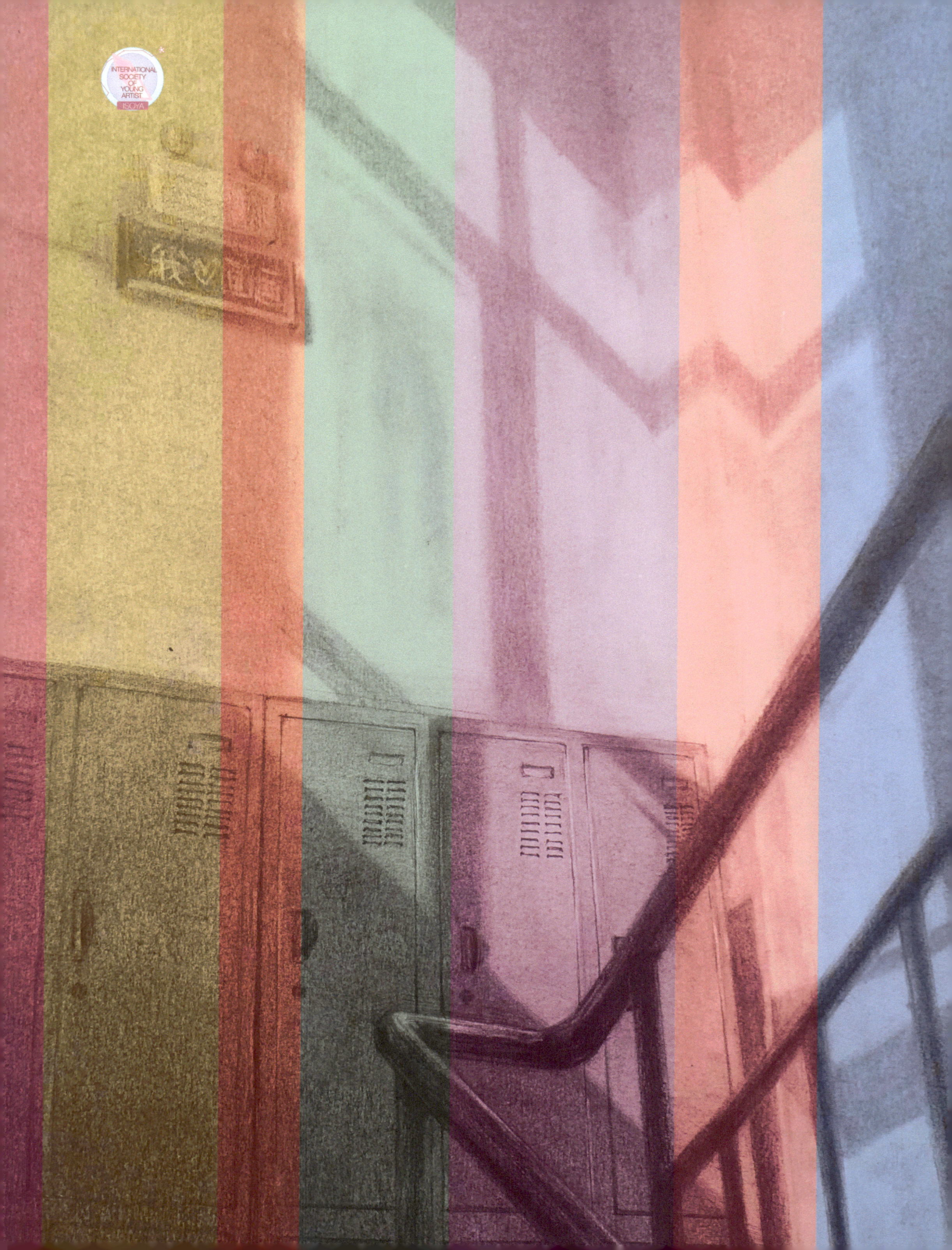

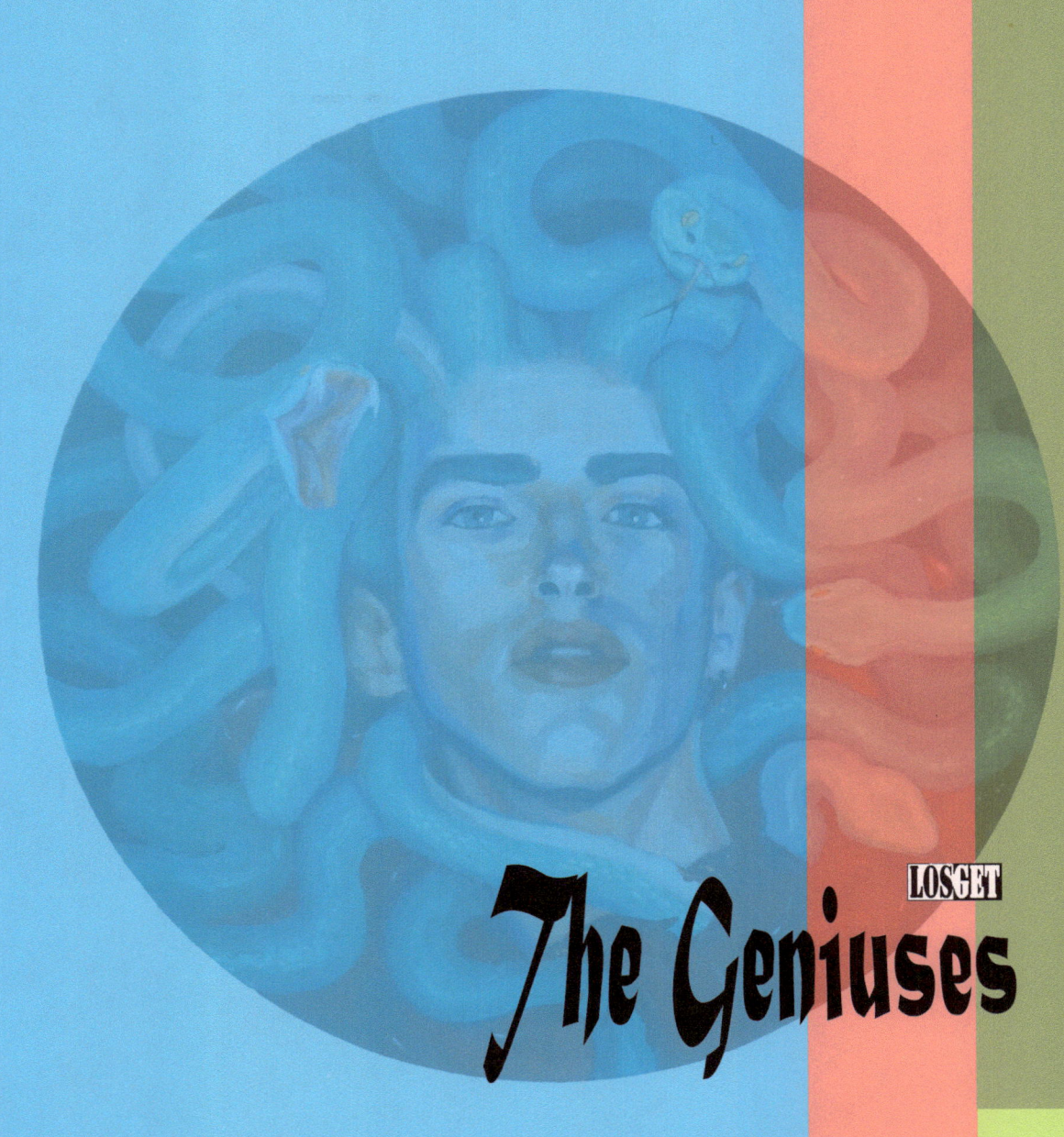

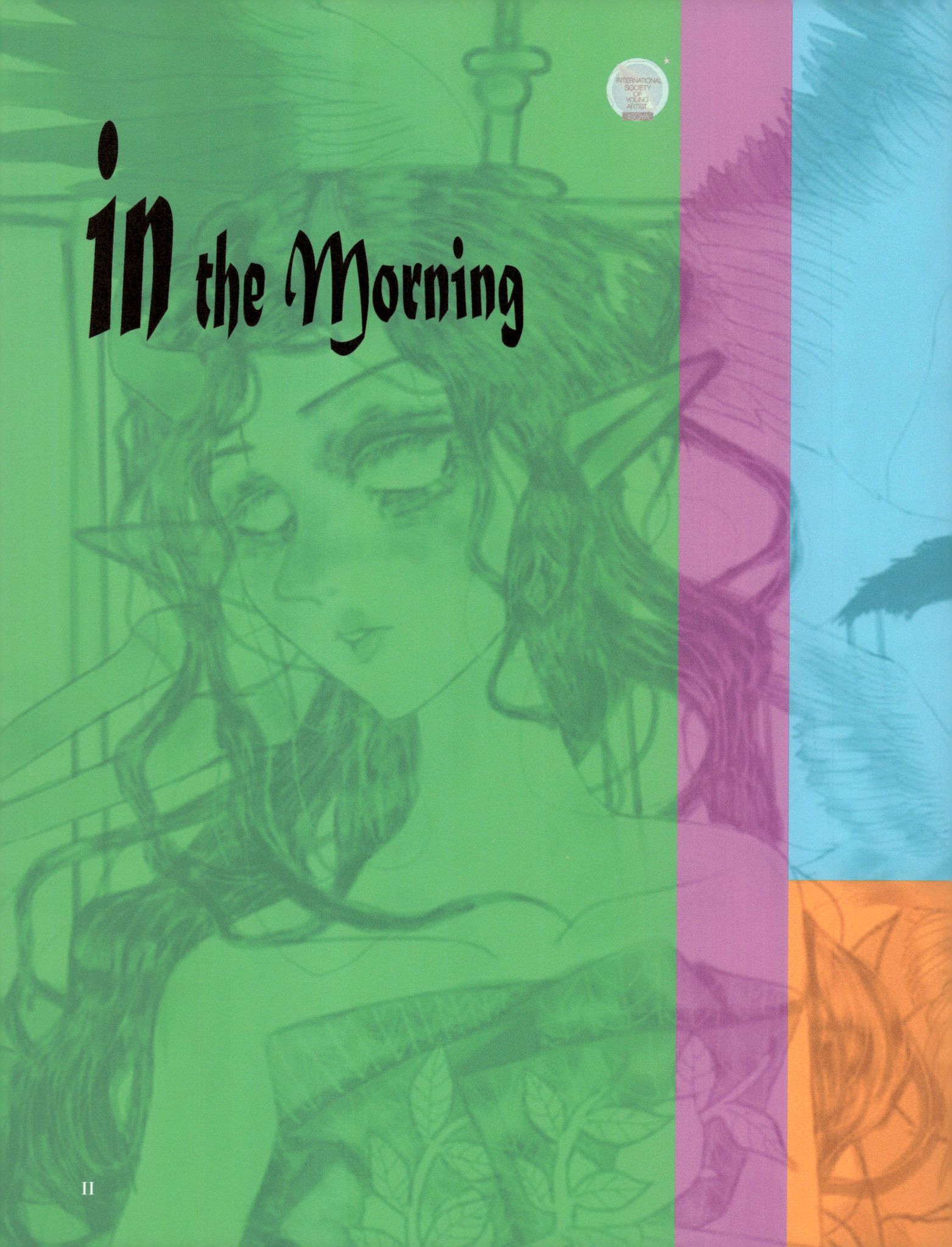

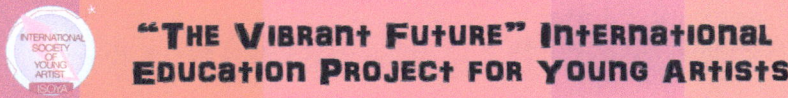 "THE VIBRANT FUTURE" INTERNATIONAL EDUCATION PROJECT FOR YOUNG ARTISTS

The Geniuses in the Morning
International Youth Artist Artwork Series -1

CHIEF EDITOR YEMEN CHEN
ASSOCIATE EDITOR XIAOJING HONG
EDITORIAL BOARD XUNYAN KUANG, RONG HONG, FANGYU REN, PEIYU WU, SUNBOYU WANG, ZIYAN CHEN, JIAXIN LENG, JINGLIN GUO
EXECUTIVE COORDINATORS YUTING HE, NAN LI, JIAN CHEN
COVER AND INTERIOR DESIGN BY TIGER HUPO, CALEB R. WU
ARTISTS BOYANG JIAO, CALEB R. WU, CHANGLU XU, FANGYU REN, GEFEI WANG, HOULIN WANG, JIAJUN CHEN, JIAJUN DENG, JIAXIN LENG, JIA ZHONG, JINCHANG ZHANG, JINGHAN XU, JINGLIN GUO, JINGXUAN YU, JINGYI YANG, JUNKAI GONG, KUN WANG, LEYI YANG, LIYU ZHANG, PEIYU WU, QINGXIA SONG, RONG HONG, RUI LI, SHUO PANG, TIMOTHY X. WU, WANCHEN ZHANG, XIKAI XU, XIN WEN, XUNYAN KUANG, YIFEI WANG, YIFEI XIAO, YIHAN ZHANG, YUE WANG, YU JIANG, YUNING YANG, YUTING HE, ZIQI MENG, ZIYAN CHEN

LOSGET
LOSGET PRESS
2020

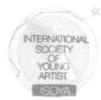

The publication of this book is part of a benevolent program - "The Vibrant Future" International Education Project for Young Artists, sponsored by the International Society of Young Artists. All of the earnings from the publication of this book will be donated to improve education for young artists.

CHIEF EDITOR Yemen Chen
ASSOCIATE EDITOR Xiaojing Hong
EDITORIAL BOARD Xunyan Kuang, Rong Hong, Fangyu Ren, Peiyu Wu, Sunboyu Wang, Ziyan Chen, Jiaxin Leng, Jinglin Guo
EXECUTIVE COORDINATORS Yuting He, Nan Li, Jian Chen
ARTISTS Boyang Jiao, Caleb R. Wu, Changlu Xu, Fangyu Ren, Gefei Wang, Houlin Wang, Jiajun Chen, Jiajun Deng, Jiaxin Leng, Jia Zhong, Jinchang Zhang, Jinghan Xu, Jinglin Guo, Jingxuan Yu, Jingyi Yang, Junkai Gong, Kun Wang, Leyi Yang, Liyu Zhang, Peiyu Wu, Qingxia Song, Rong Hong, Rui Li, Shuo Pang, Timothy X. Wu, Wanchen Zhang, Xikai Xu, Xin Wen, Xunyan Kuang, Yifei Wang, Yifei Xiao, Yihan Zhang, Yue Wang, Yu Jiang, Yuning Yang, Yuting He, Ziqi Meng, Ziyan Chen

LOSGET

Copyright © 2020 by Losget Press
All rights reserved.
Published in the United States by Losget Press, Los Angeles
Originally published in Paperback in the United States by Losget Press, in 2020
Title: The Geniuses in the Morning: International Youth Artist Artwork Series -1
Description: First Edition. | Los Angeles: Losget Press, 2020.
Identifiers: ISBN-13: 978-1-951364-05-2 | ISBN-10: 1-951364-05-8
www.losget.com
E-mail: contact@losget.com
Book design by Tiger Hupo
First Printing. 2020.

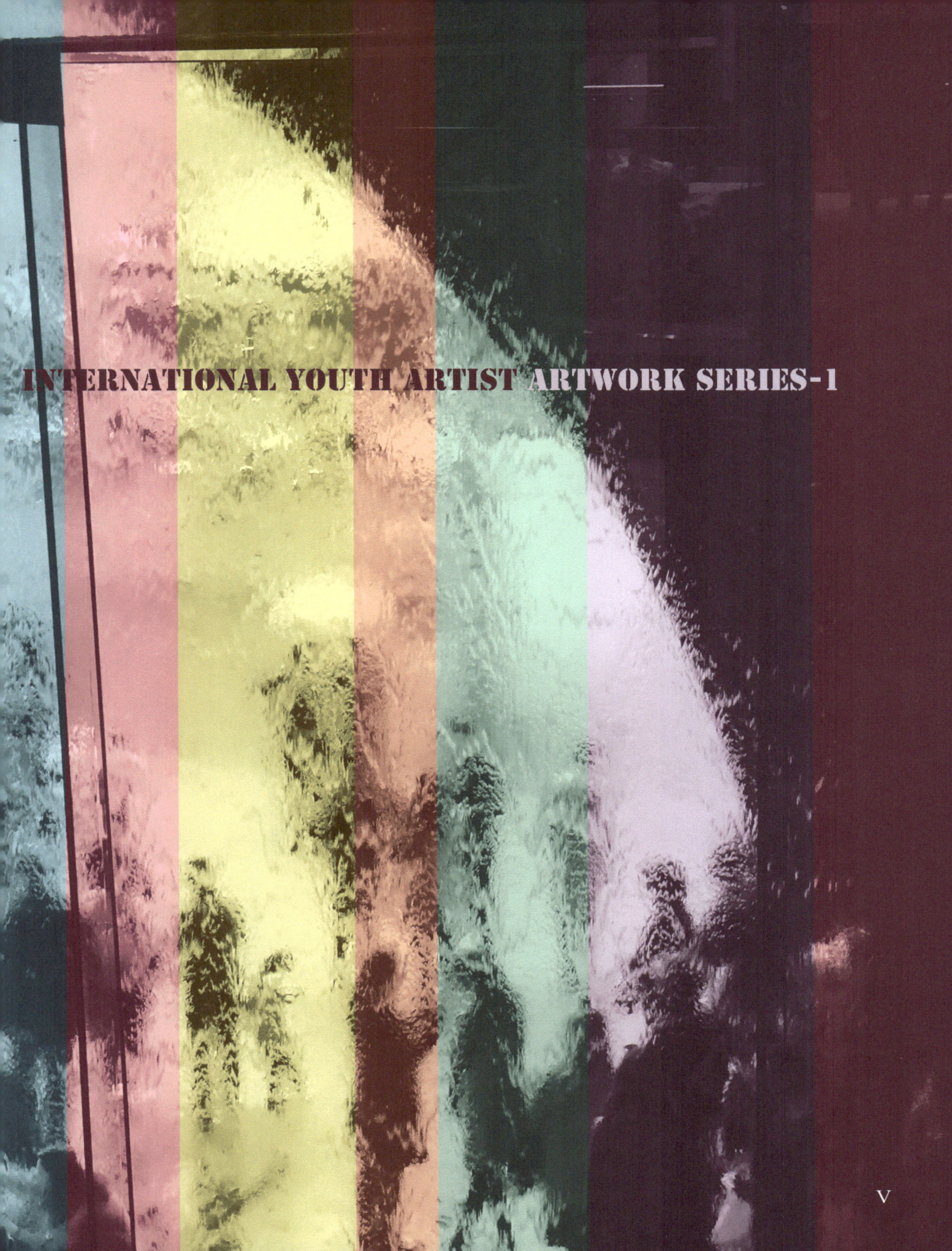

Children Who Love Art Will

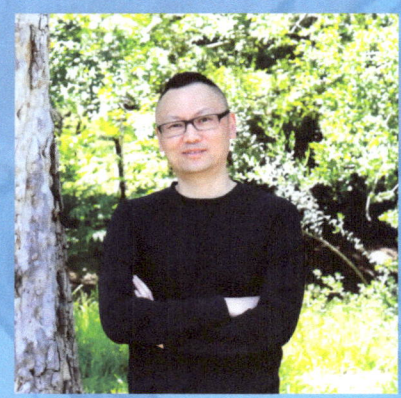

YEMEN CHEN
President
International Society of Young Artists

FOREWORD

The International Society of Young Artists, established on August 18, 2018, with its headquarters in Los Angeles, is a non-profit organization aims to provide a platform for young artists to develop their creative talents.

The rapid advancement of technology has changed the way the world operates. Today's young generation is faced with unprecedented opportunities, and of course, temptations. Without proper guidance, they will easily fall into the trap of consumerism. Bombarded with commercials, they can easily lose track of what's important and what's not. With this in mind, the International Society of Young Artists aims to remind young people that life is more than what is presented in the media. The reason why they are so attracted to consumerism just because the artistic design hidden within the advertisements themselves. It is the intentional design that makes one thirsty just from looking at a soda can. It is the laborious industry behind the scenes, in which hundreds of artistic professions are involved, that makes movie stars appear glamorous on movie screens.

For a long time, art has been misconceived by the public as something reserved for minority artists, while it is, in fact, profoundly relevant to our daily lives. Art is a superior form of language. It expresses emotions that verbal language fail to describe. The language of art, like all other languages, can only be perfected through extensive practice. Art is everything, and everything is art. Art is an expanding keyhole through which humans perceive the world. Thus, the International Society of Young Artists dedicates itself to improving young people's sensibility of art. We believe that art has no boundaries, art includes everything that can be perceived through our senses, and it encompasses existing art forms such as painting, music, dance, photography, drama and movie, as well as those that are yet to be created. Therefore, the only boundary of art lies at the endpoint of the imaginative realm of the human mind.

The International Society of Young Artists welcomes everyone between the age of 8 and 28. Whether or not you have the intention of pursuing an artistic career, we would like to plant the aesthetic seed of art in the rich soil deep in your heart, hoping that one day it

Become the Future Peace-lovers

will sprout and thrive, so that you may become a doctor who knows how to comfort your patients by performing a surprising music, a banker who places a vase of blooming flowers next to your computer, a housewife who creates cute cartoon characters with fried eggs and sausages...

The purpose of learning art is not merely to acquire a useful skill, but to strengthen our cerebral function. As a significant form, visual art provides training for the parietal lobe in charge of creativity and spatial relations. The nature of aesthetics lies in the overall cohesion and unity. Through studying art, one is trained to notice the details without losing sight of the big picture, which is an essential skill for personal development of individuals as well. The sensibility and attentiveness formed in artistic training will become the backbone that supports a person in all enterprises, from career management to creative proposals, and much more.

The magical power of art education does not limit itself to making a person elegant. It also has the ability to make one competitive. Art is the key ingredient of competitiveness in today's commercial world. Steve Jobs accomplished his milestone achievements because he knew that the consumers love the art behind the product that captives them.

Most importantly, the process of creating art exerts a positive impact on individuals' psychological and sentimental health. The universal love towards humanity is a common theme underlying many renowned artworks in history. Creating and appreciating art stimulates the natural tenderness within children and artists, which motivates them to explore the positive side of human nature. Therefore, we say that art is an indispensable component in the growth of a child. Children who love art will become the future peace-lovers.

The International Society of Young Artists will gather young people worldwide who share the same passion for art, and offer them opportunities to learn, communicate and explore. We welcome volunteers and donors from all parts of the world to contribute to this career that will make a difference in the future of humanity. We encourage every young person to become a member of the International Society of Young Artists, and we would sincerely appreciate any help given to us to assist our ultimate goal – to cultivate the love and appreciation for arts in the young generation, and to make the world a better place.

January 2019

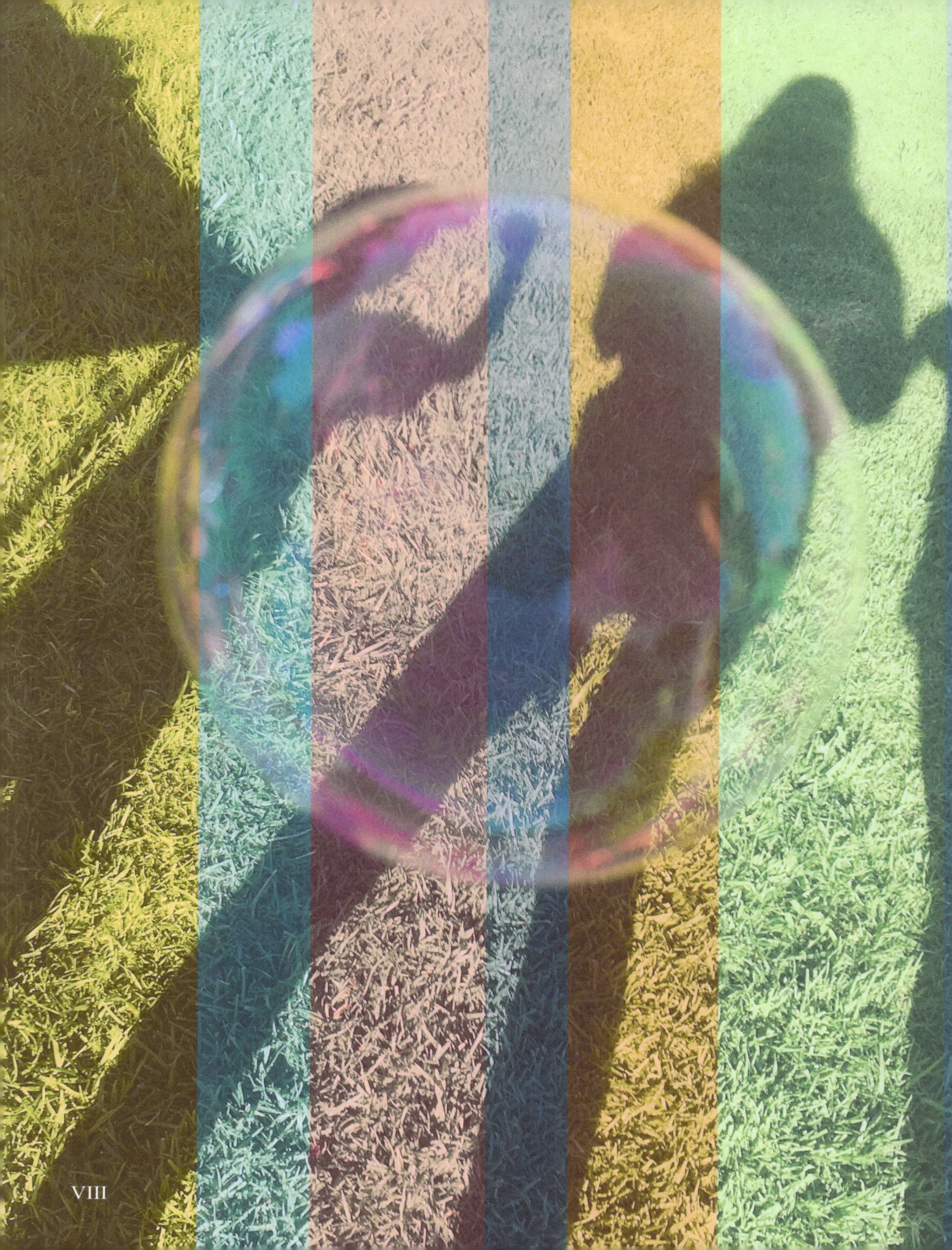

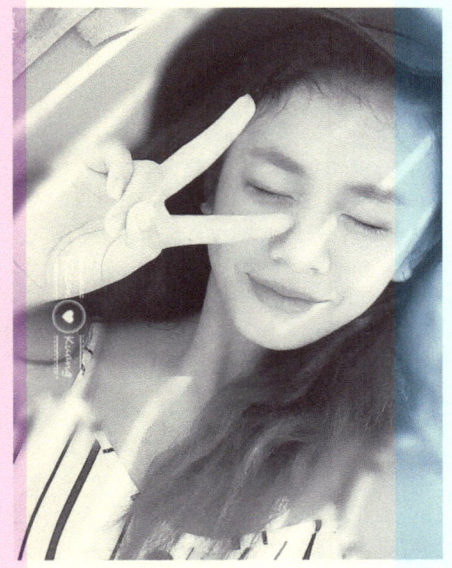

I would first like to thank the International Society of Young Artists for selecting me as the PERSON OF 2019. I am sincerely grateful to have the honor of being awarded with this title and for the recognition that I have received.

Here, my deepest appreciations and respect goes to Mr. Chen for giving me the opportunity to become ISOYA's chief representative of Los Angeles. He saw through the best of me and invariably provided me with incessant support.

With my new role, I had the opportunity to assist and work with many of our members and experienced the duties of a representative in our society. I want to thank them all for their support and feedbacks that challenged me to become a better representative.

Thank you from the bottom of my heart to everyone who have helped me get to where I am today. I promise to only improve in the future and become a better self. Thank you.

XUNYAN KUANG
Chief Representative of Los Angeles
International Society of Young Artists
December 28, 2019, USA

Contents

Boyang Jiao......................1
Caleb R. Wu......................3
Changlu Xu......................7
Fangyu Ren......................11
Gefei Wang......................15
Houlin Wang......................19
Jiajun Chen......................21
Jiajun Deng......................23
Jiaxin Leng......................25
Jia Zhong......................31
Jinchang Zhang......................37
Jinghan Xu......................41
Jinglin Guo......................45
Jingxuan Yu......................51
Jingyi Yang......................53
Junkai Gong......................59
Kun Wang......................63
Leyi Yang......................67
Liyu Zhang......................71
Peiyu Wu......................73
Qingxia Song......................77
Rong Hong......................81
Rui Li......................85
Shuo Pang......................89
Timothy X. Wu......................93
Wanchen Zhang......................97
Xikai Xu......................99
Xin Wen......................101
Xunyan Kuang......................103
Yifei Wang......................109
Yifei Xiao......................113
Yihan Zhang......................115
Yue Wang......................117
Yu Jiang......................121
Yuning Yang......................125
Yuting He......................129
Ziqi Meng......................133
Ziyan Chen......................137

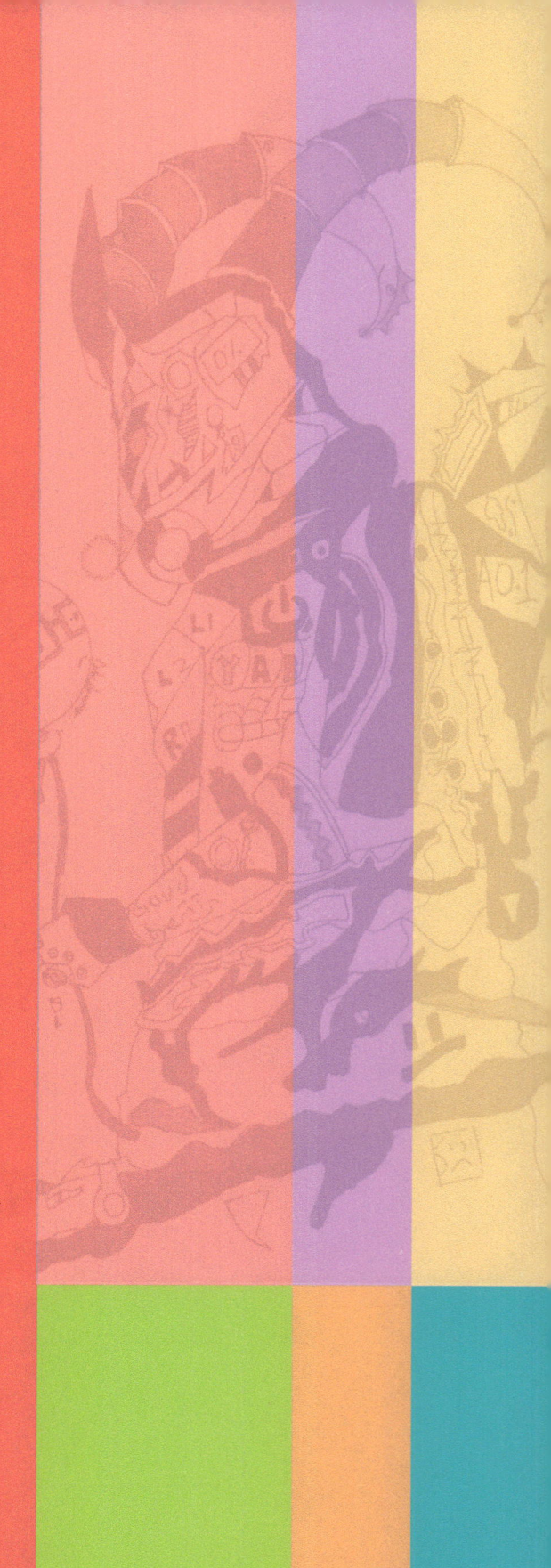

The Geniuses in the Morning

LOSGET

International Youth Artist Artwork Series-1

XI

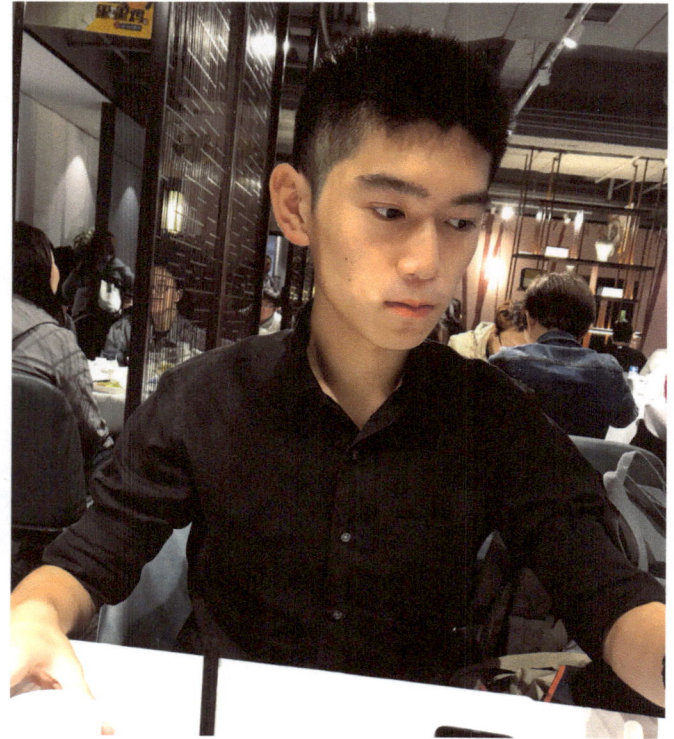

BOYANG JIAO
Beijing University of Chinese Medicine, China

Silver Award for Art, 2nd Liberty Awards, International Society of Young Artists, 2019
Silver Award for Art, 1st Liberty Awards, International Society of Young Artists, 2018
1st Prize & Team 1st Prize, National Junior Aeromodelling Championship, 2016

The Geniuses in the Morning

BOYANG JIAO

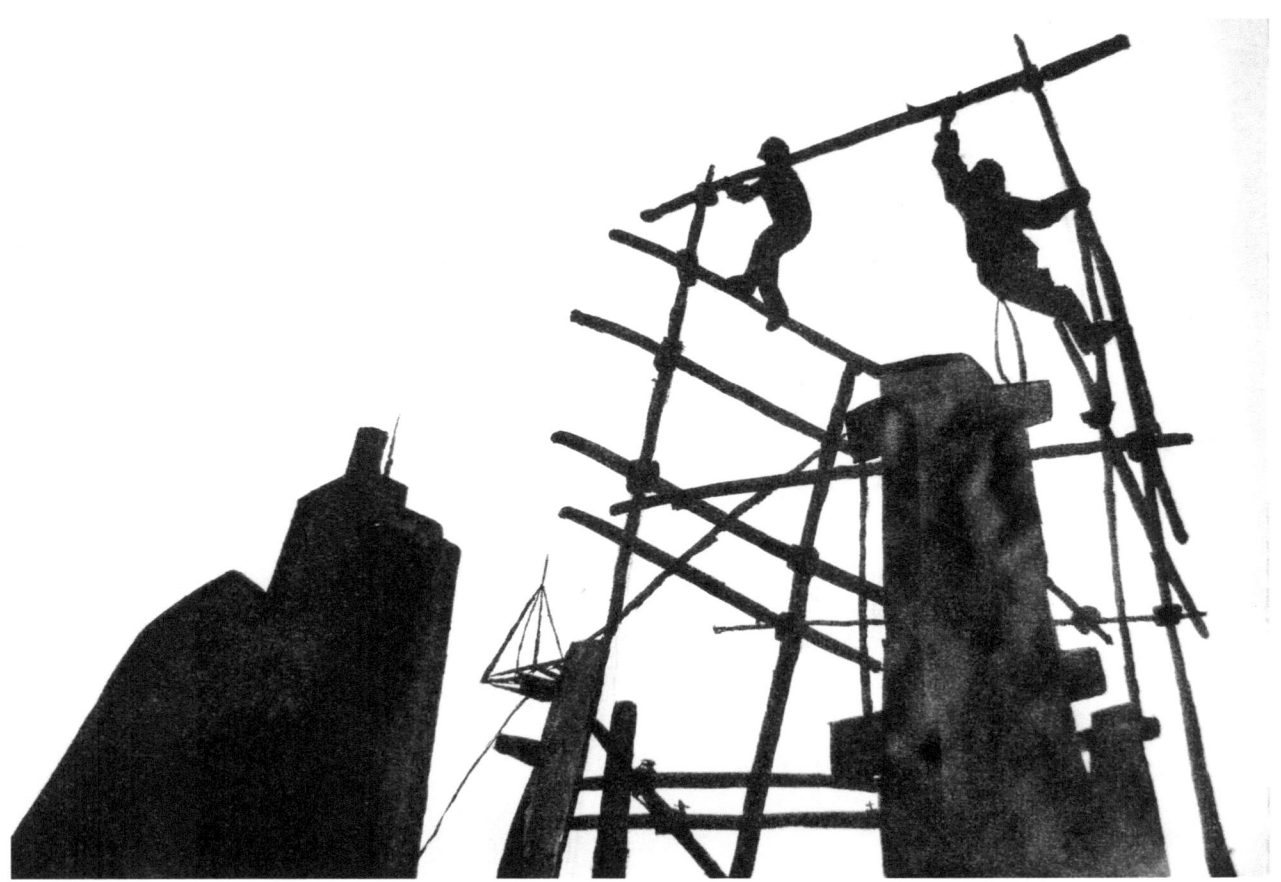

Constrution, ink on paper, 2012

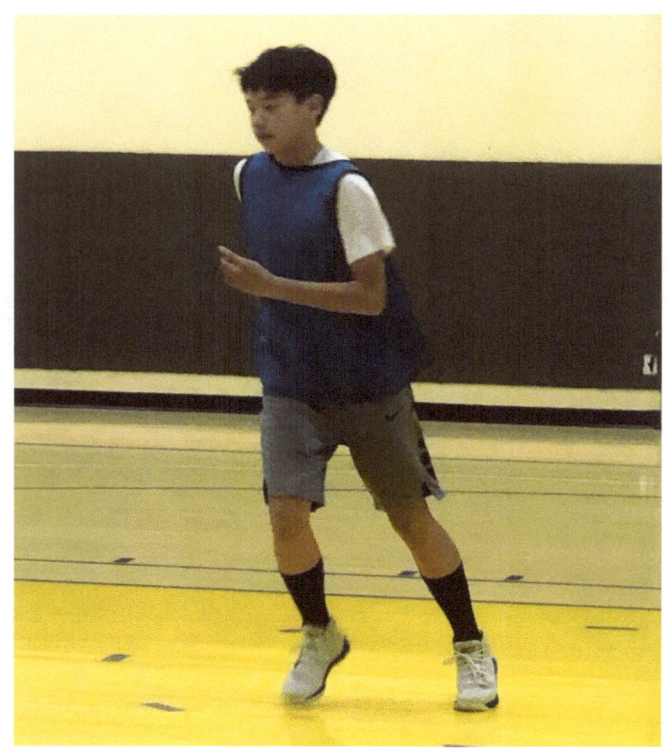

CALEB R. WU
Robert O. Townsend Junior High, USA

Gold Award for Art, 2nd Liberty Awards, International Society of Young Artists, 2019
Bronze Award for Art, 1st Liberty Awards, International Society of Young Artists, 2018

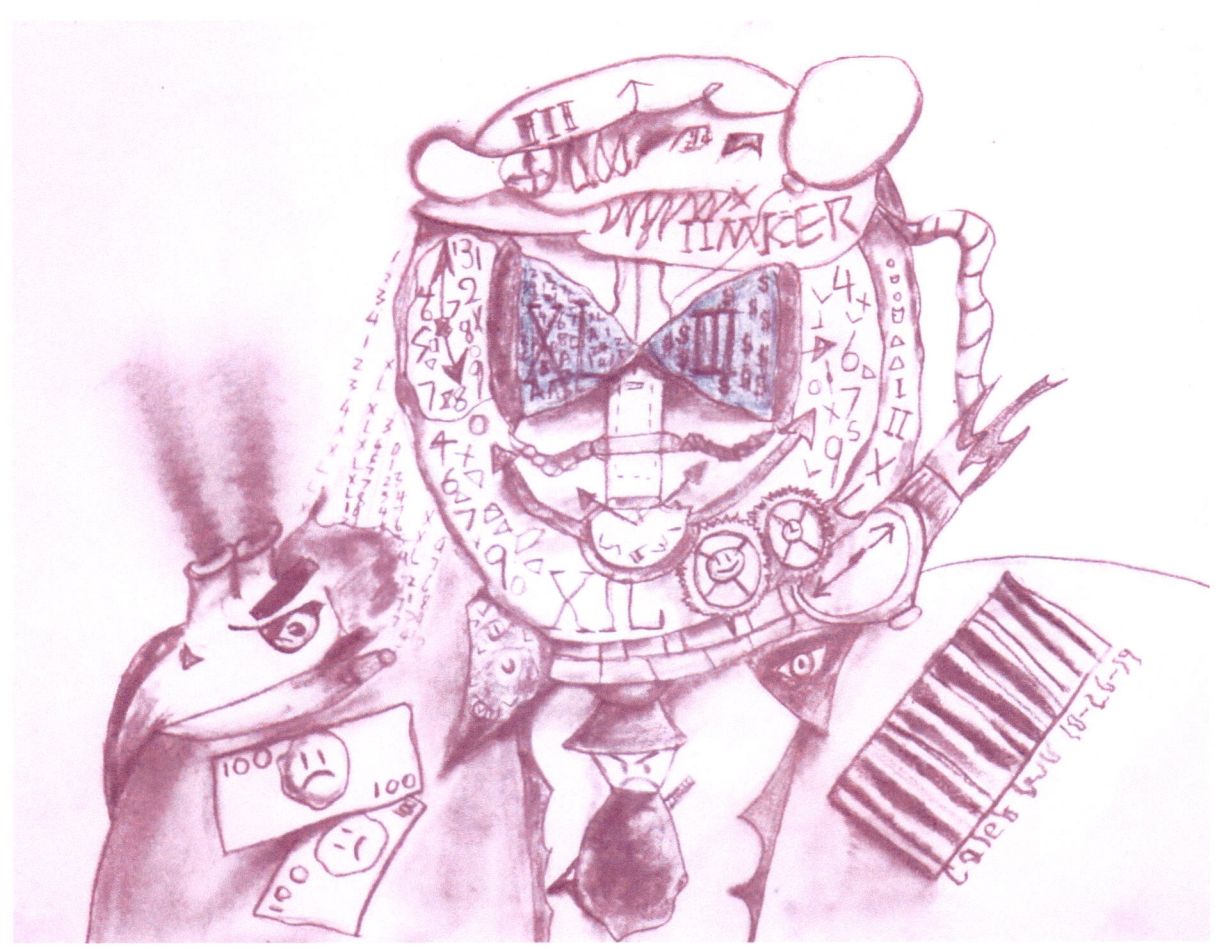

Modern, pencil and colored pencil on paper, 2019

CALEB R. WU

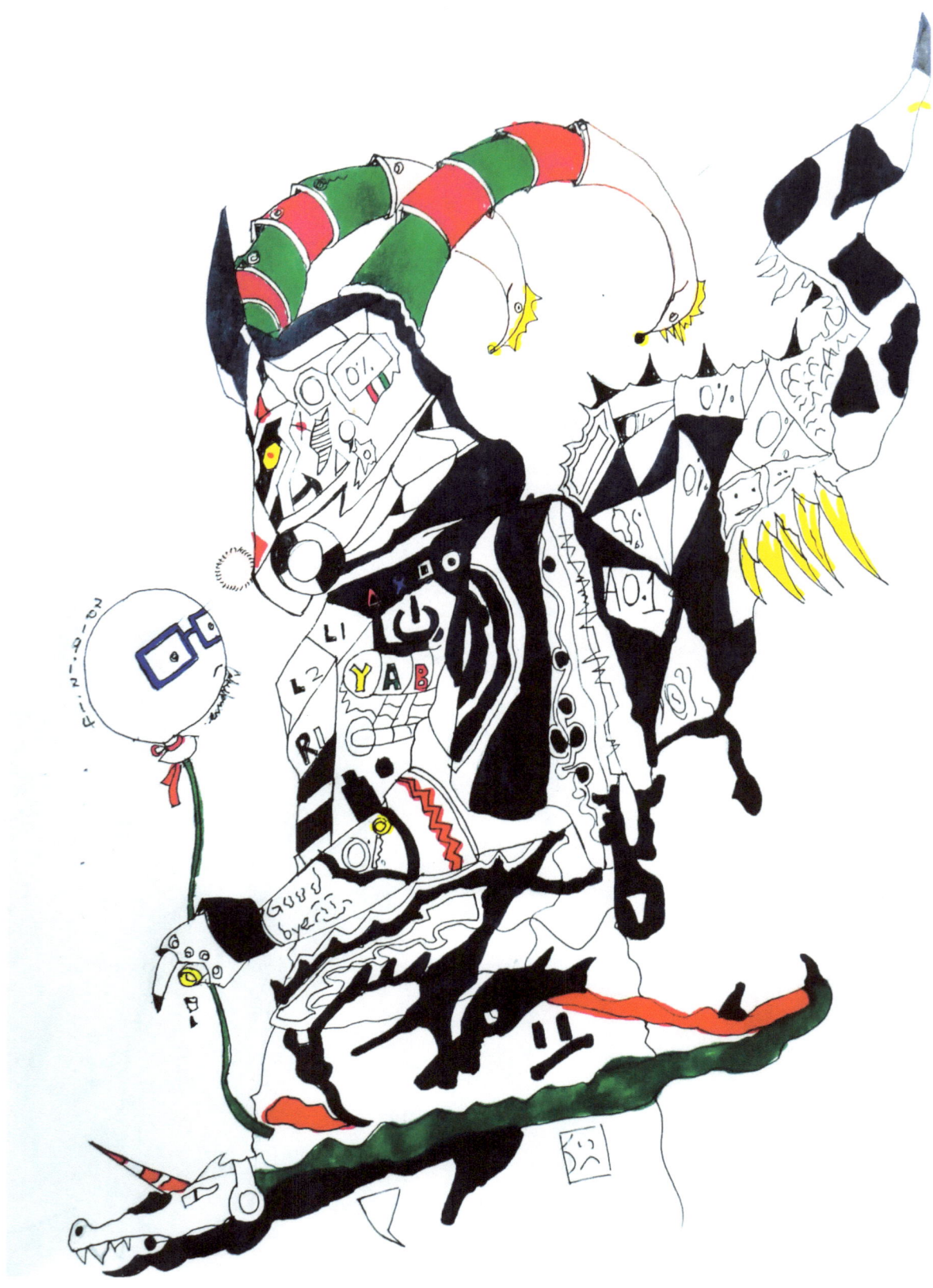

Mutt, pen and coloring marker on paper, 2019

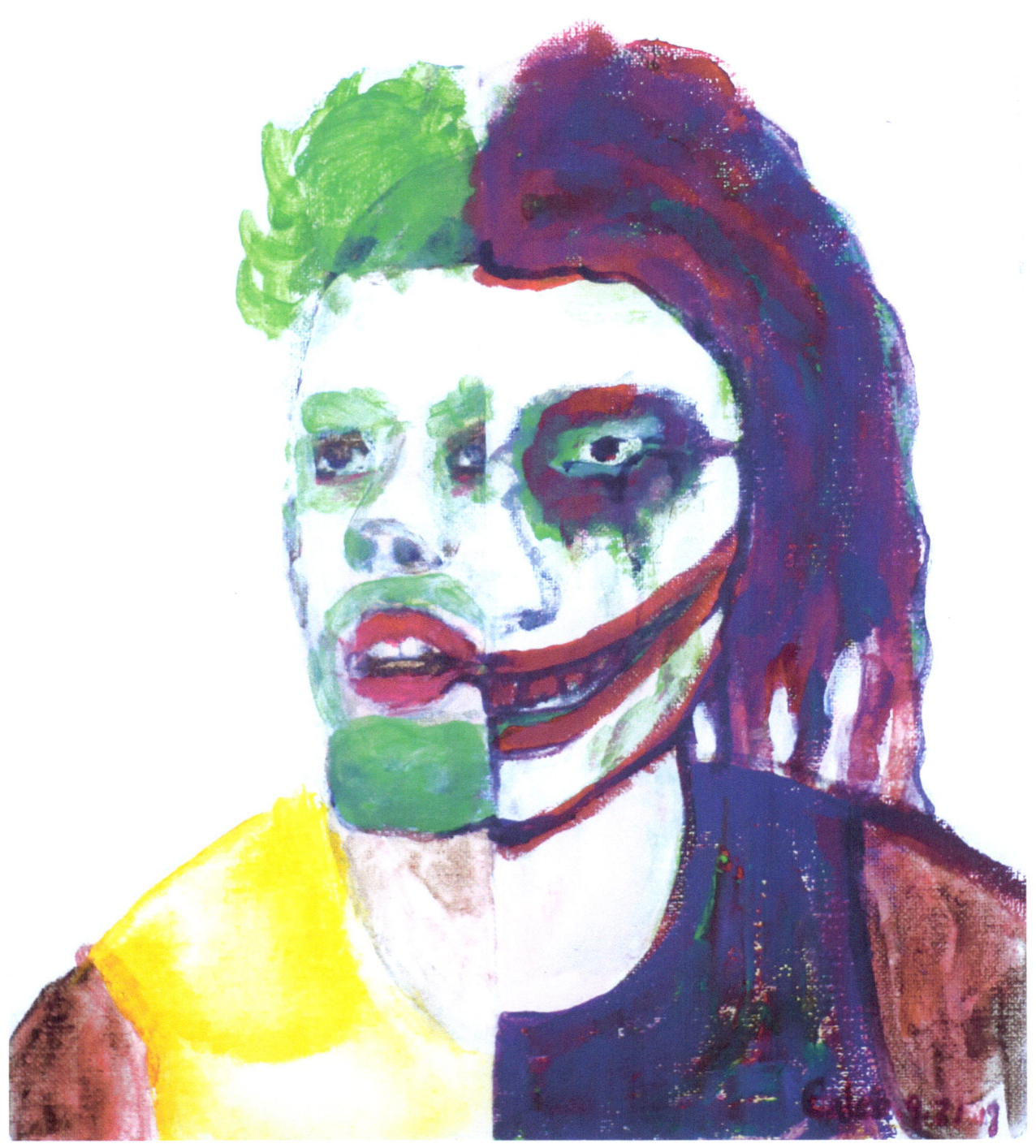

Two-sides, acrylic on canvas, 2019

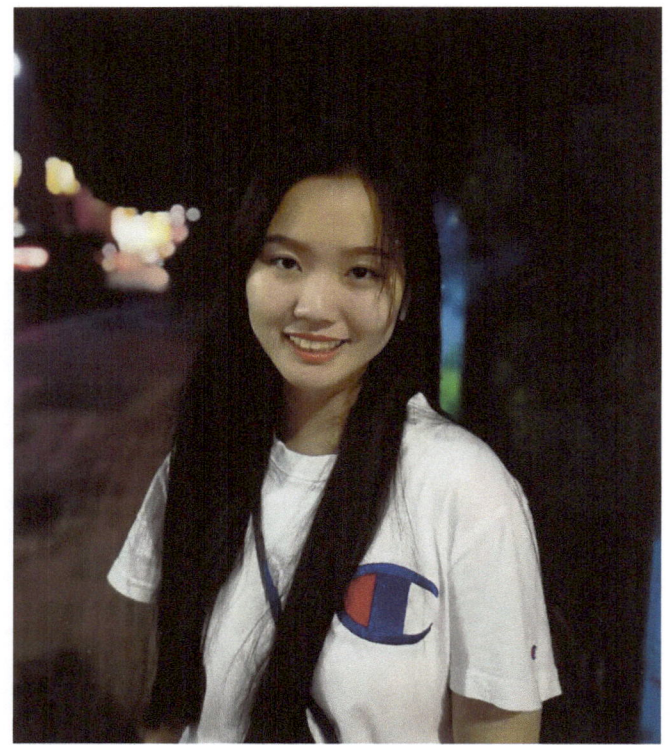

CHANGLU XU
Qingdao Haishan School, China

Rising Star Award, 2nd Liberty Awards, International Society of Young Artists, 2019
Rising Star Award, 1st Liberty Awards, International Society of Young Artists, 2018

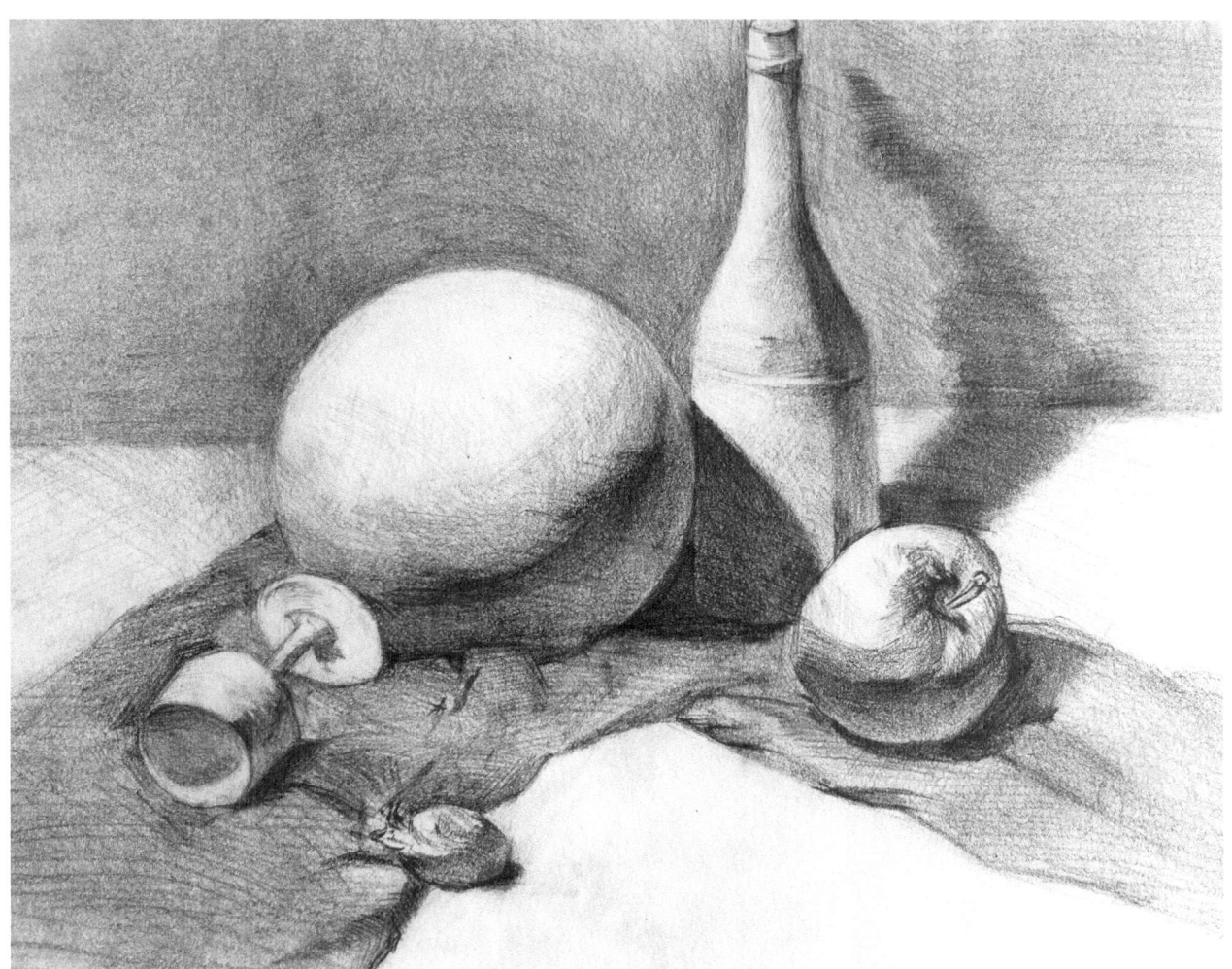

Still Life, pencil on paper, 2019

CHANGLU XU

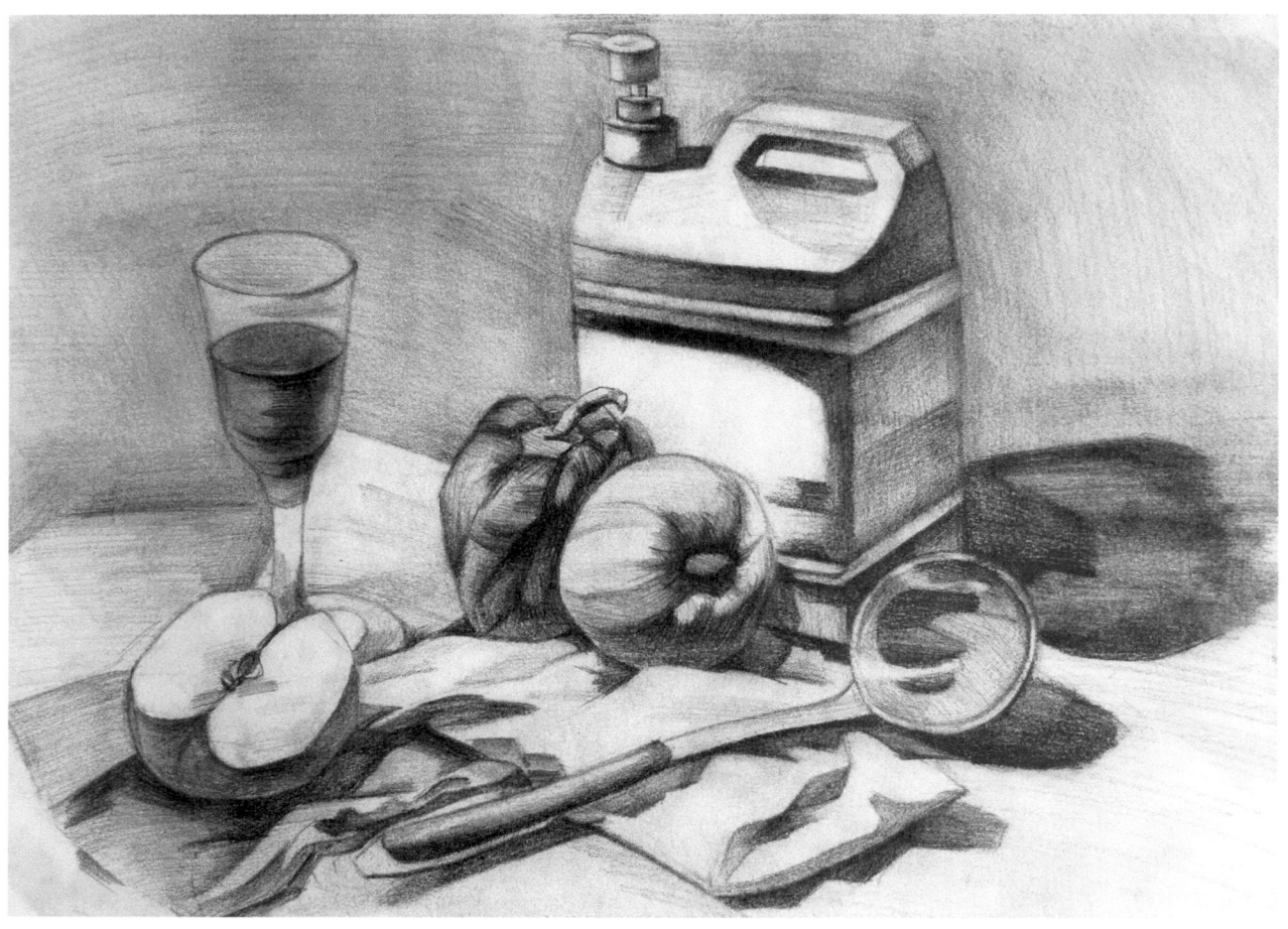

Still Life, pencil on paper, 2019

CHANGLU XU

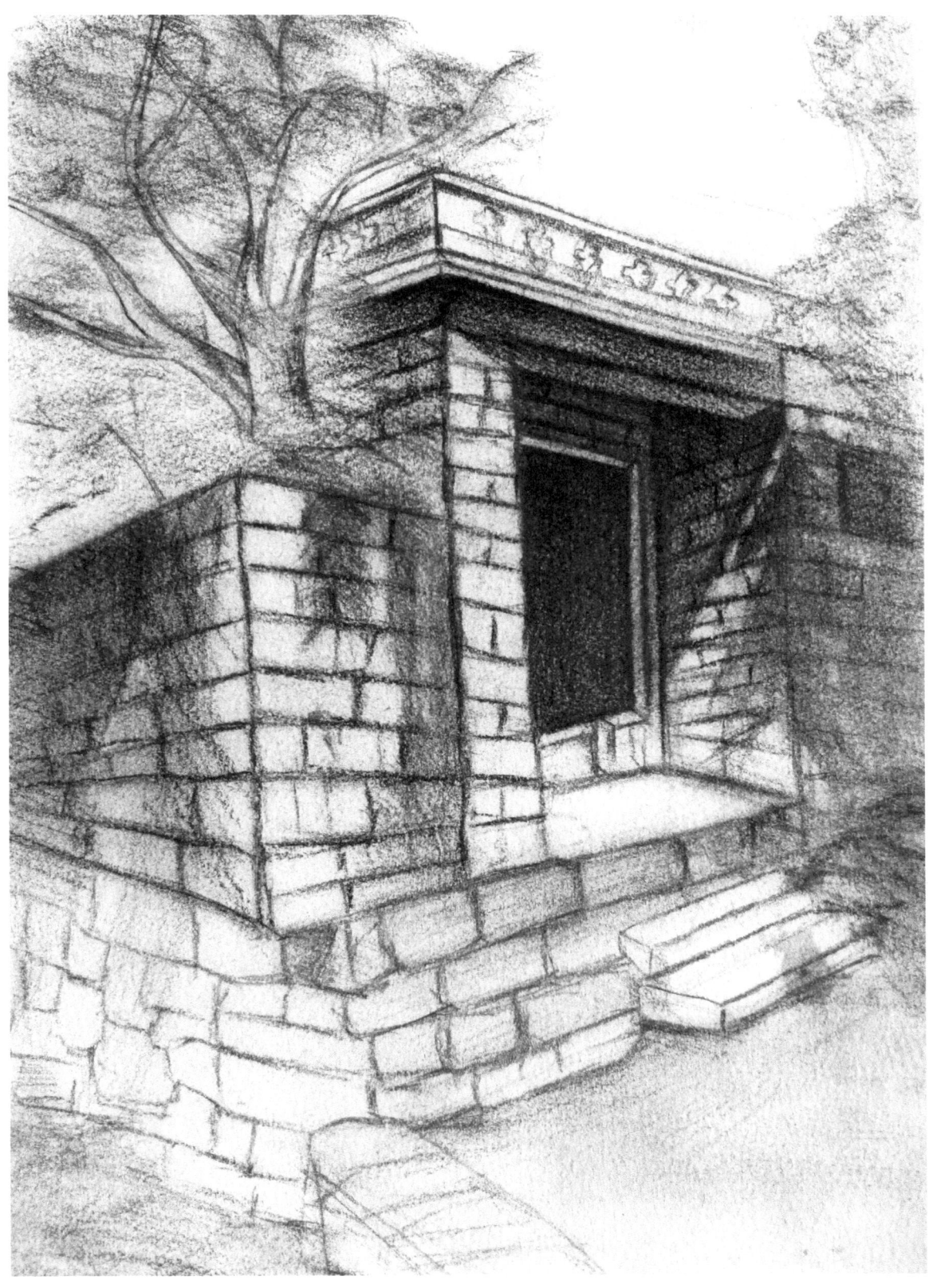

Dwelling, pencil on paper, 2019

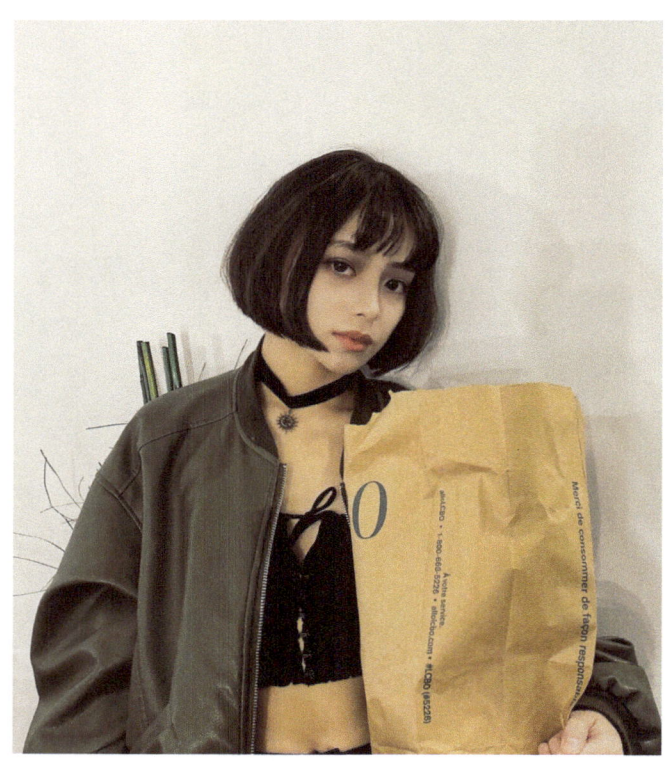

FANGYU REN
University of Toronto, Canada

Gold Award for Art, 2nd Liberty Awards, International Society of Young Artists, 2019
Gold Award for Art, 1st Liberty Awards, International Society of Young Artists, 2018
Excellence in Teaching Award, Losget Academy, 2018
Excellence Press Award, Losget Press, 2018
Excellence in Mentoring, "The Colorful Peace" Art Project Honoring the 100th Anniversary of the WWI Armistice, International Society of Young Artists, 2018

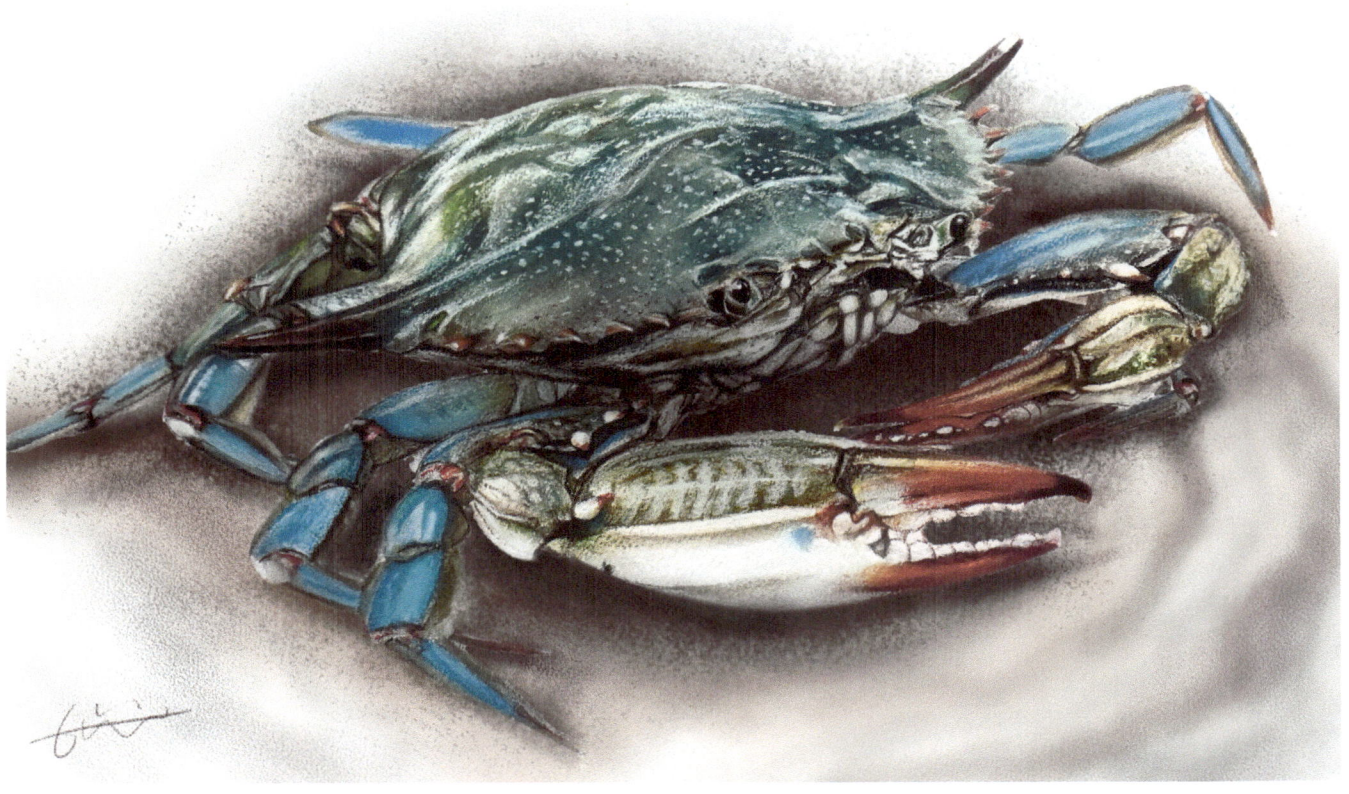

Rainbow Crab, watercolor and colored pencil on paper, 2019

FANGYU REN

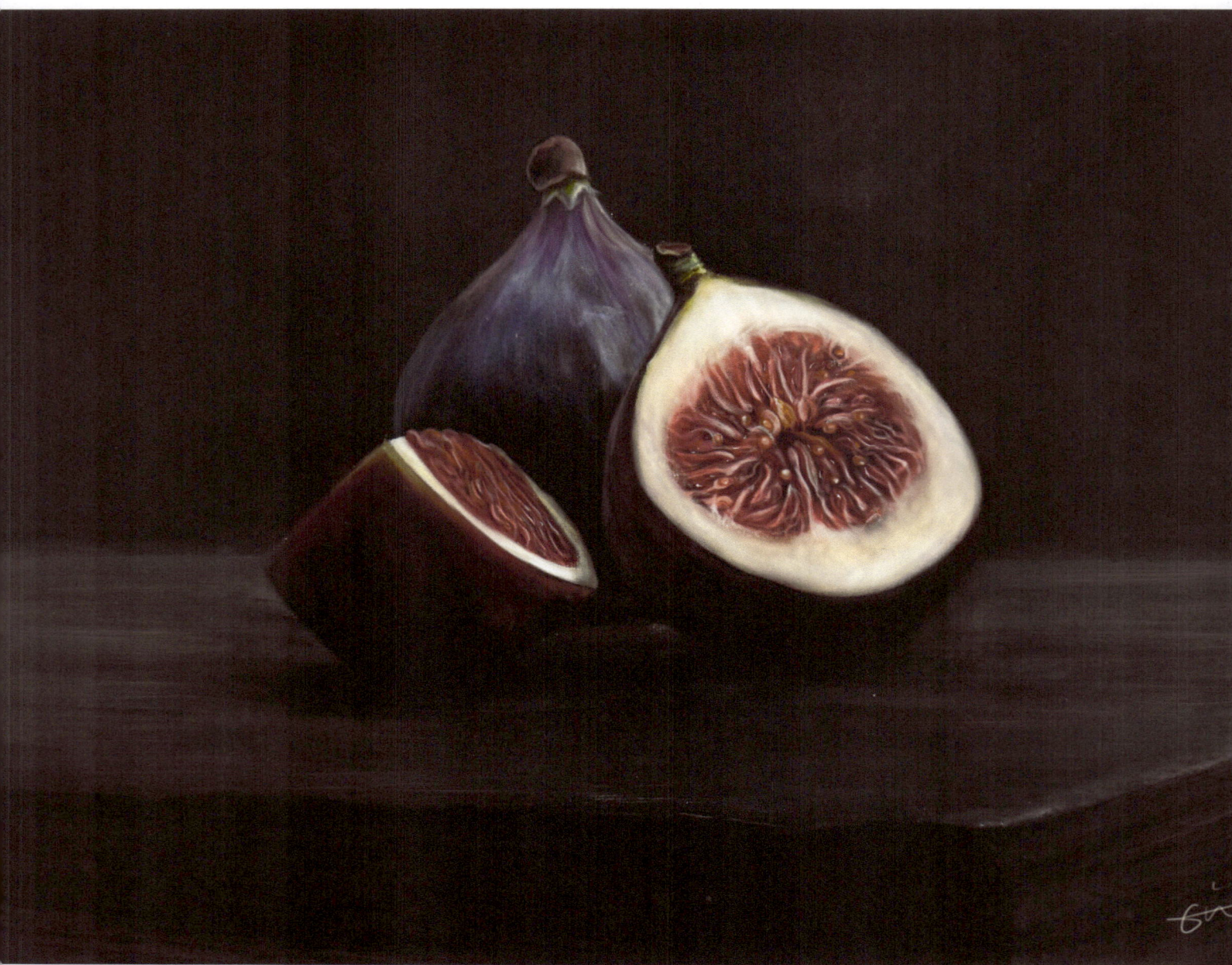

Figs, acrylic on canvas with digital rendering, 2019

FANGYU REN

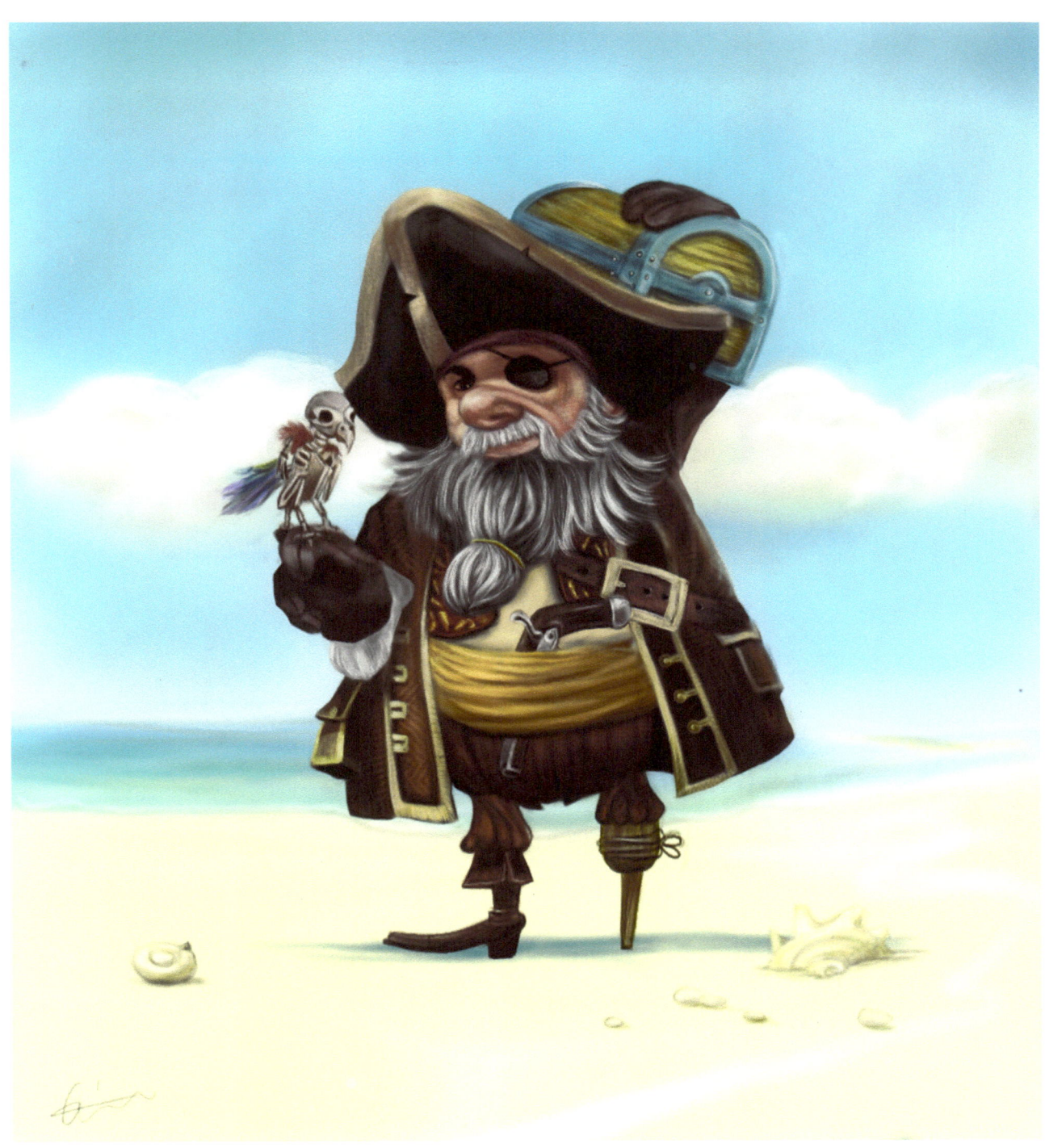

Captain Eyepatch, digital, *2019*

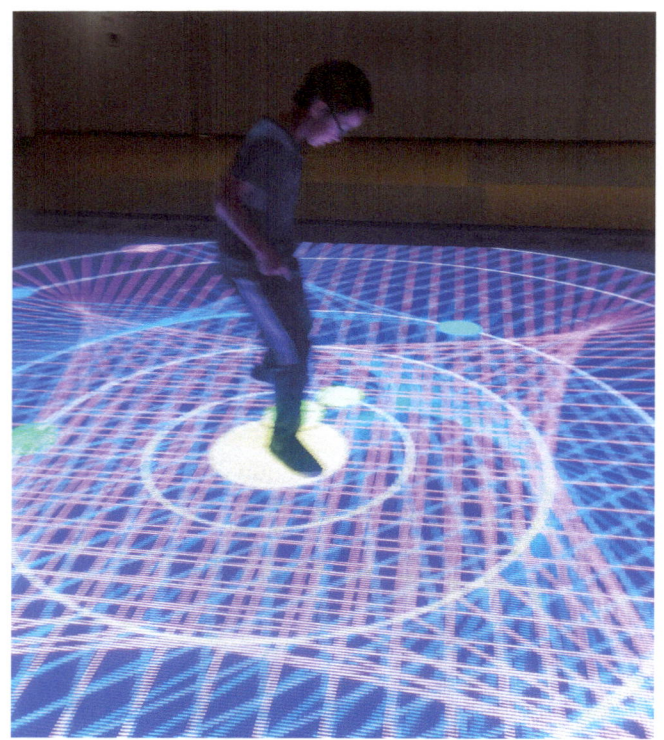

GEFEI WANG
Brookdale Elementary School, USA

Bronze Award for Art, 2nd Liberty Awards, International Society of Young Artists, 2019
Rising Star Award, 1st Liberty Awards, International Society of Young Artists, 2018

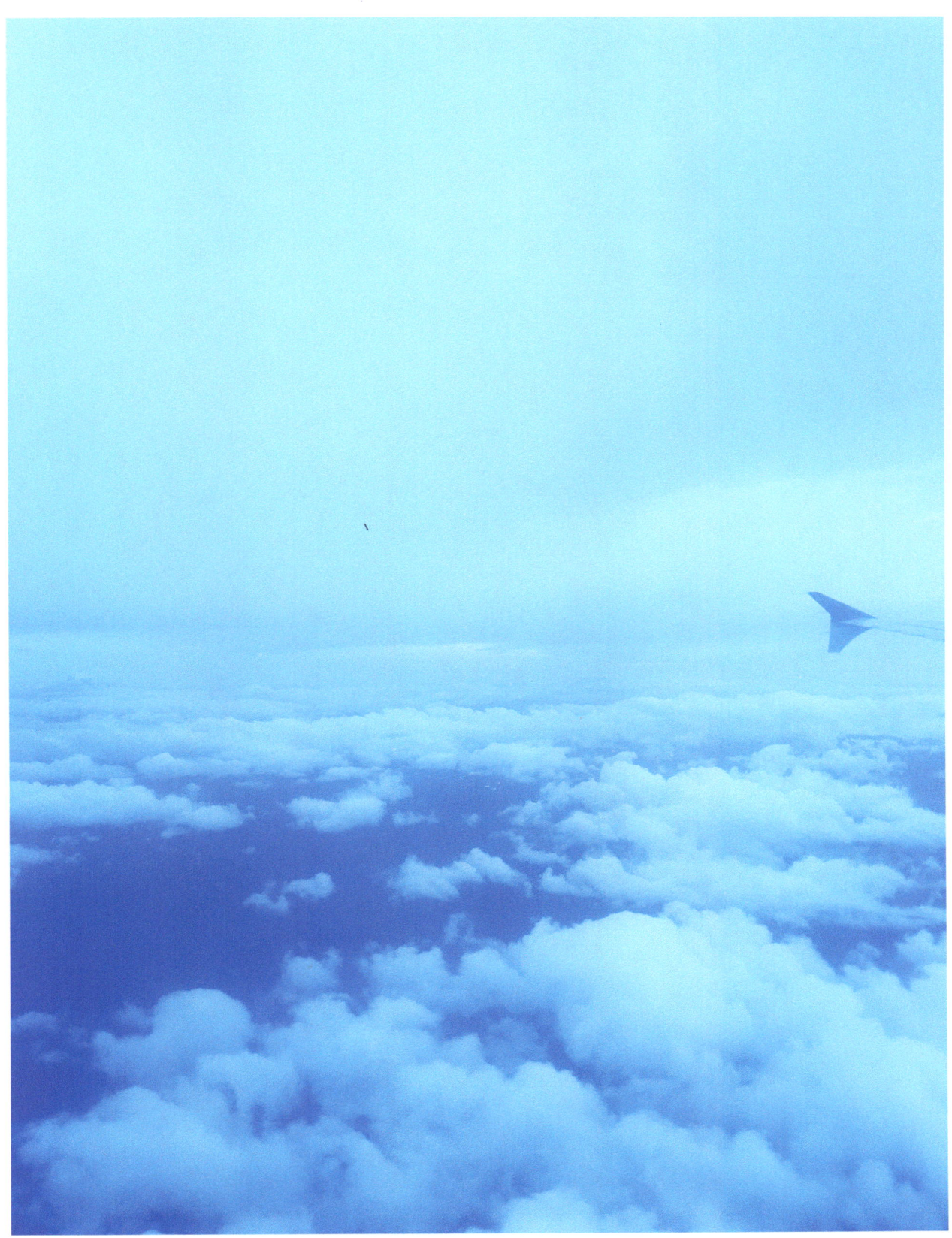

Clouds over New York City, photography, 2019

GEFEI WANG

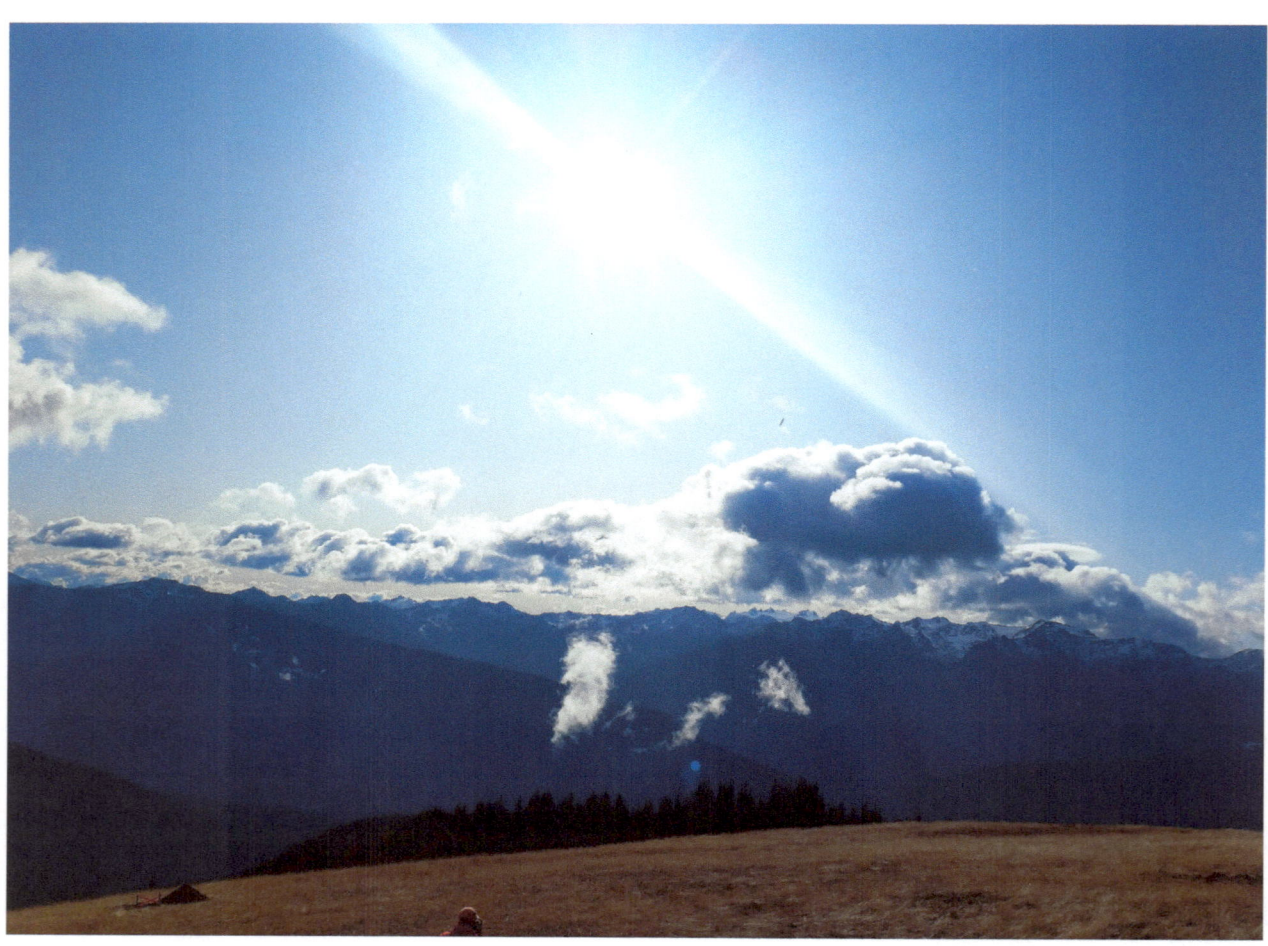

Clouds in Olympic National Park WA -1, photography, 2019

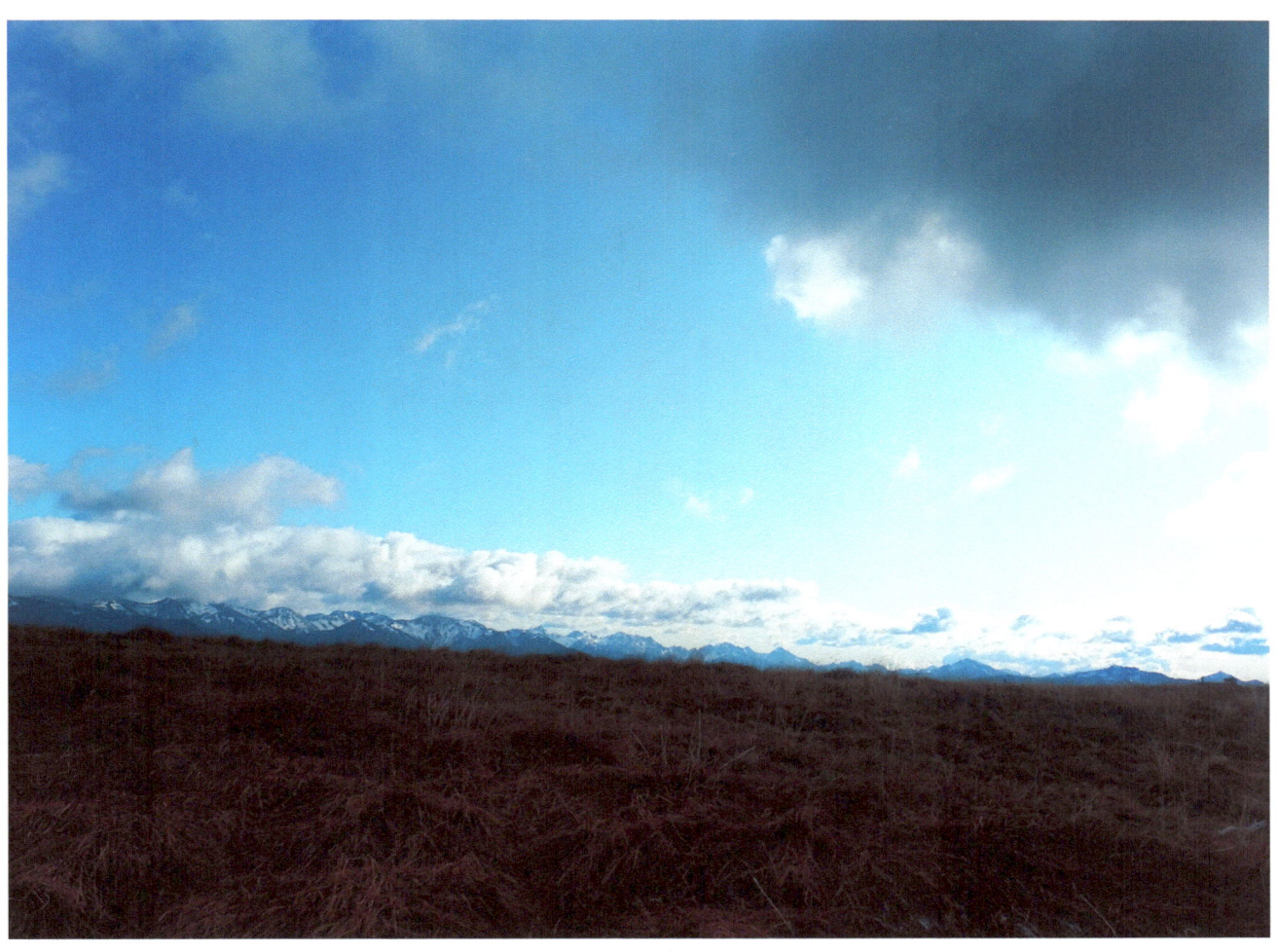

Clouds in Olympic National Park WA -2, photography, 2019

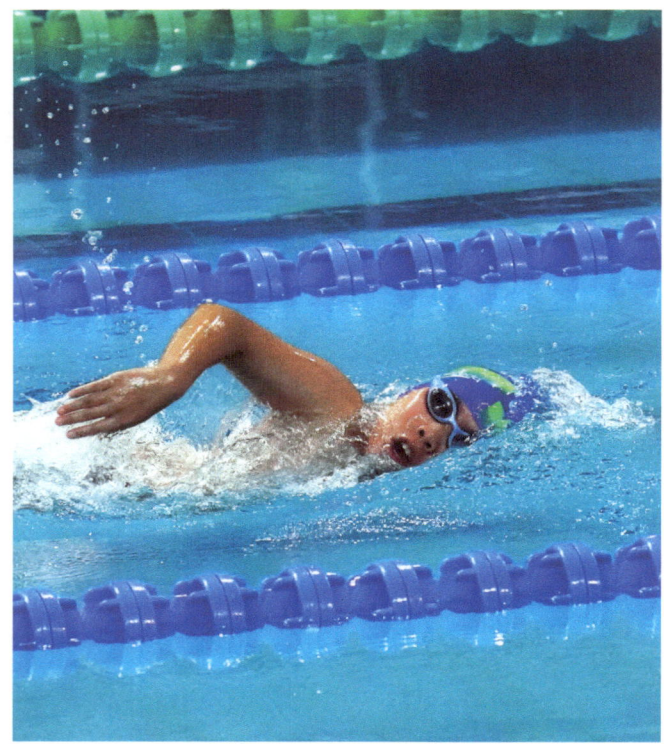

HOULIN WANG
Ocean University of China Affiliated Middle School, China

Rising Star Award, 1st Liberty Awards, International Society of Young Artists, 2018
1st Place, 4x100m Relay in Freestyle, Swimming Competition of 4th Qingdao Games, 2017
1st Place, Butterfly Stroke, Swimming Competition of 4th Qingdao Games, 2017
1st Prize, 2016 WER World Championships Bricks Robotics Contest, 2016
1st Prize, WER Engineering Innovation Competition of 2016 Shandong Robotics Contest, 2016

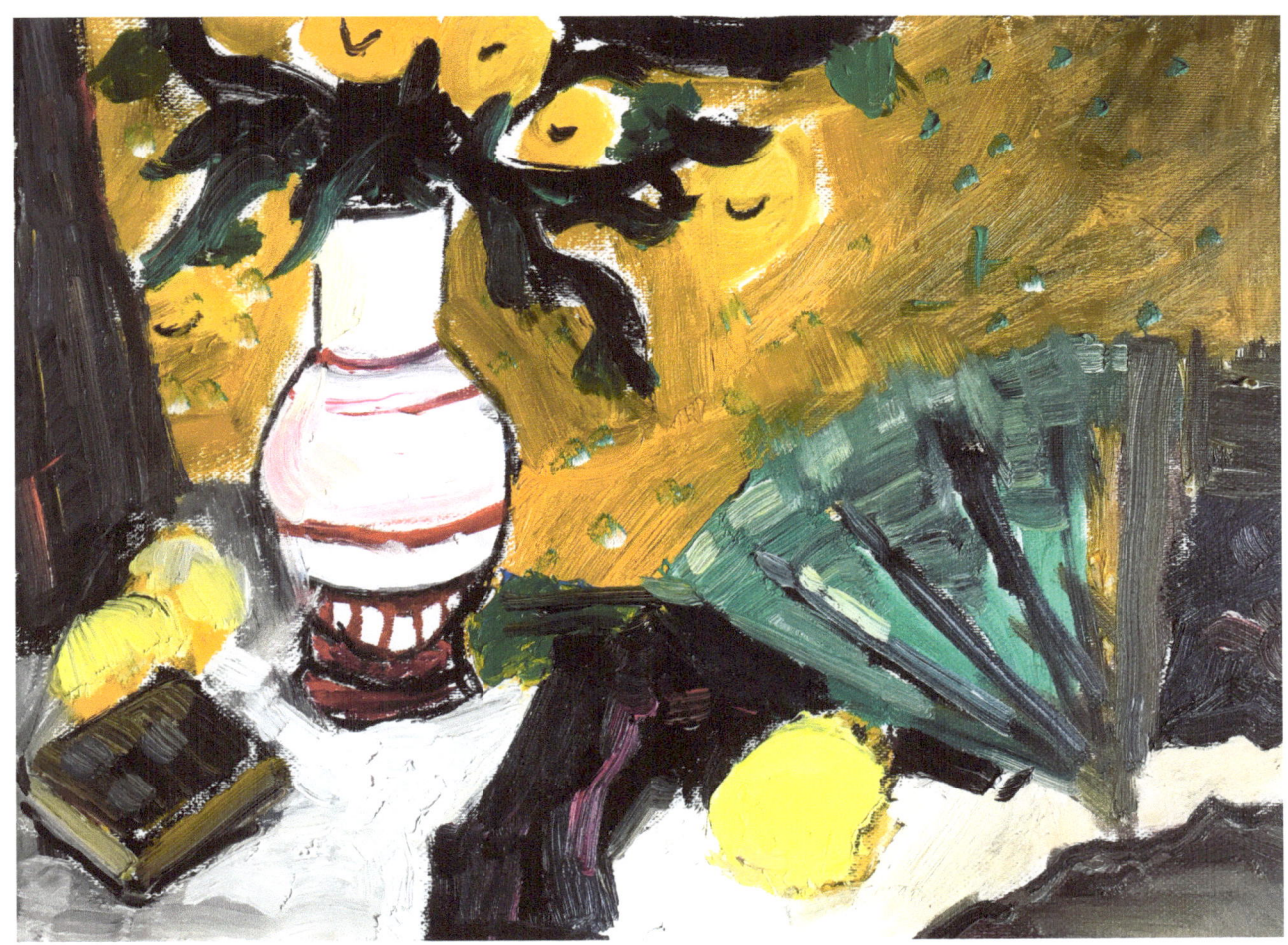

Still Life, oil on canvas, 2018

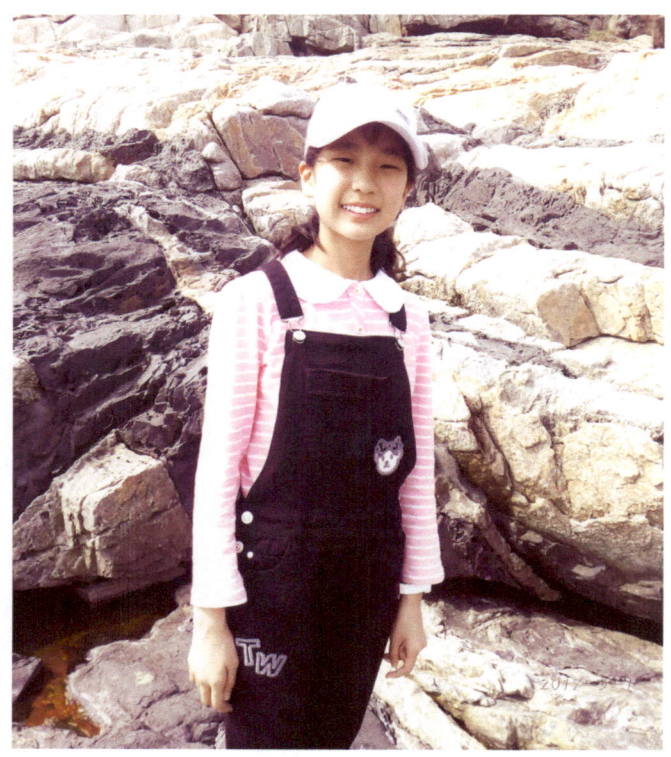

JIAJUN CHEN
Qingdao No.17 High School, China

Bronze Award for Art, 2nd Liberty Awards, International Society of Young Artists, 2019
Rising Star Award, 1st Liberty Awards, International Society of Young Artists, 2018

JIAJUN CHEN

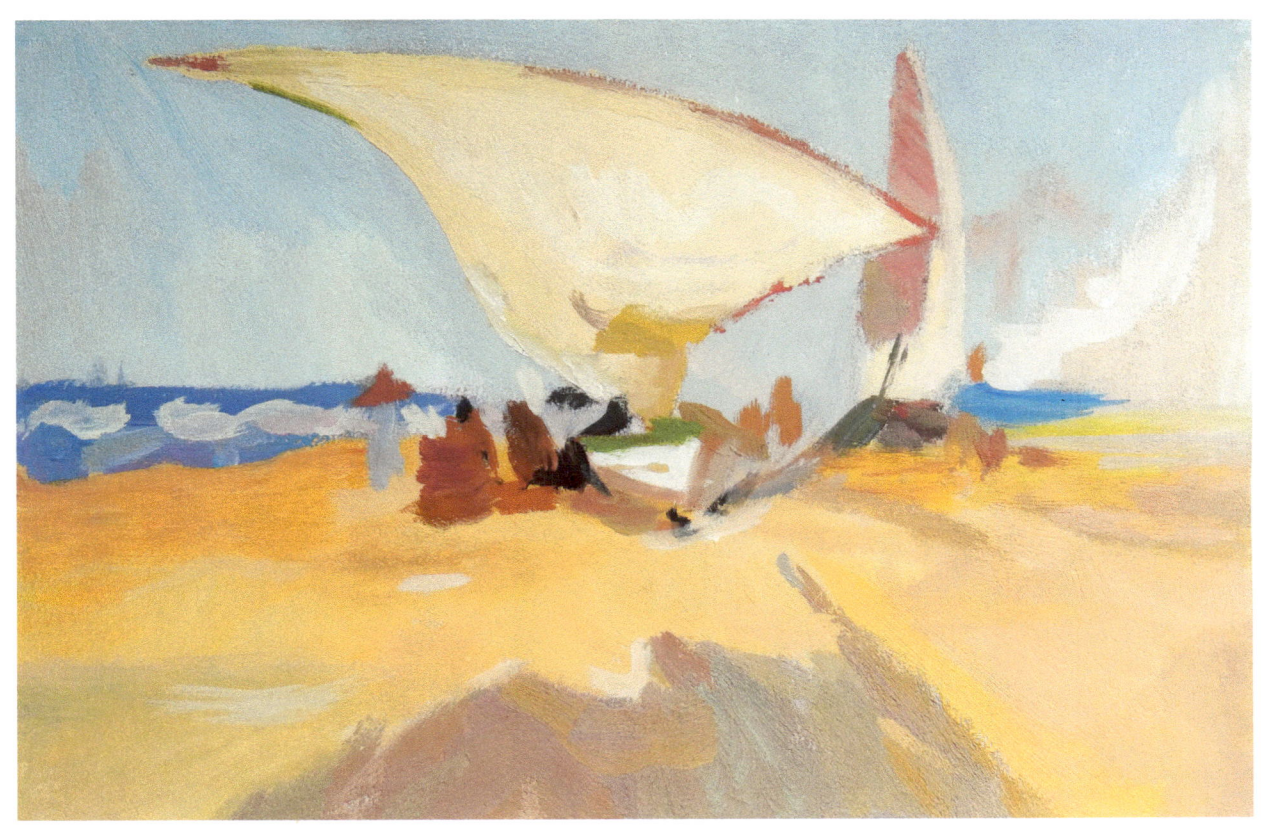

Beach, gouache on paper, 2019

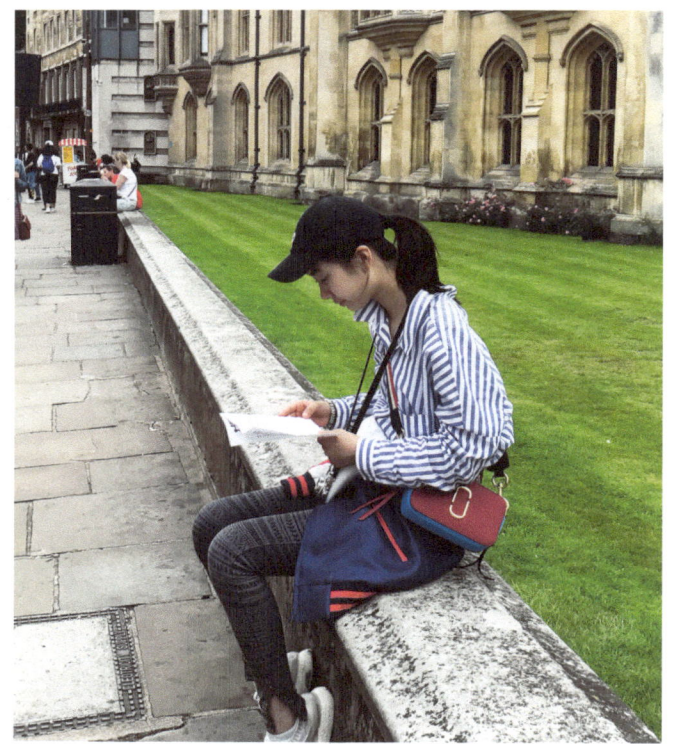

JIAJUN DENG
Qingdao No.17 High School, China

Silver Award for Art, 2nd Liberty Awards, International Society of Young Artists, 2019
Gold Award for Art, 1st Liberty Awards, International Society of Young Artists, 2018
Gold Award, "The Colorful Peace" Art Project Honoring the 100th Anniversary of the WWI Armistice, International Society of Young Artists, 2018

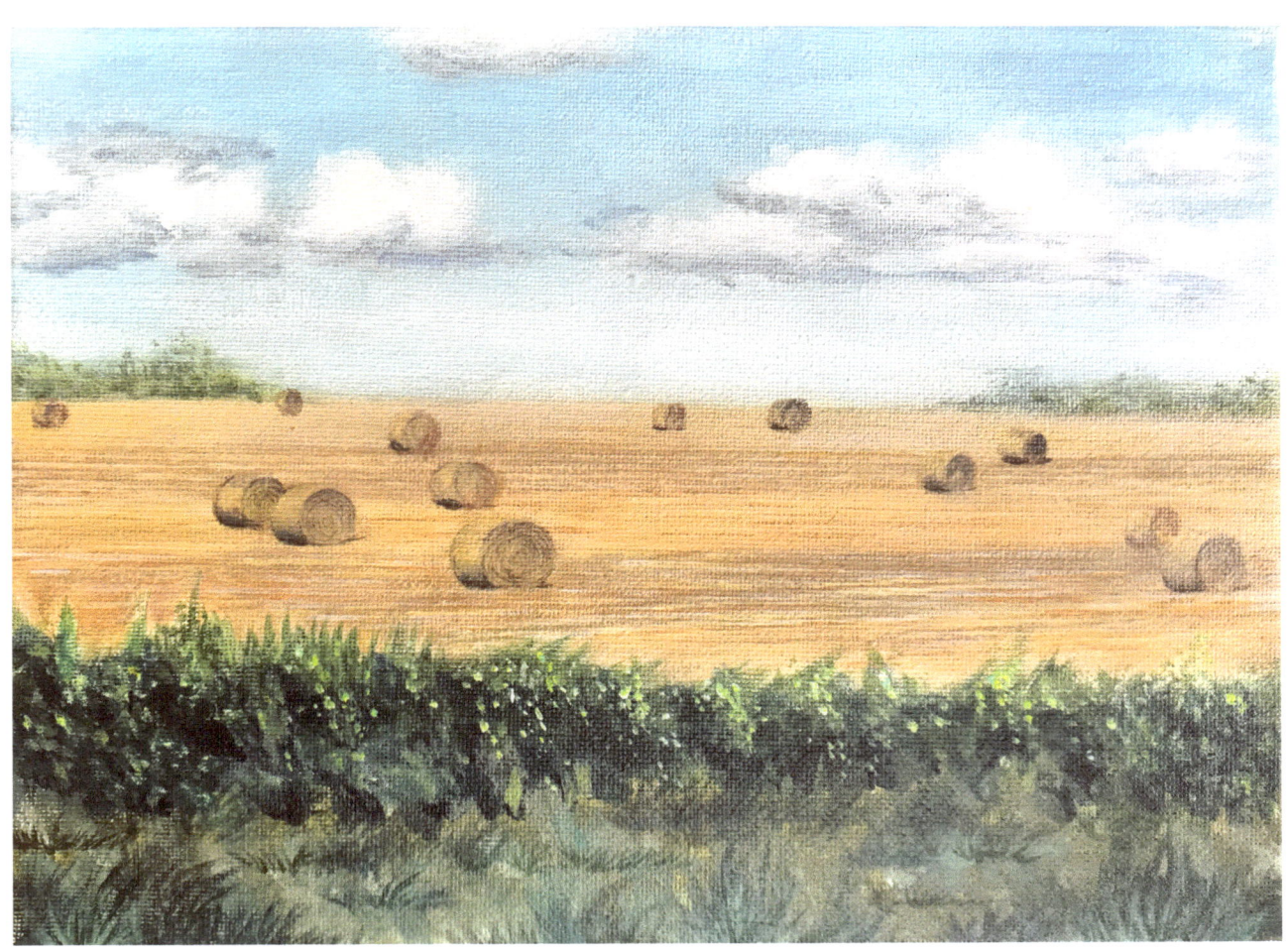

Amesbury, acrylic on canvas, 2018

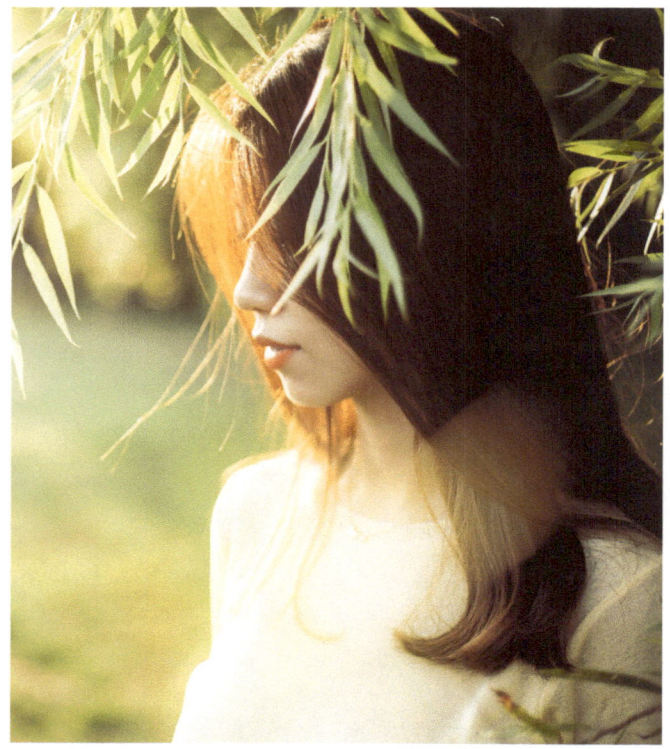

JIAXIN LENG
Fashion Designer in Jane Express, China

Gold Award for Art, 2nd Liberty Awards, International Society of Young Artists, 2019
Gold Award for Art, 1st Liberty Awards, International Society of Young Artists, 2018

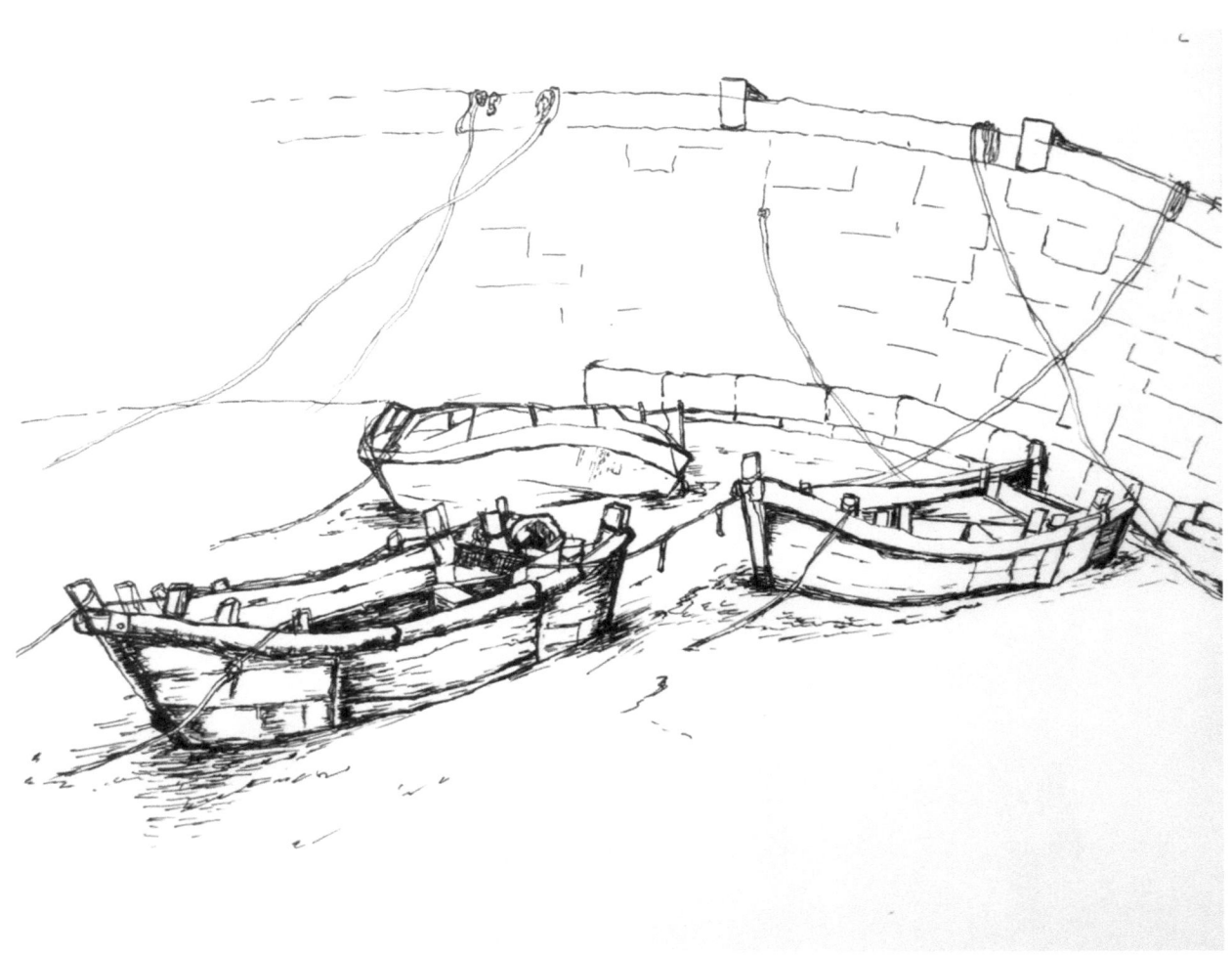

Tied In, pencil on paper, 2014

JIAXIN LENG

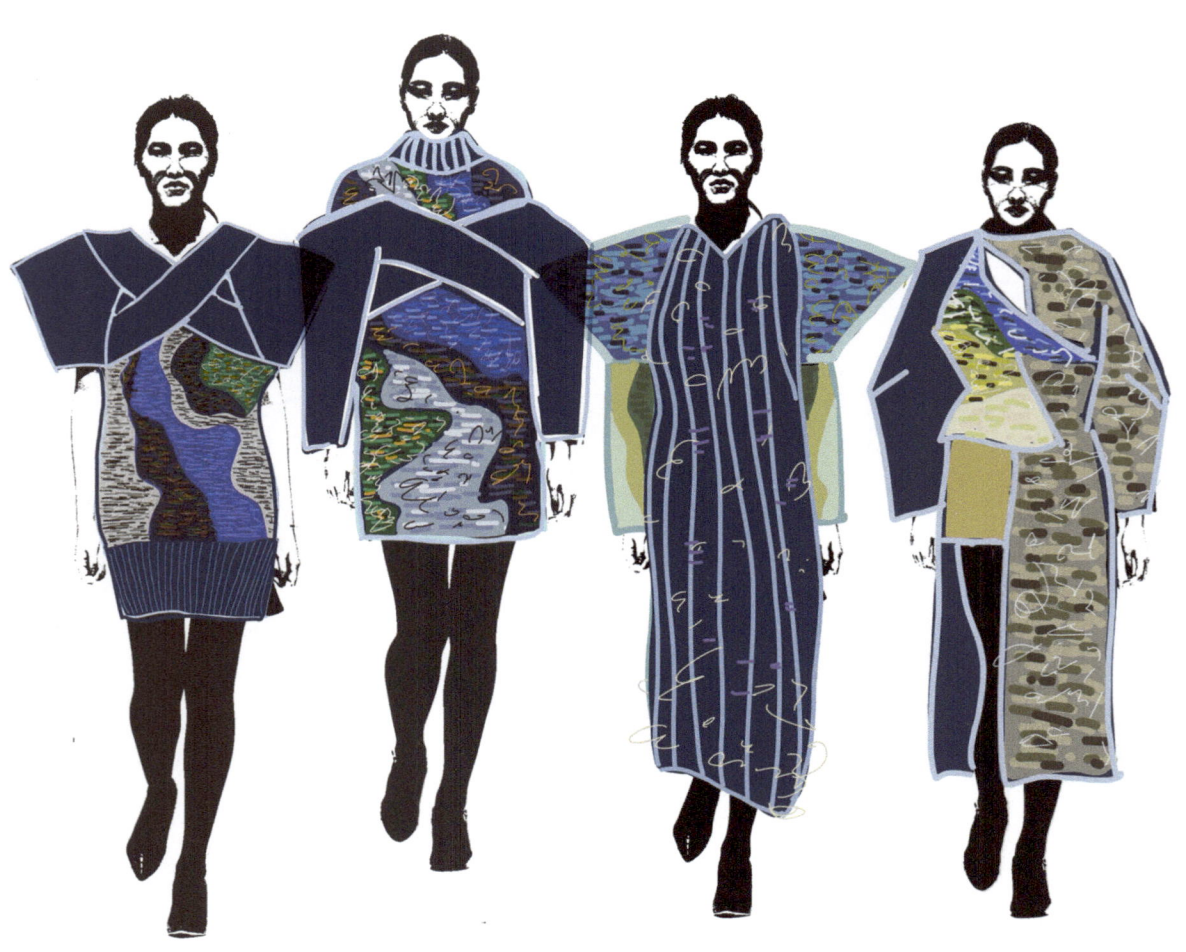

Costume Design, digital, 2018

INTRODUCTION

The production is adopted the unique craft of the Korean paper, to present the dimensional effect by layers of overlapping, and reflect ombre effect of the fire by color rendering.

The fire is made of wool fiber, which is integrated with the Korean paper. Moths are made of both the Korean paper and wool fiber. The Korean paper is unprocessed and only adopted cutting in workmanship. The wool fiber is used to shape the bodies of moths.

By utilizing two kinds of material to work in concert with each other, the whole piece of production reflects the harmony between fire and moths.

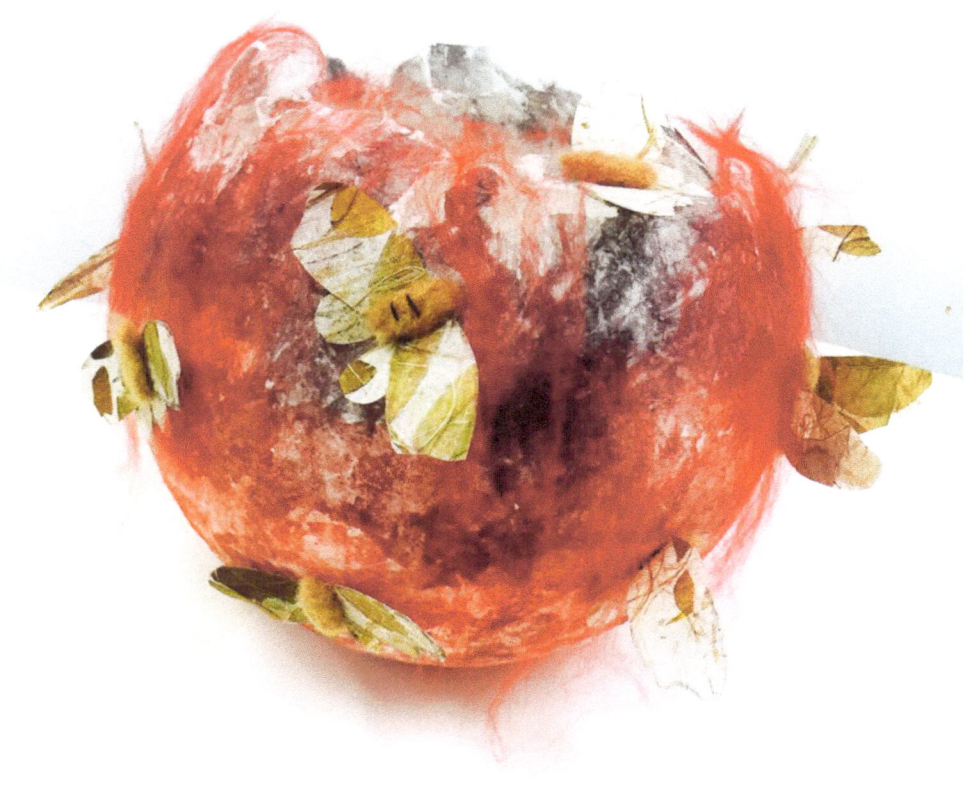

Fire and Moths, synthesized material, 2018

JIAXIN LENG

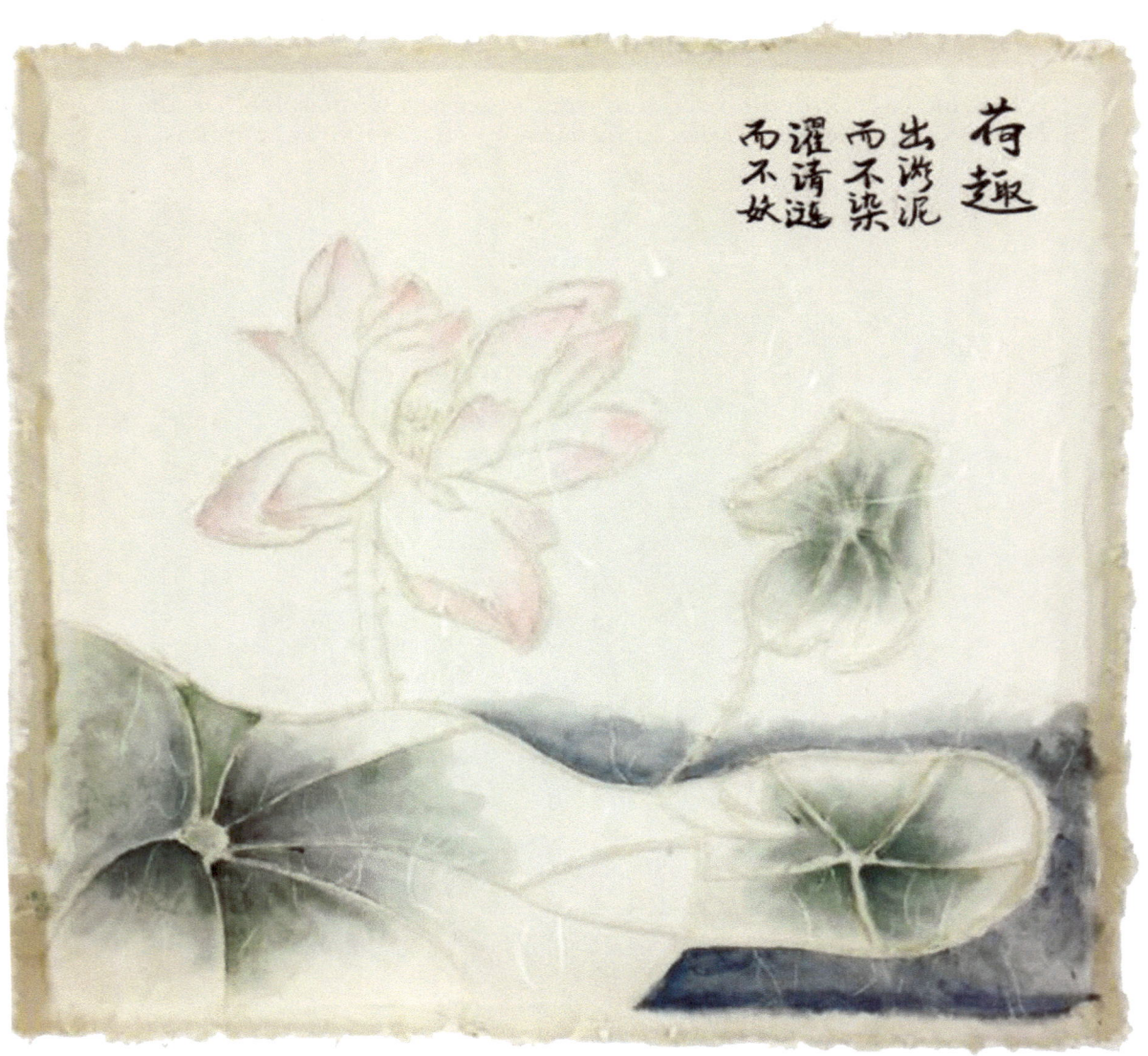

Lotus, dyestuffs on Korean paper, 2018

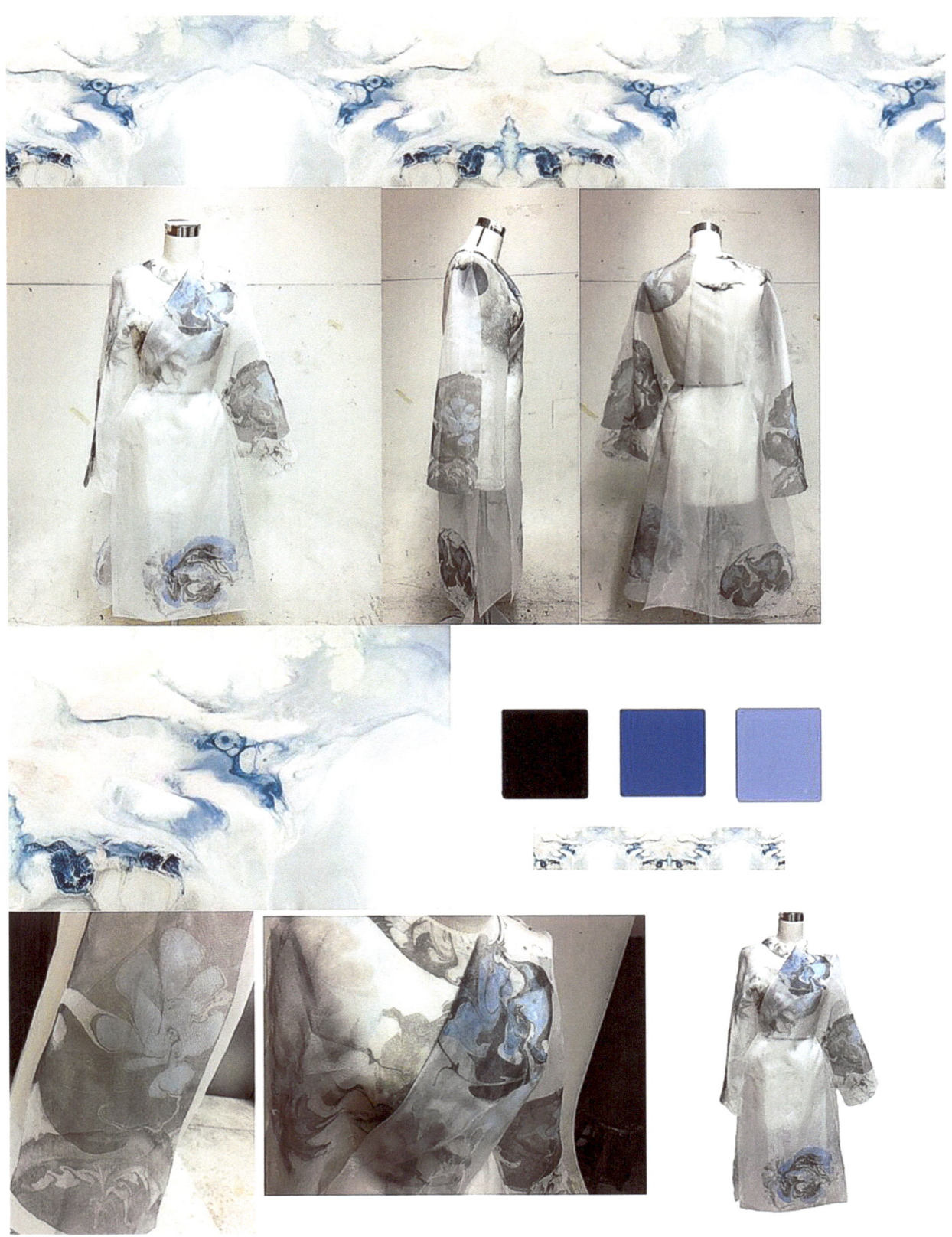

Costume Design, dyestuffs on silk, 2018

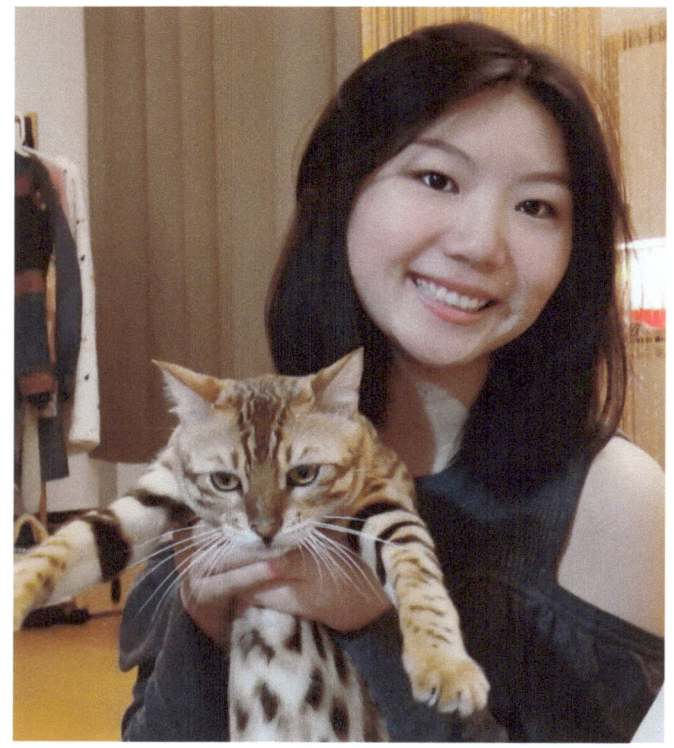

JIA ZHONG
School of Visual Arts, USA

Gold Award for Art, 2nd Liberty Awards, International Society of Young Artists, 2019
Gold Award for Art, 1st Liberty Awards, International Society of Young Artists, 2018
3rd Prize, 10th "Earth Doctor" National Geographic Science and Technology Competition, the Geographical Society of China, 2016

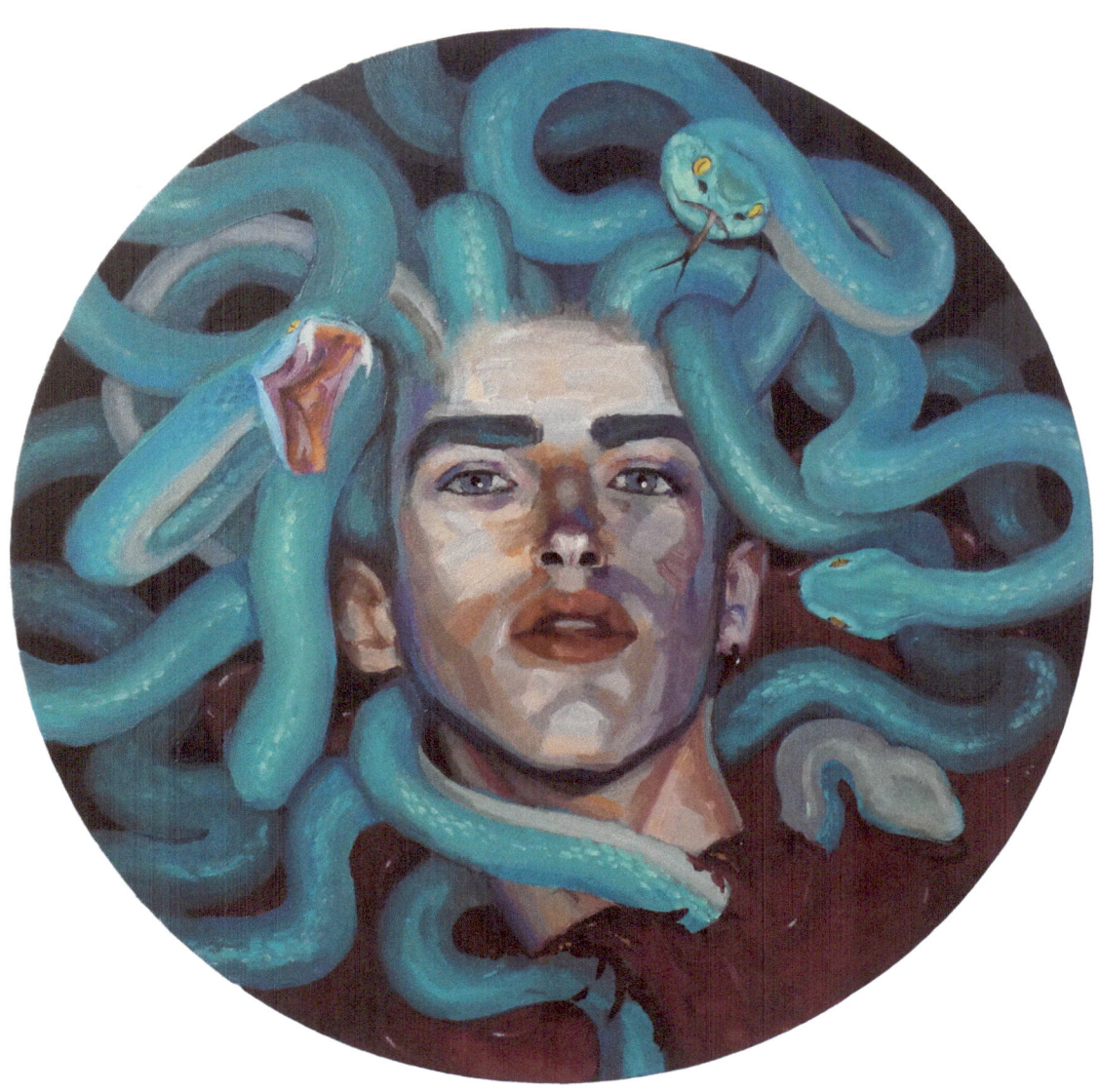

Medusa, oil on canvas, 2019

JIA ZHONG

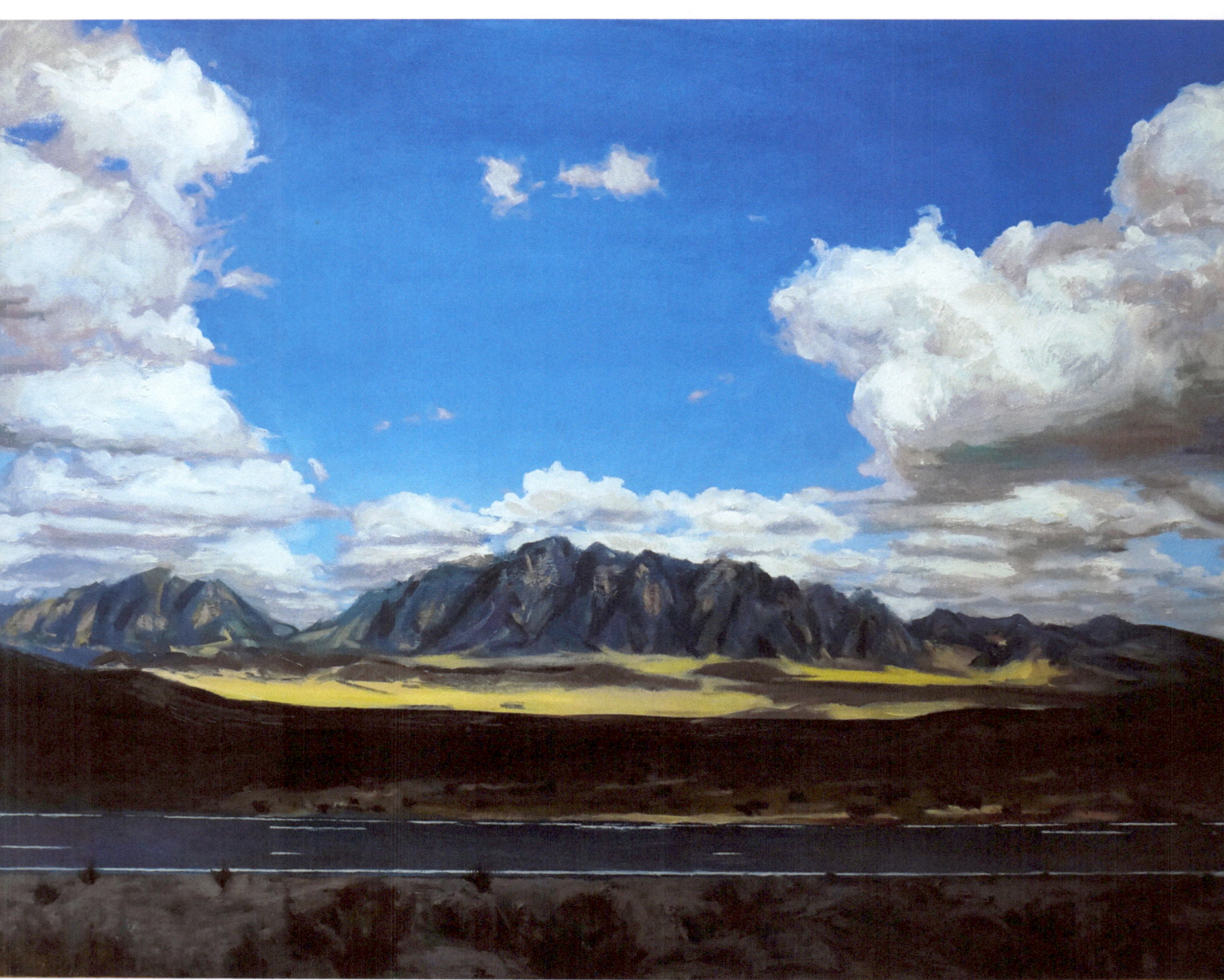

Haixi Mongol and Tibetan Autonomous Prefecture, oil on canvas, 2019

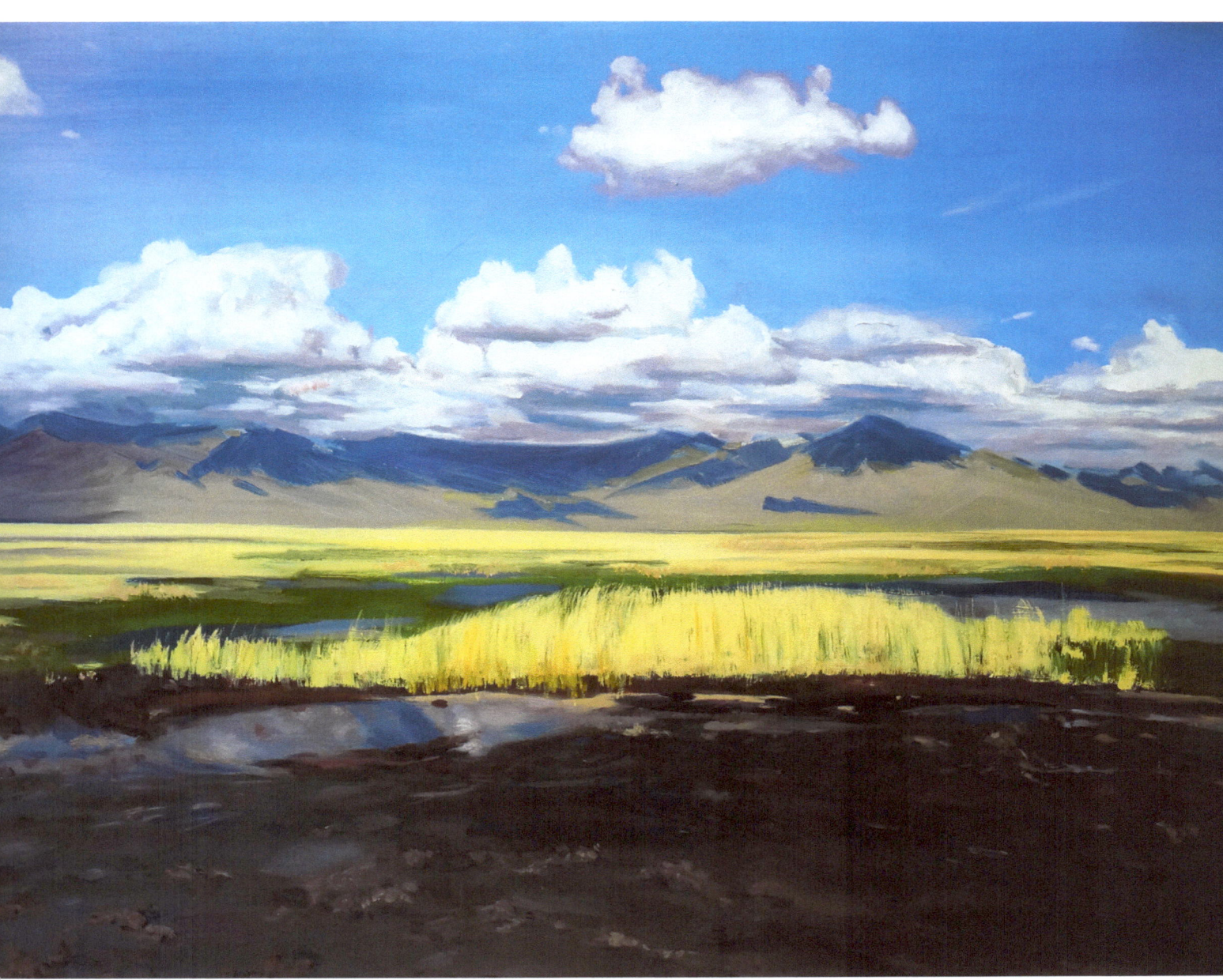

On the Way to Dachaidamu Lake, oil on canvas, 2019

JIA ZHONG

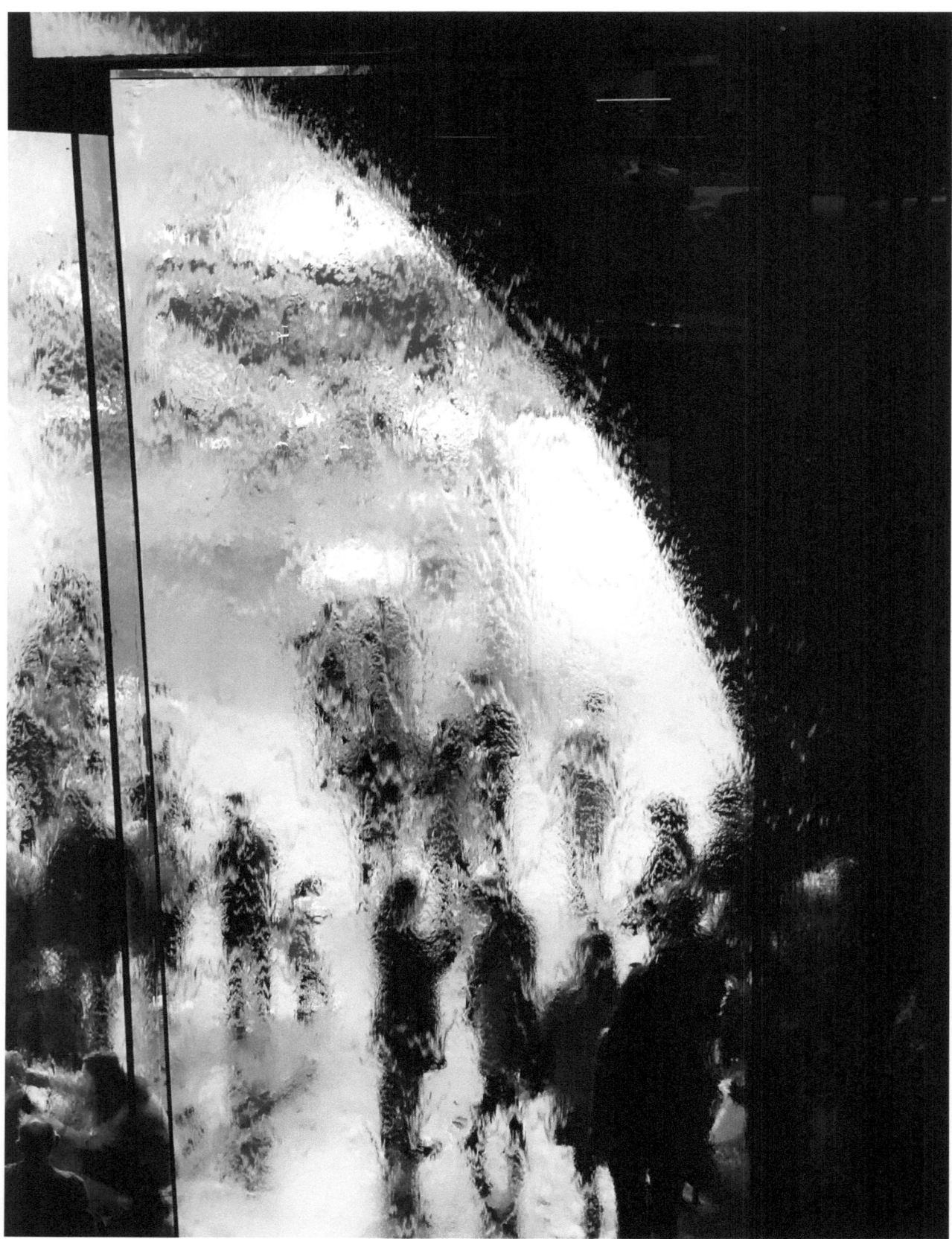

Trapped, photography, 2019

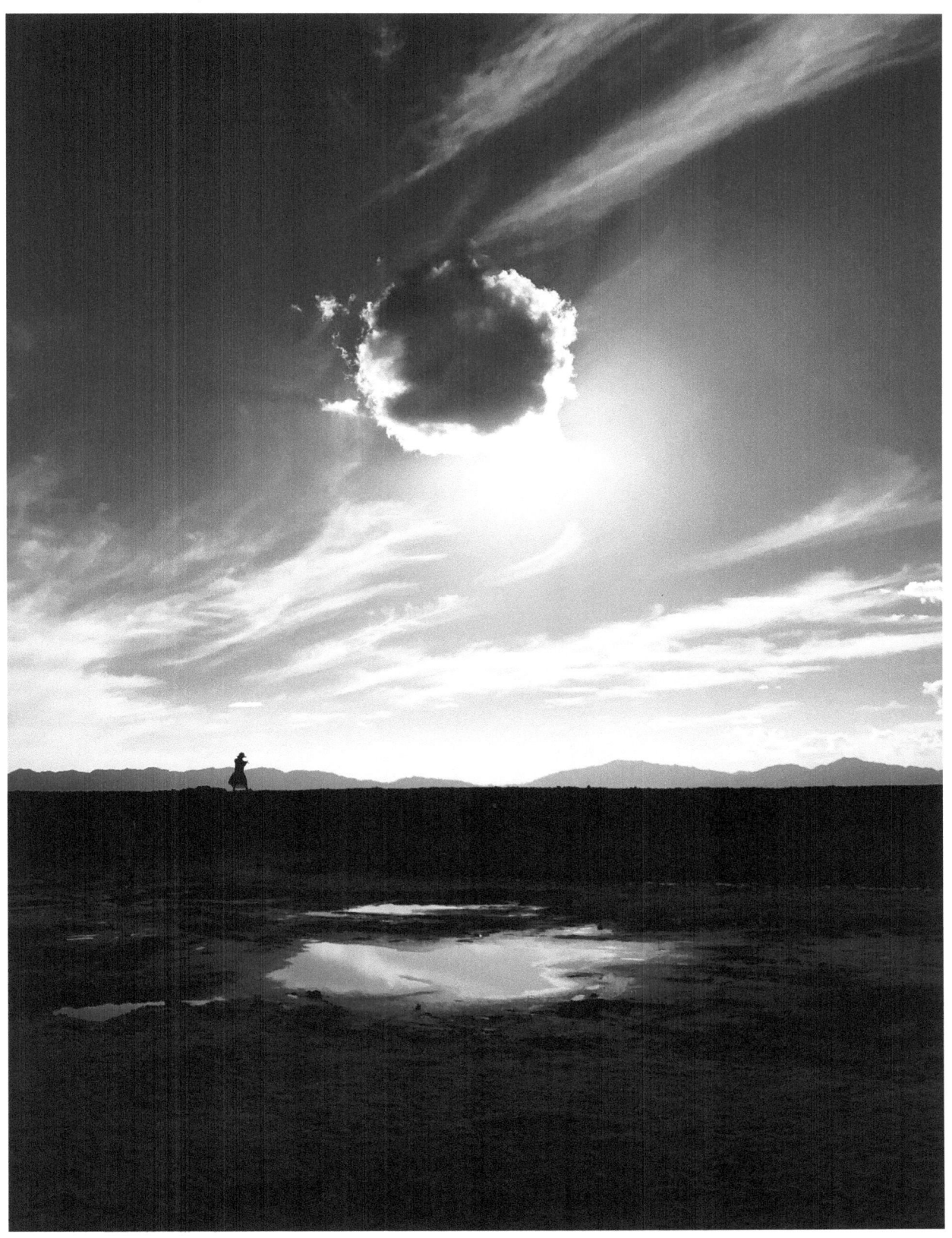

Metamorphosis, photography, 2018

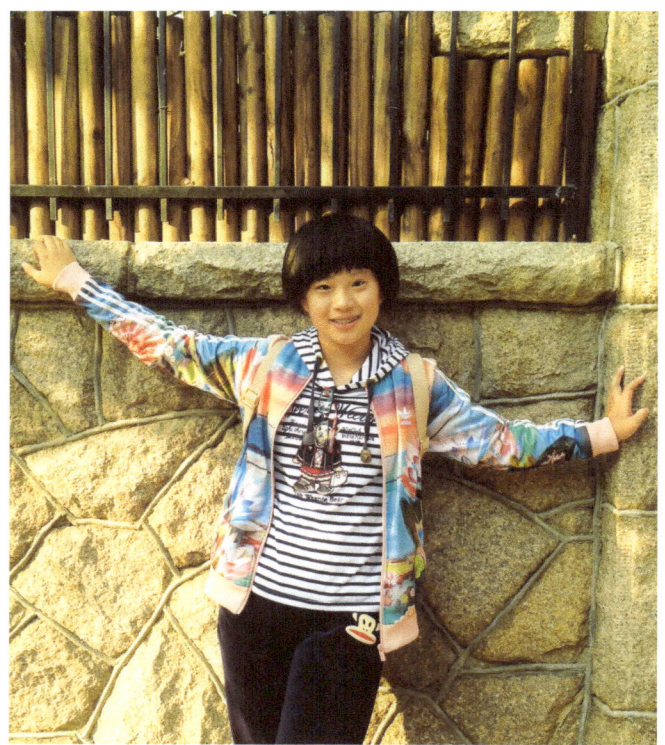

JINCHANG ZHANG
Qingdao Haishan School, China

Silver Award for Art, 2nd Liberty Awards, International Society of Young Artists, 2019
Silver Award for Art, 1st Liberty Awards, International Society of Young Artists, 2018

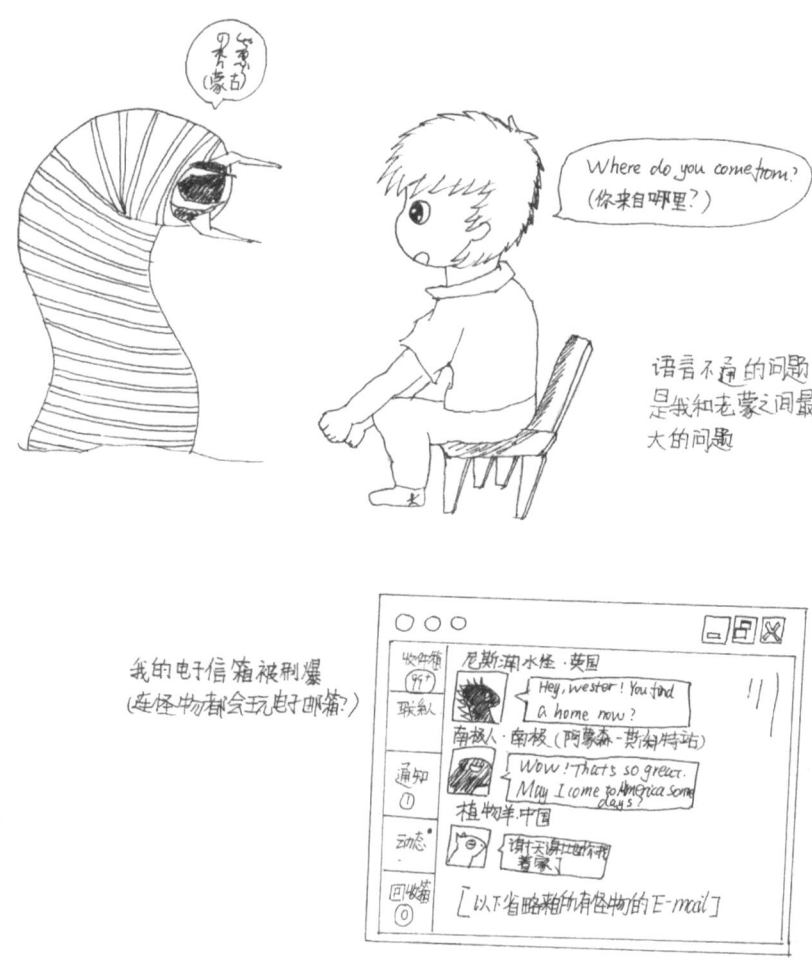

Comics Anthology *New Jersey Family*, page 9, pen on paper, 2017

JINCHANG ZHANG

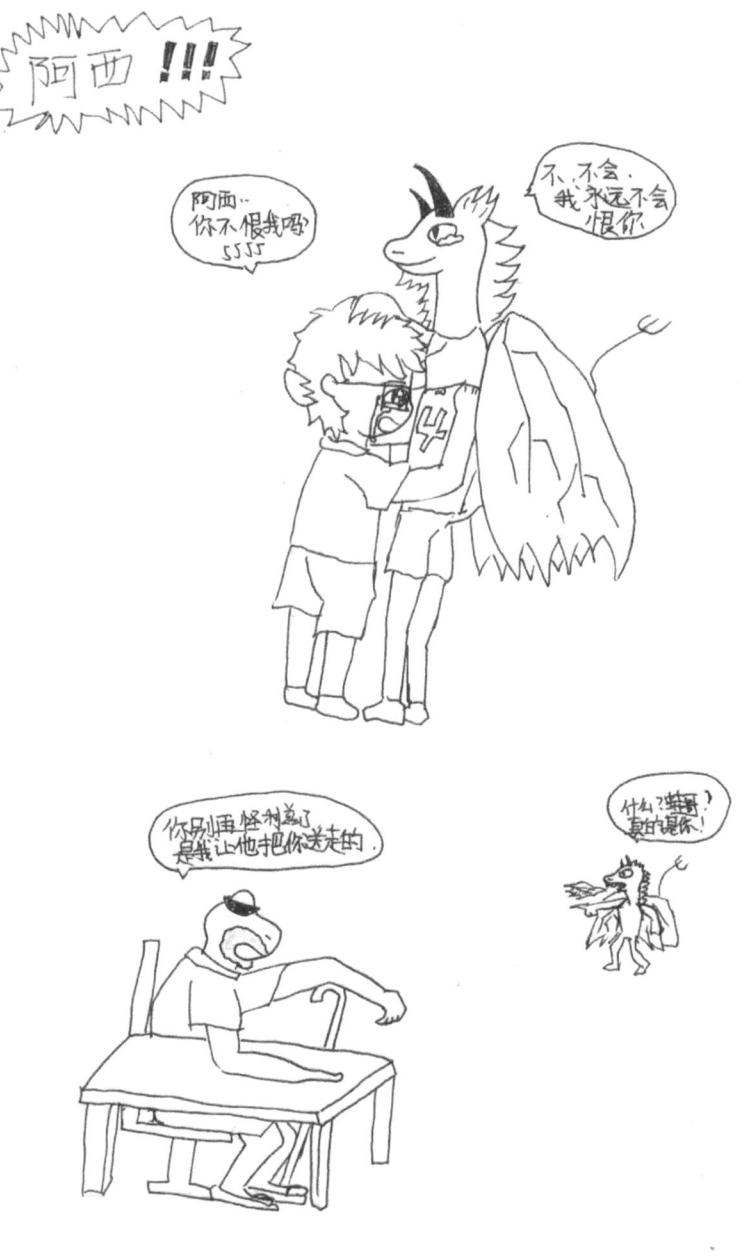

Comics Anthology *New Jersey Family*, page 24, pen on paper, 2017

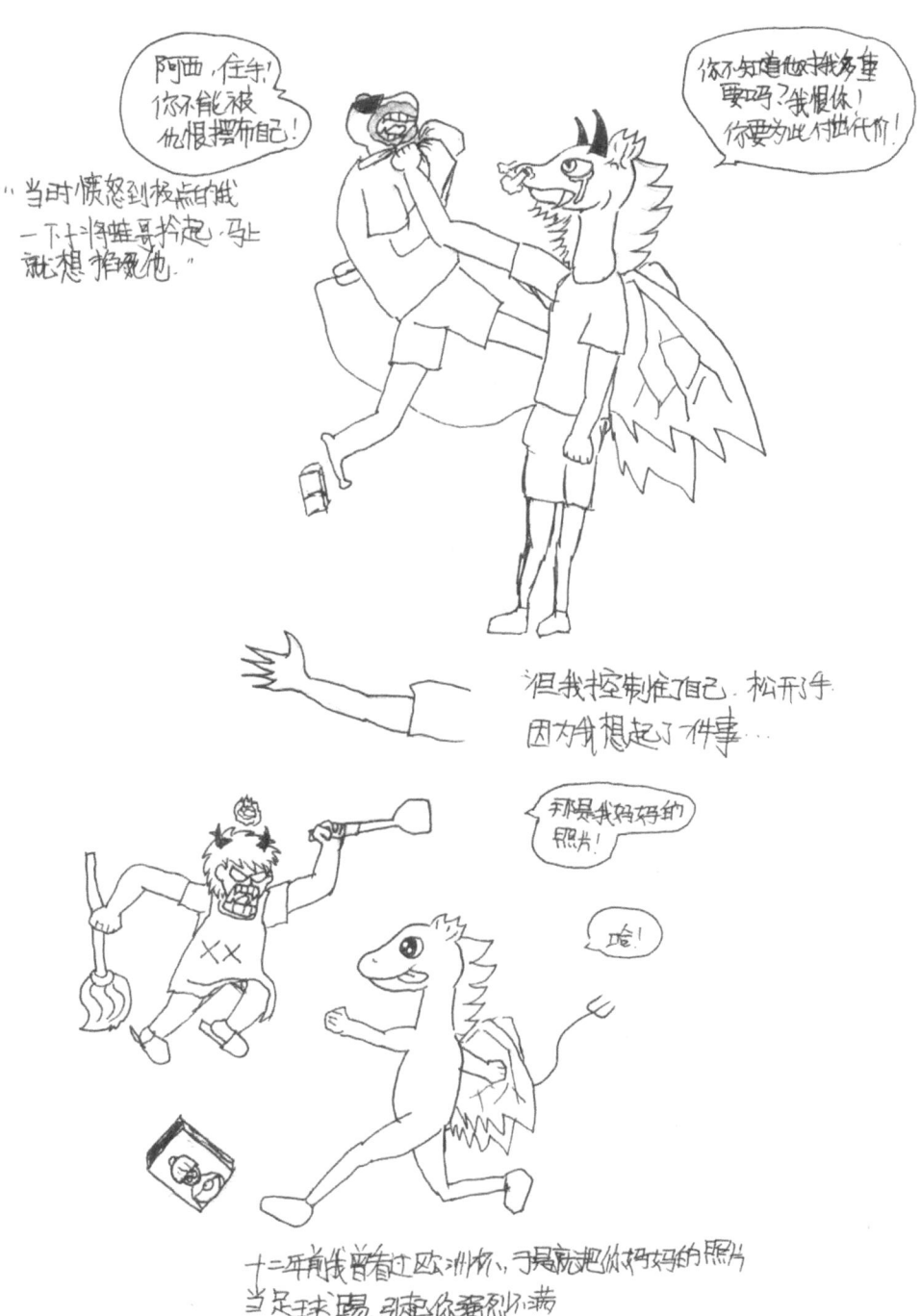

Comics Anthology *New Jersey Family*, page 25, pen on paper, 2017

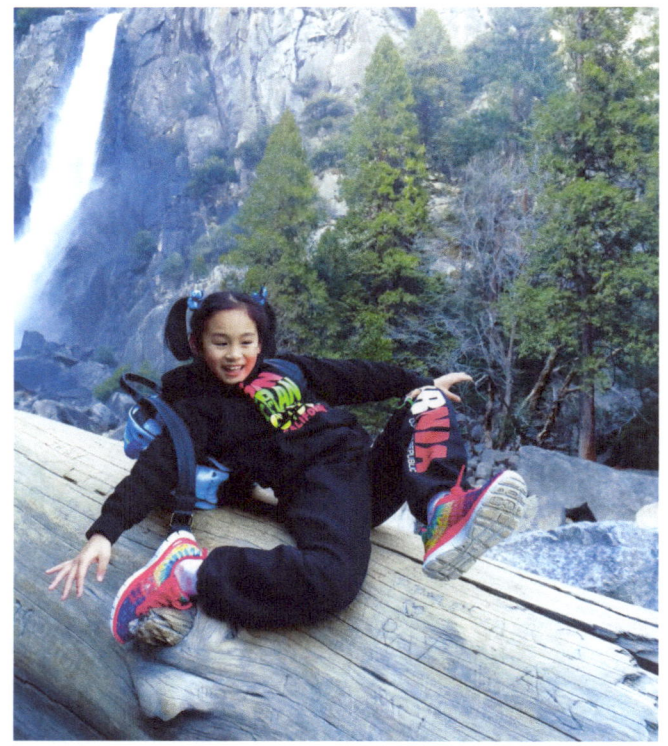

JINGHAN XU
Robert O. Townsend Junior High, USA

Silver Award for Art, 2nd Liberty Awards, International Society of Young Artists, 2019
Rising Star Award, 1st Liberty Awards, International Society of Young Artists, 2018

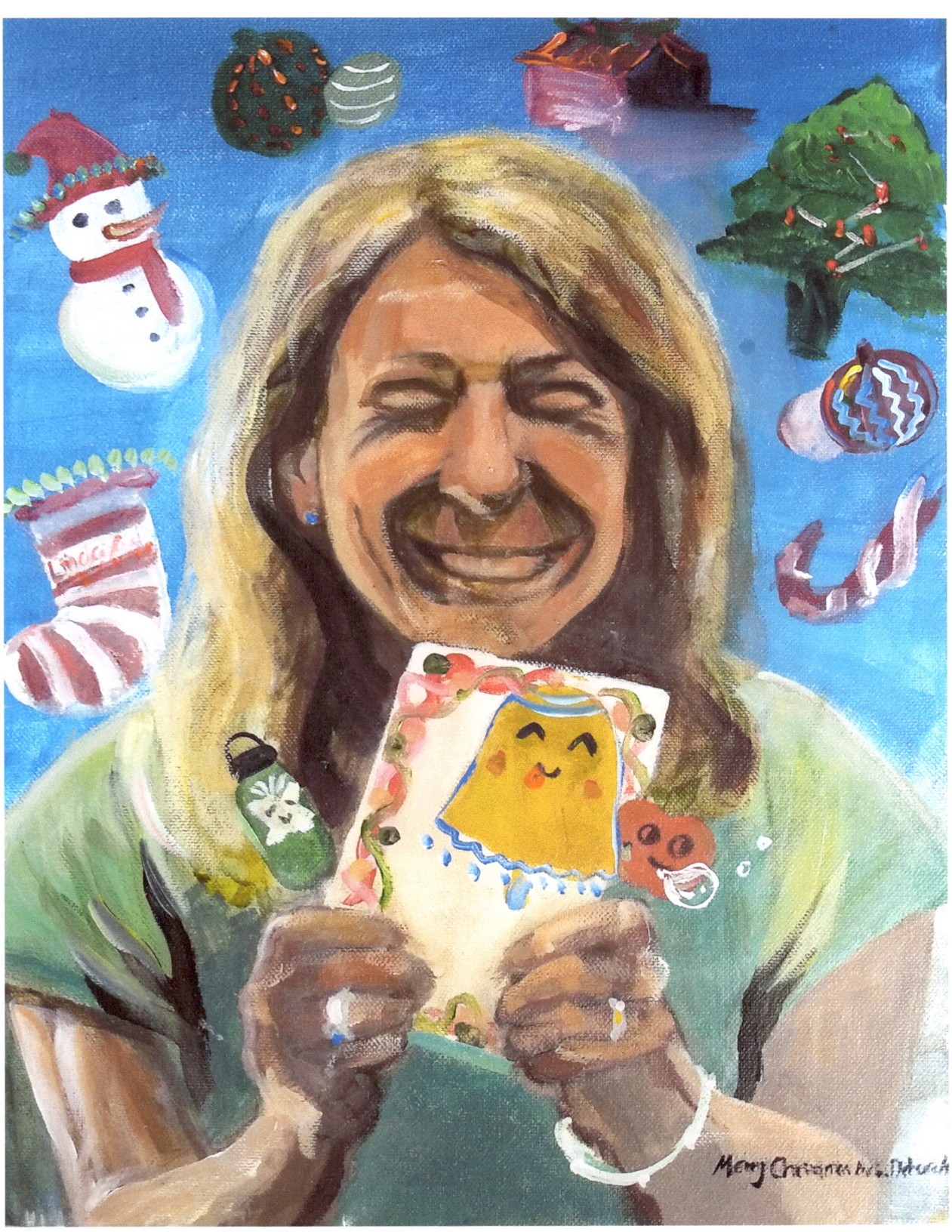

Merry Christmas, Mrs. Deborah, acrylic on canvas, 2019

JINGHAN XU

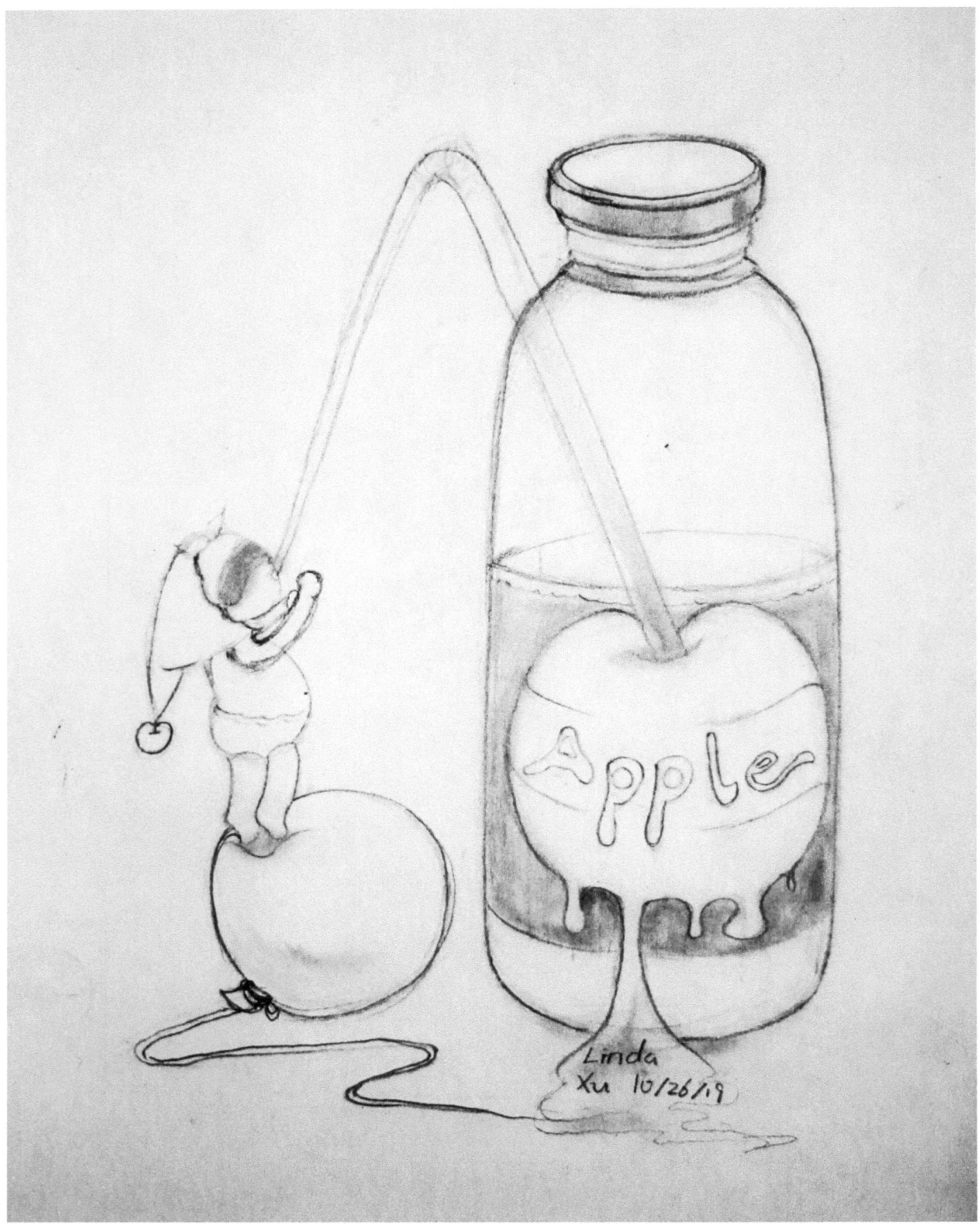

Drink, pencil on paper, 2019

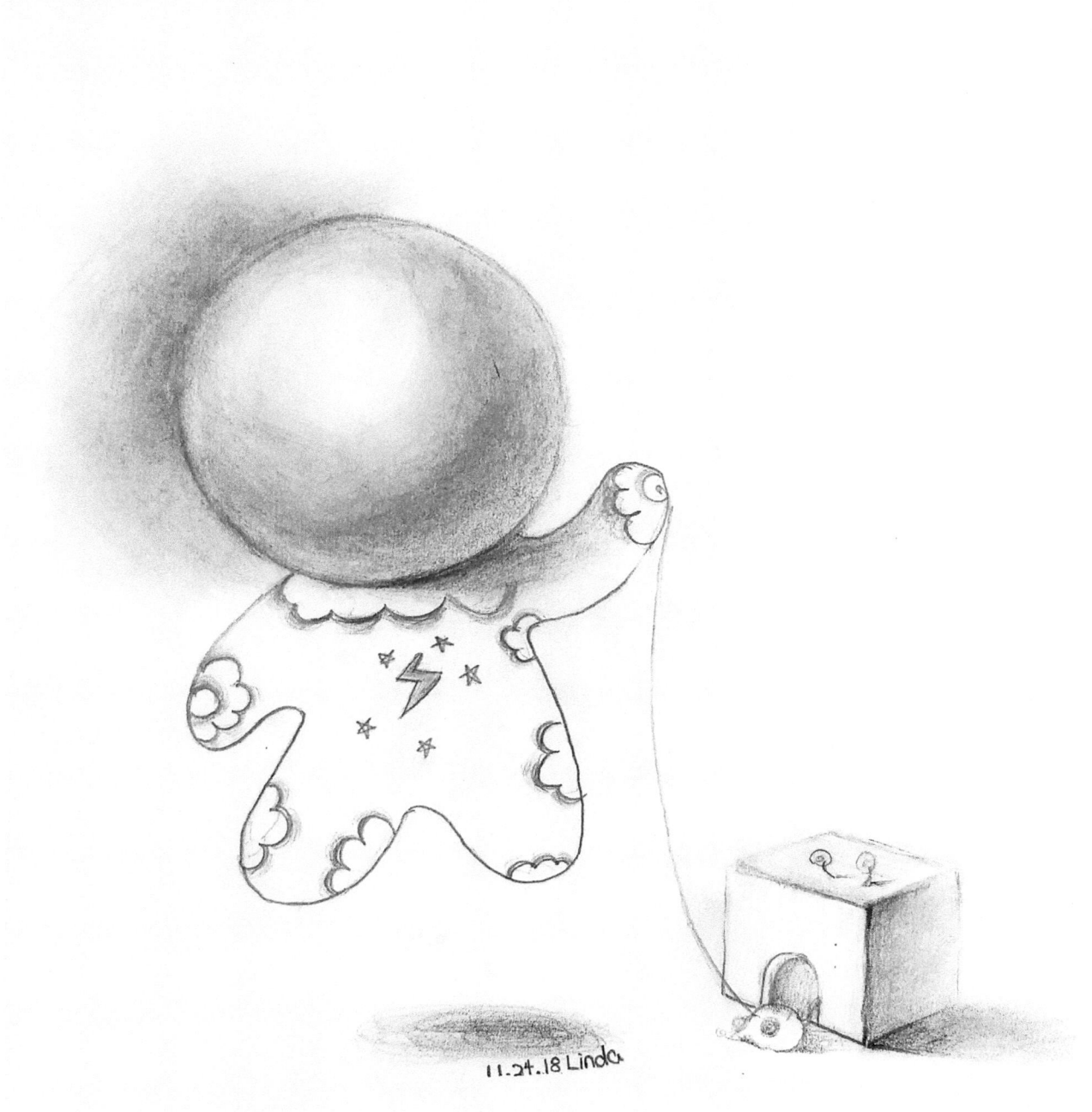

The Toy of a Toy, pencil on paper, 2018

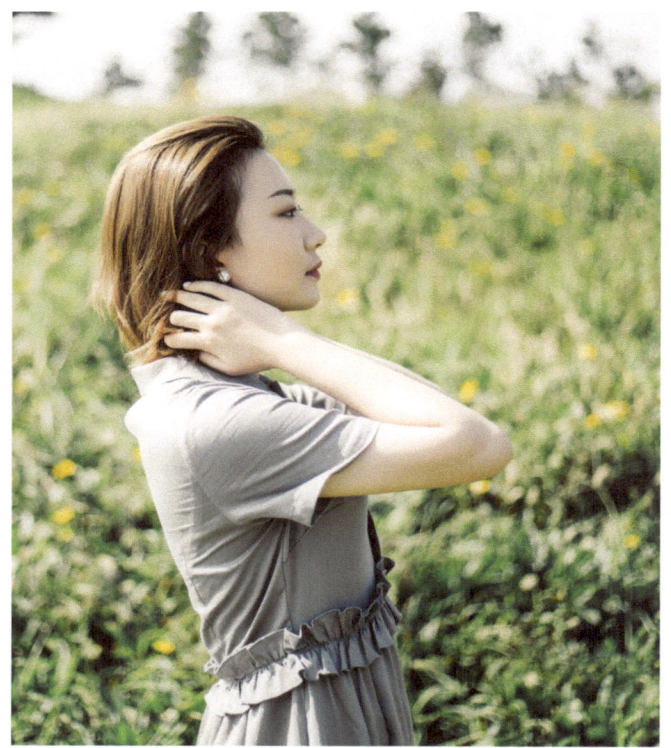

JINGLIN GUO

Gold Award for Art, 2nd Liberty Awards, International Society of Young Artists, 2019
Silver Award for Art, 1st Liberty Awards, International Society of Young Artists, 2018

JINGLIN GUO

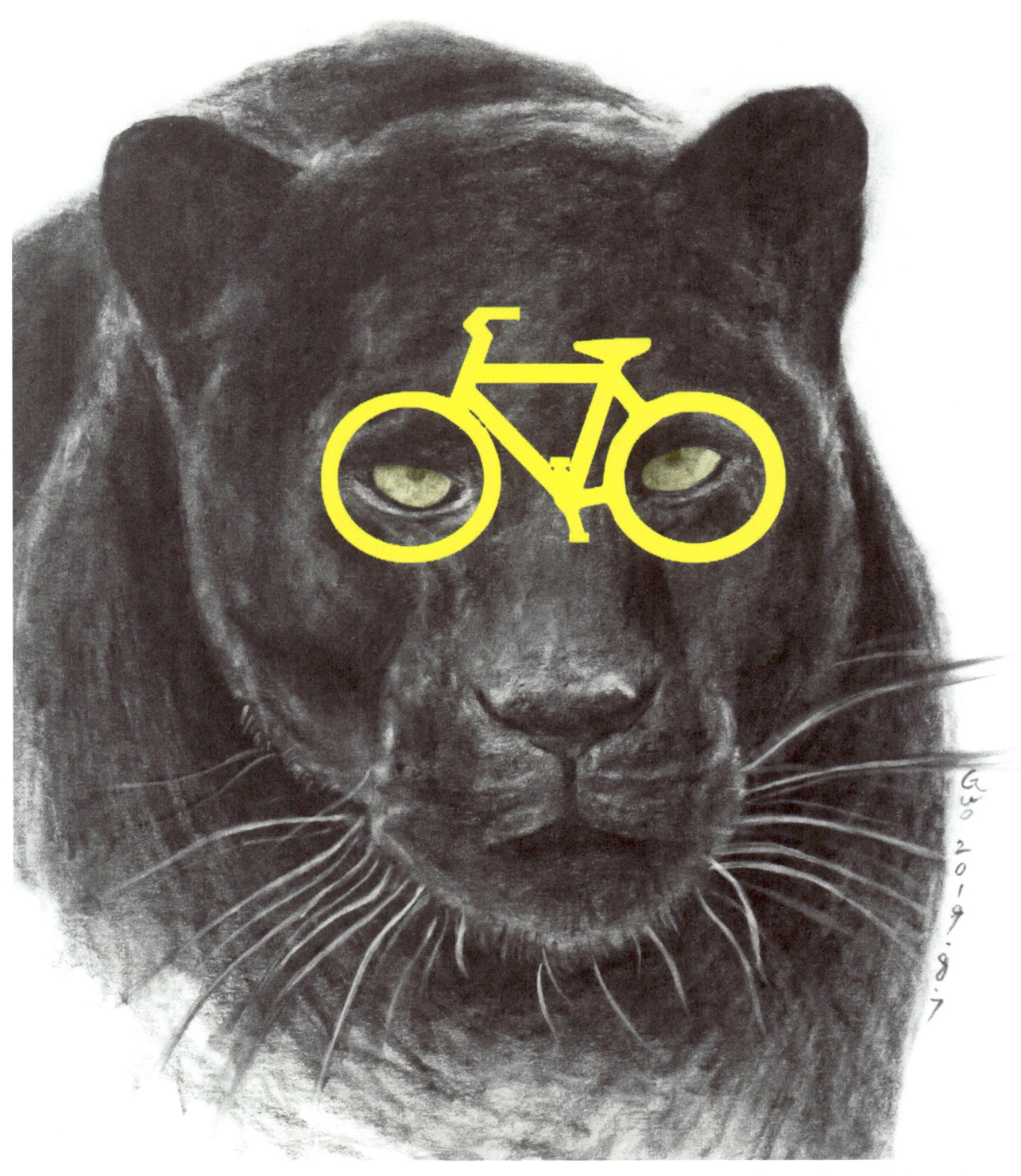

Runner, pencil, acrylic and digital, 2019

JINGLIN GUO

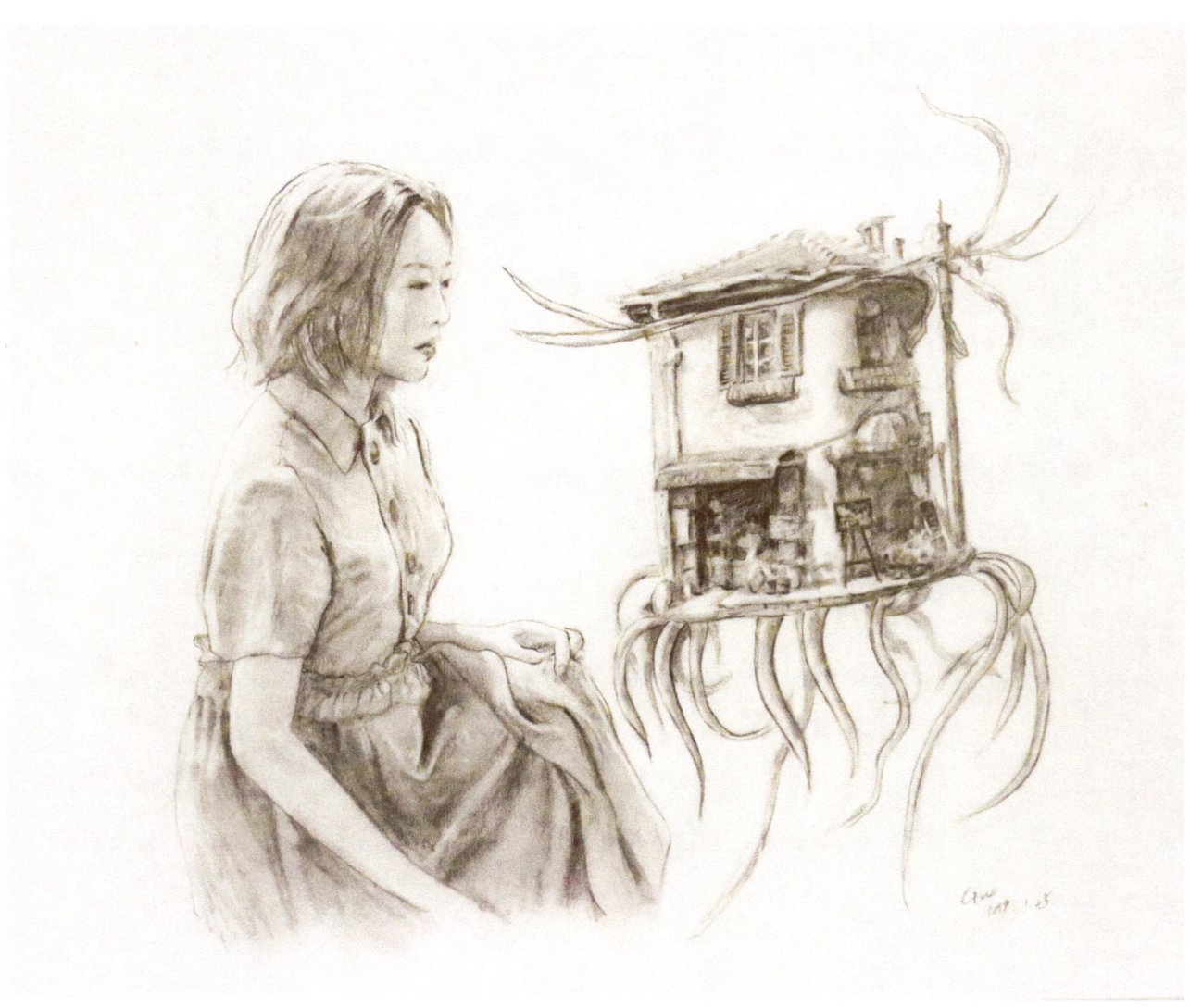

Maiden and House, pencil on paper, 2019

JINGLIN GUO

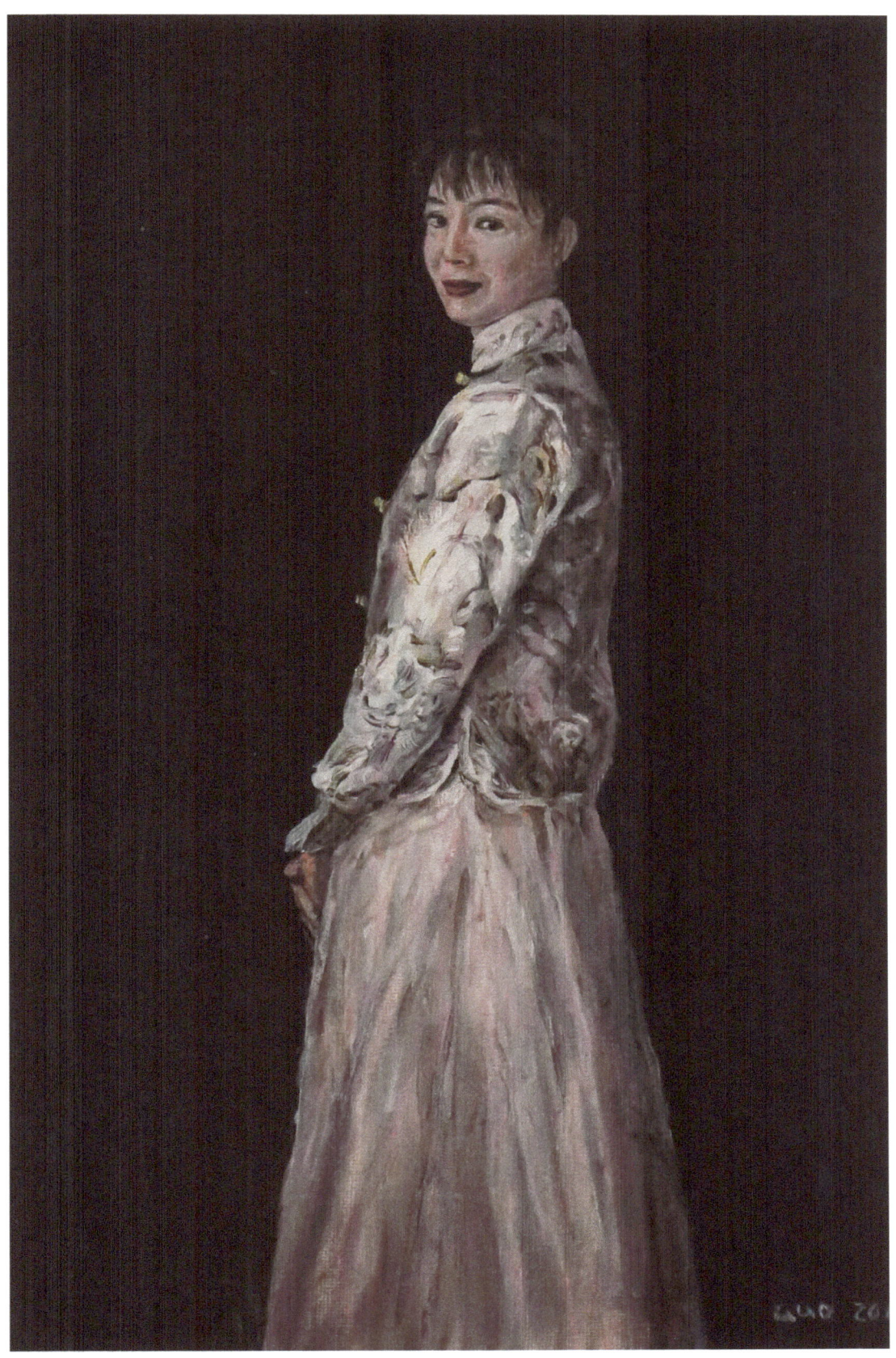

My Mother, oil on canvas, 2019

JINGLIN GUO

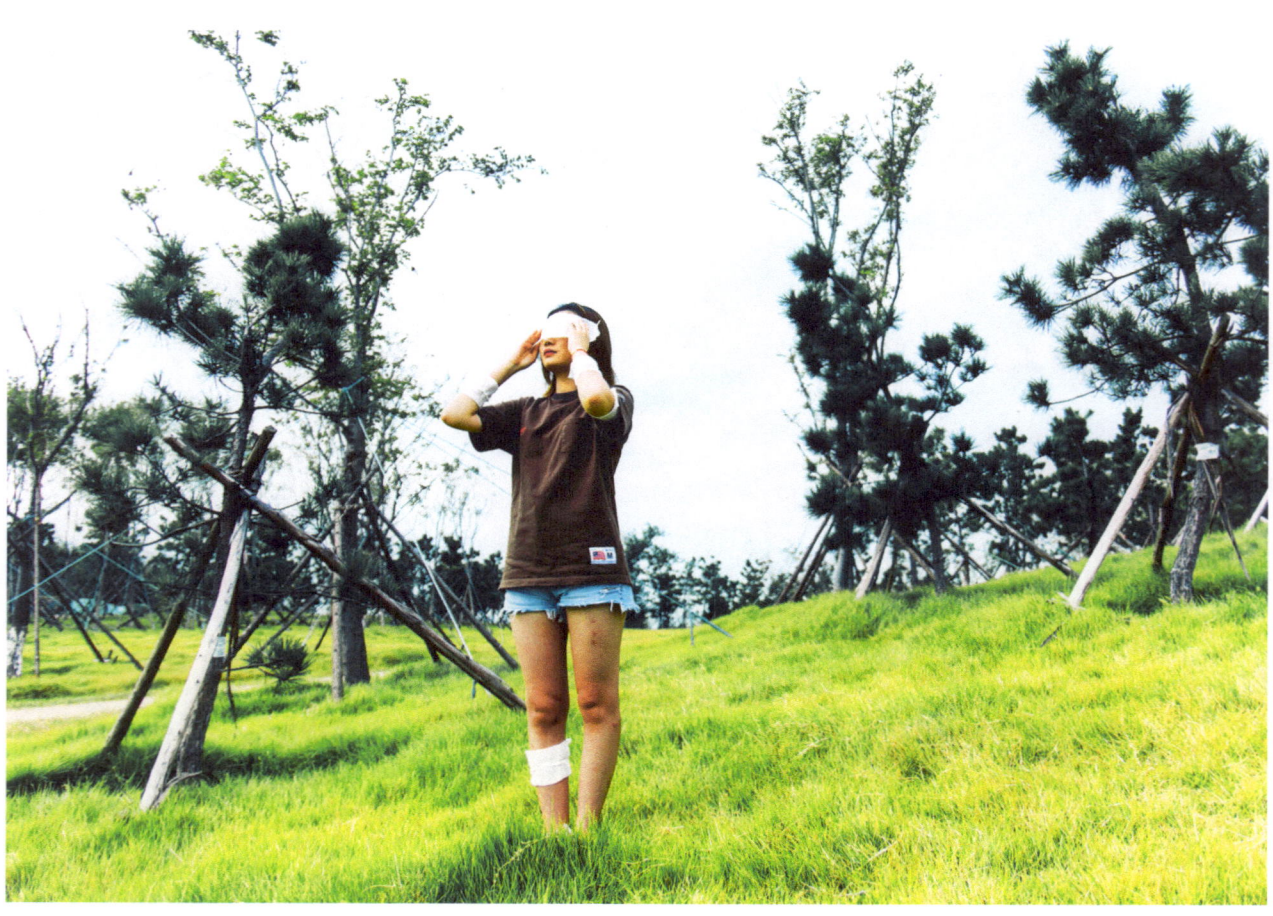

Wounded Tree——for the United Nations International Year of Plant Health 2020
Performance art, 2019

JINGLIN GUO

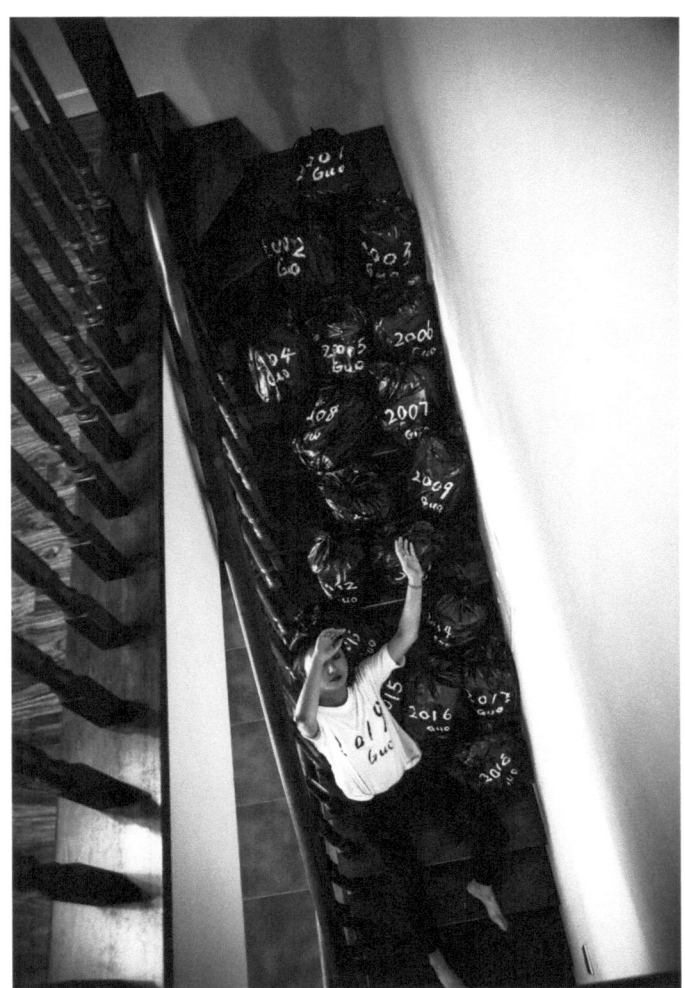

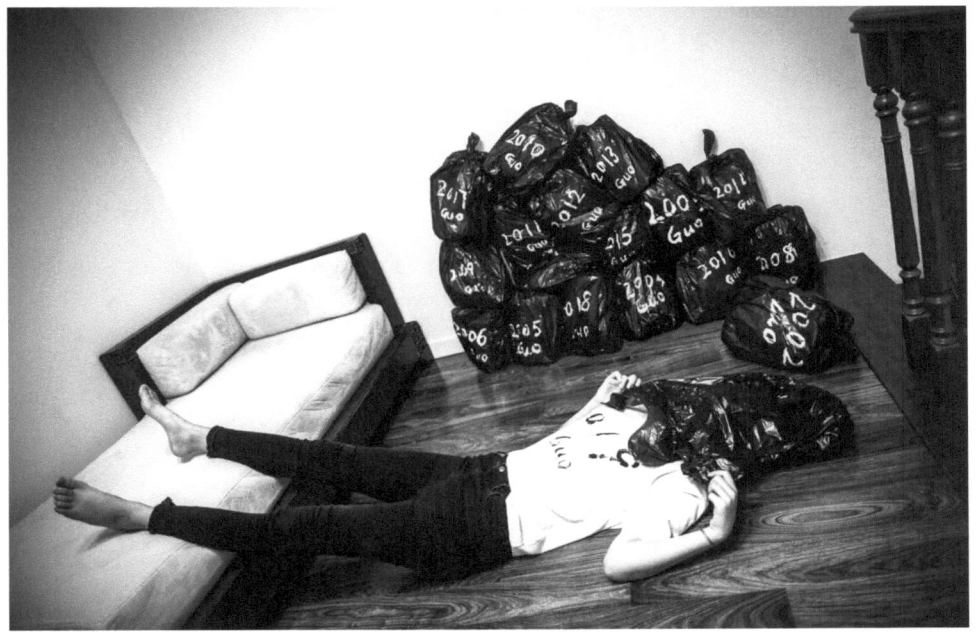

The Past Time, installation and performance art, 2019

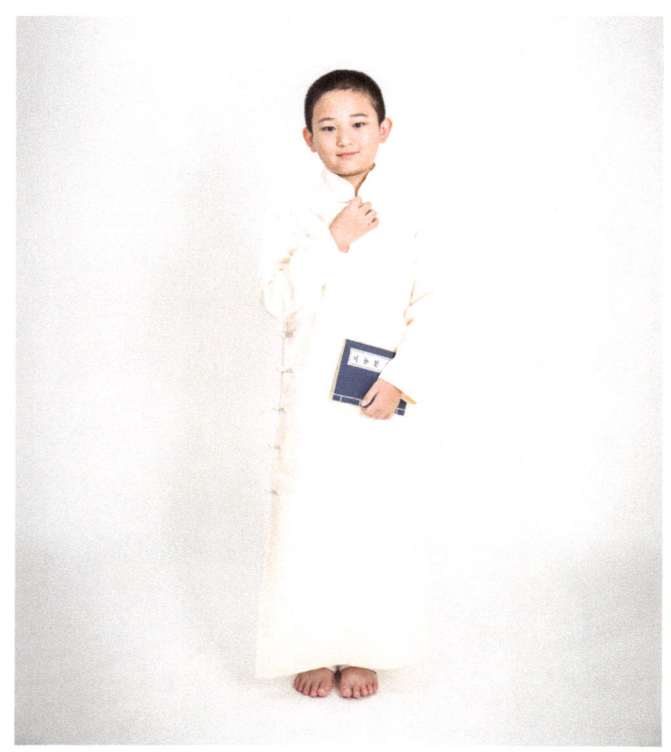

JINGXUAN YU
Qingdao No.2 Experiment Junior High School, China

Rising Star Award, 2nd Liberty Awards, International Society of Young Artists, 2019
Rising Star Award, 1st Liberty Awards, International Society of Young Artists, 2018

JINGXUAN YU

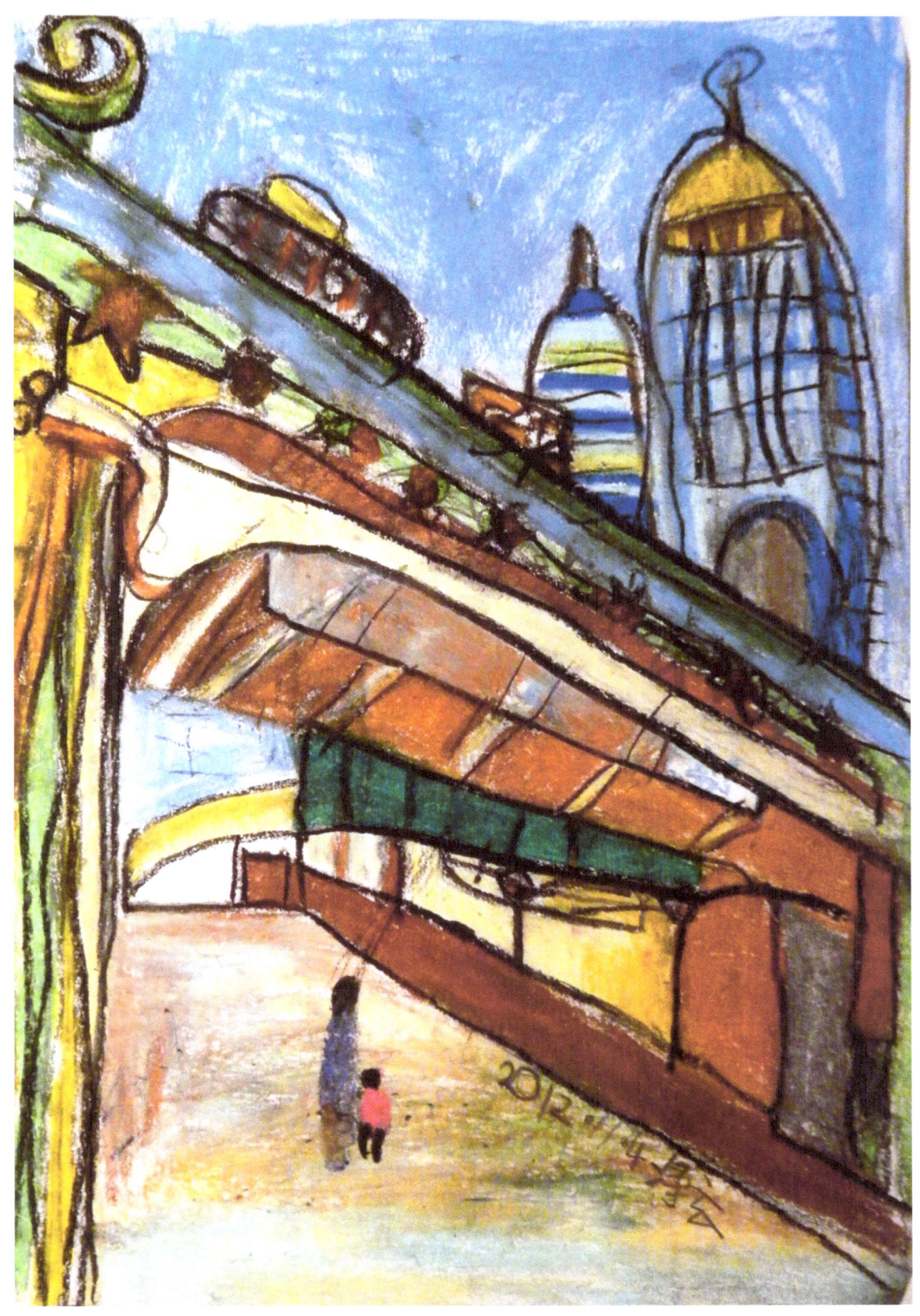

Flyover, oil pastel on paper, 2012

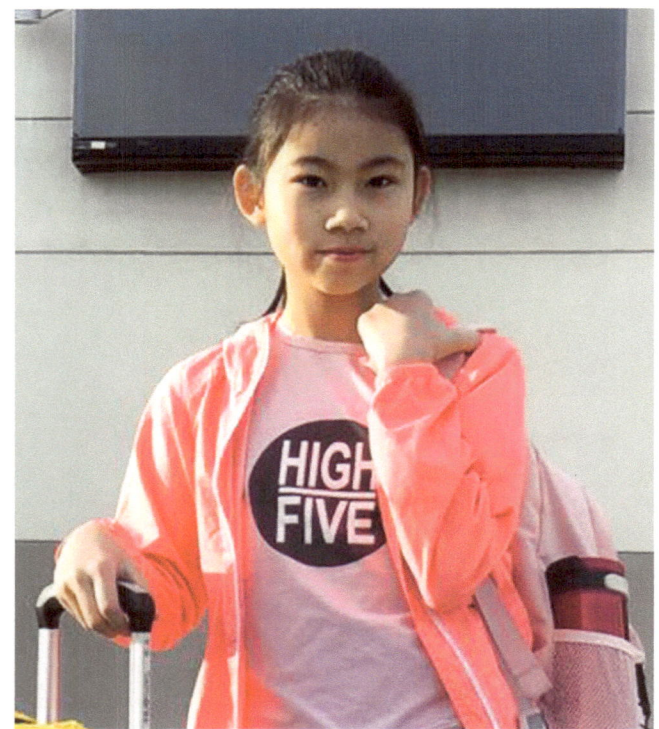

JINGYI YANG
Robert O Townsend Junior High, USA

Bronze Award for Art, 2nd Liberty Awards, International Society of Young Artists, 2019
Bronze Award for Art, 1st Liberty Awards, International Society of Young Artists, 2018

JINGYI YANG

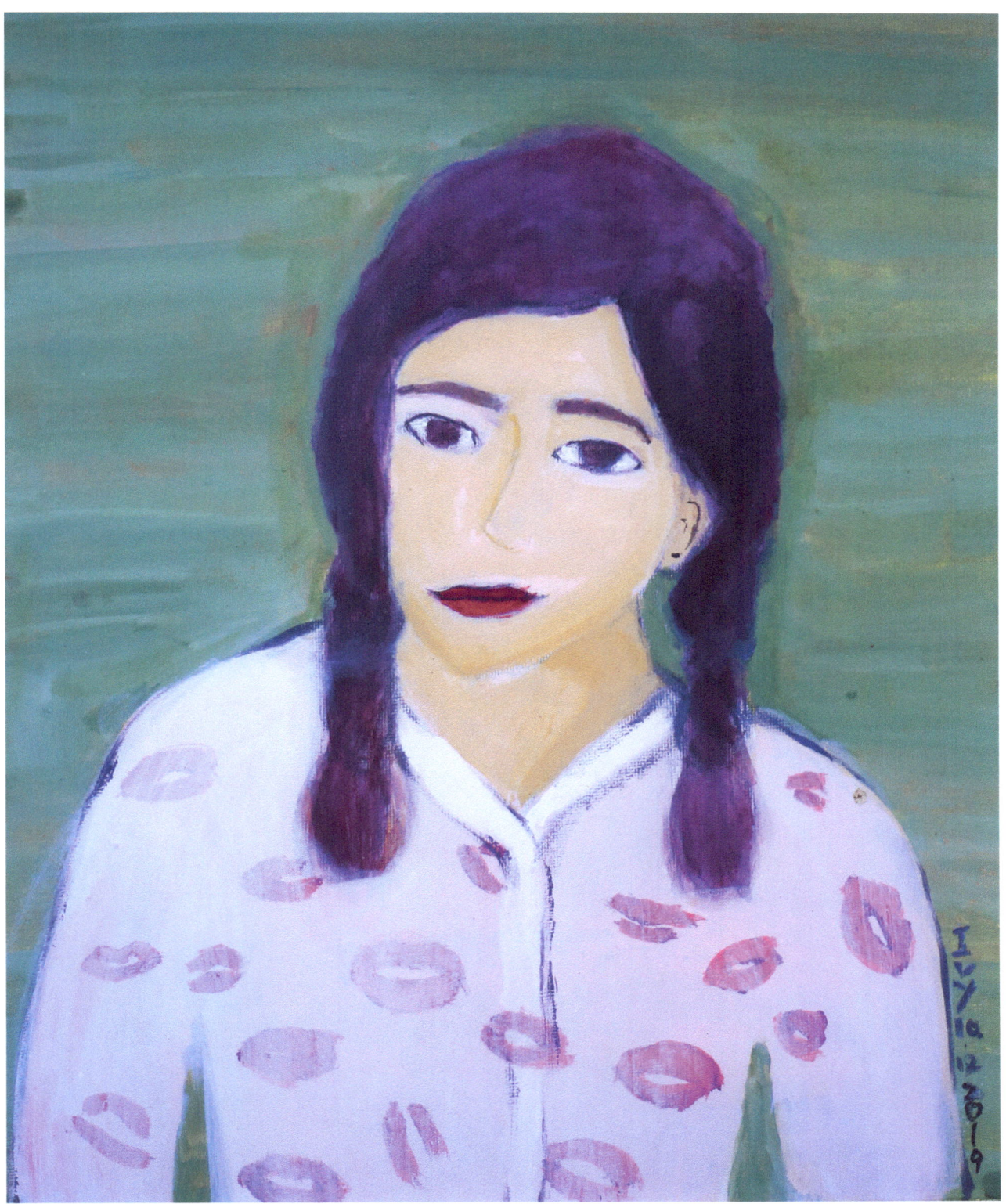

Zoe, acrylic on canvas, 2019

JINGYI YANG

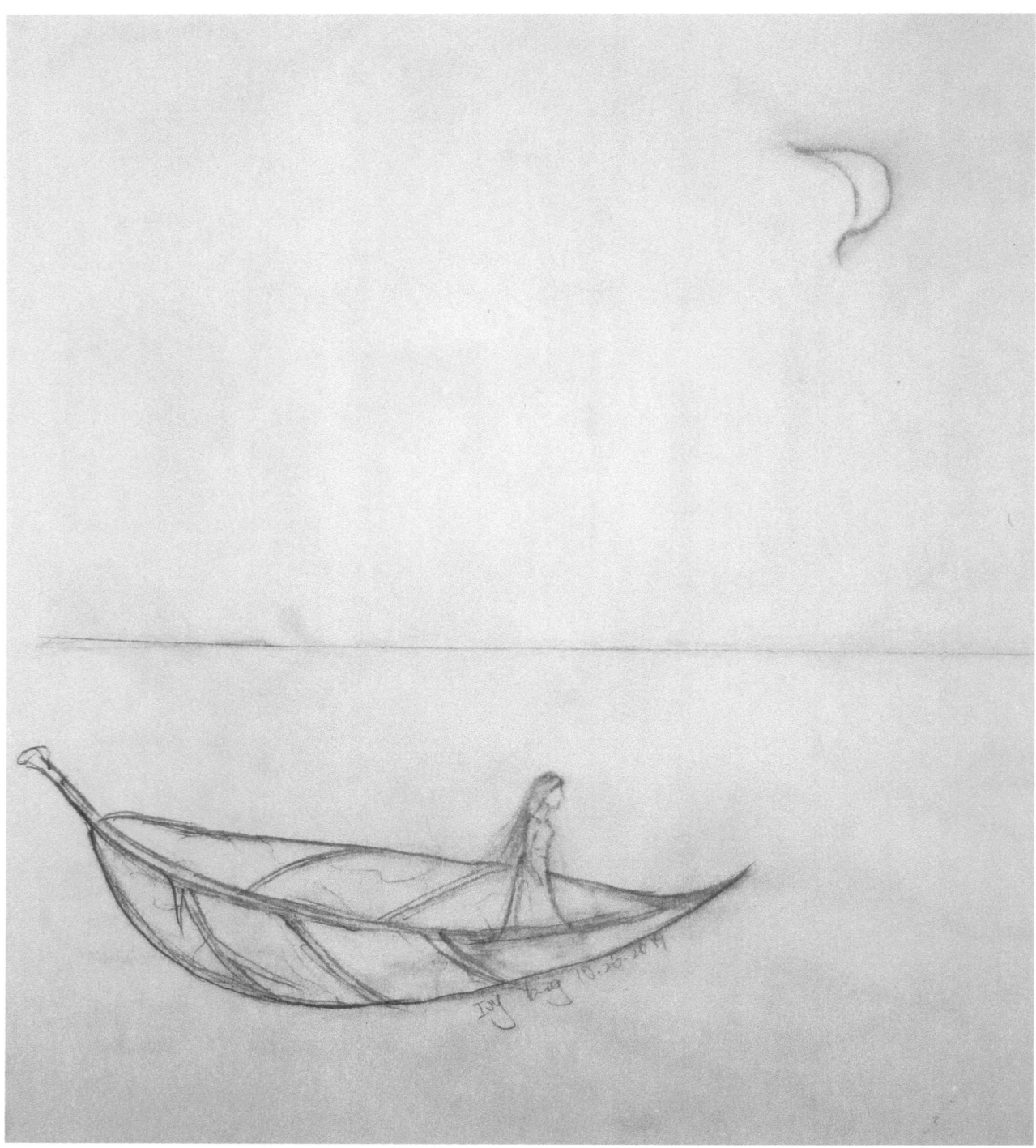

Leaf Boat, pencil on paper, 2019

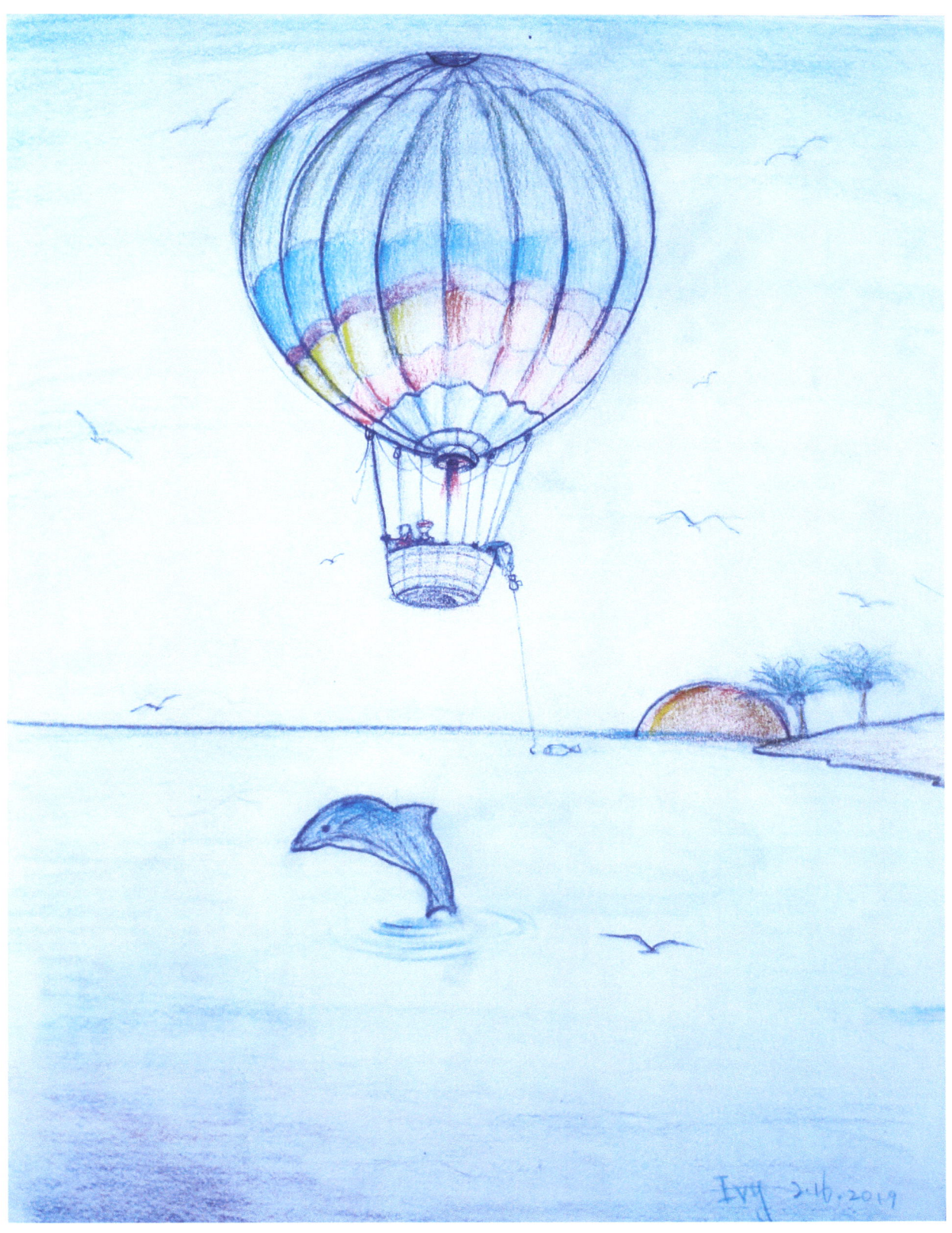

Turkish, colored pencil on paper, 2016

JINGYI YANG

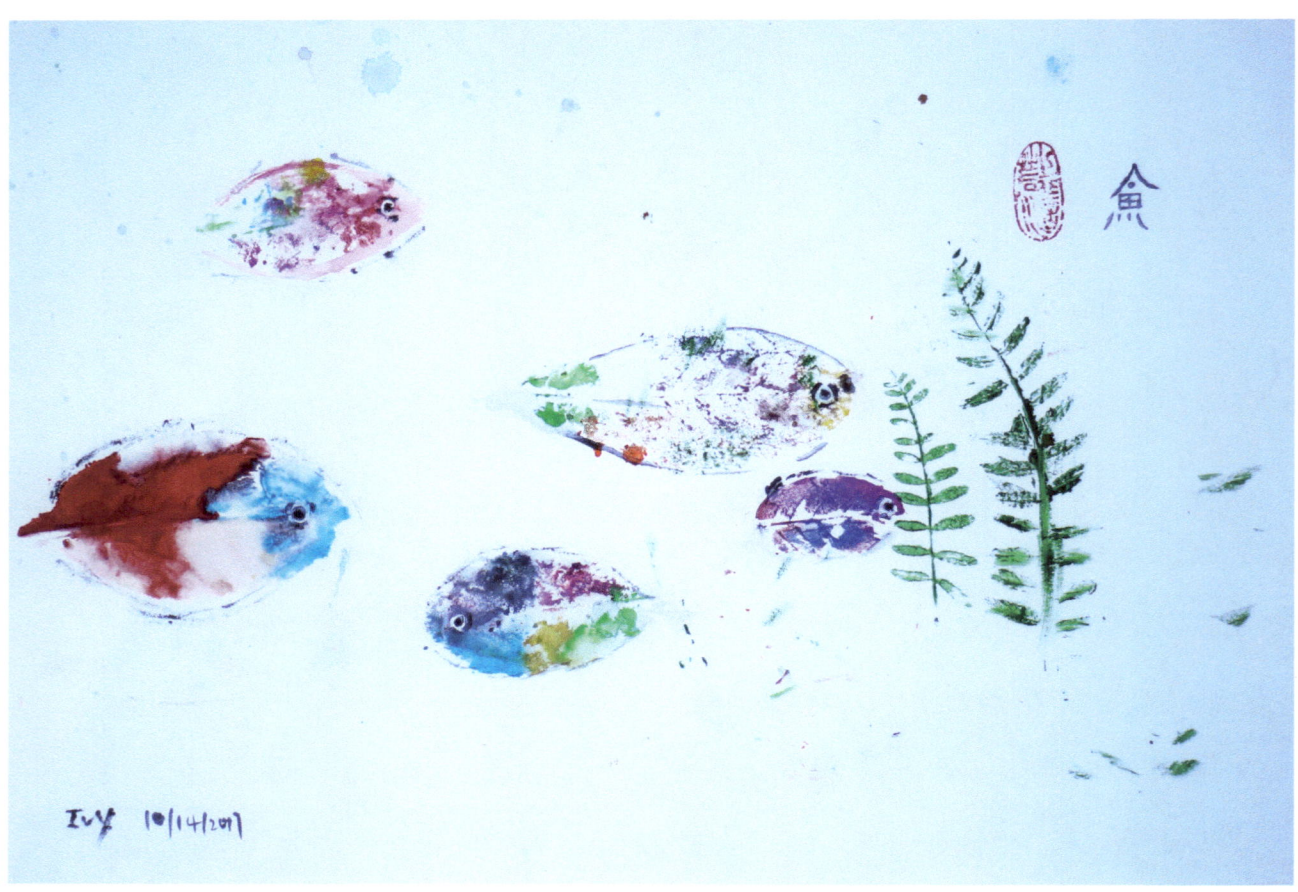

Fish, acrylic on paper, 2017

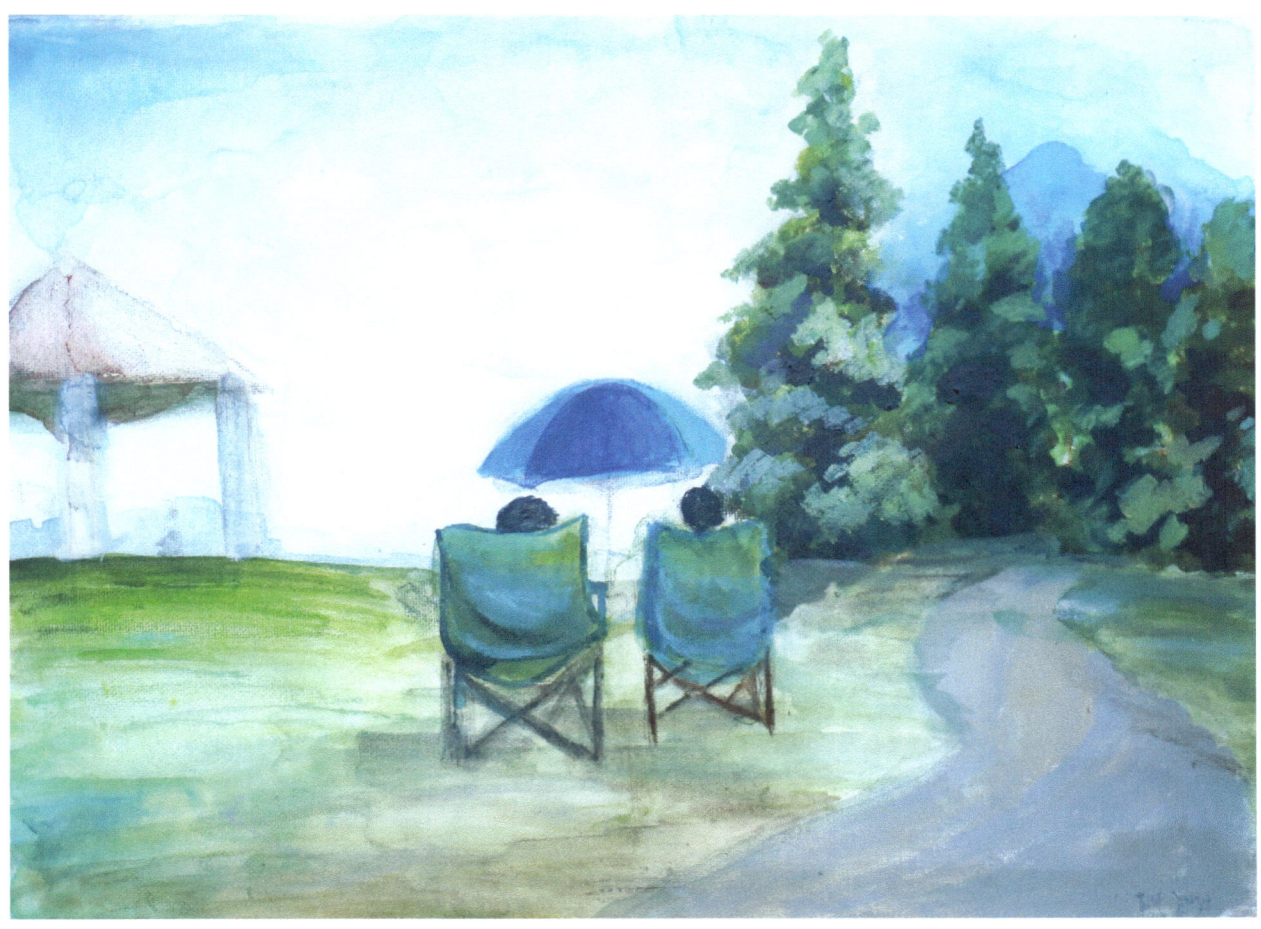

Silence, acrylic on canvas, 2018

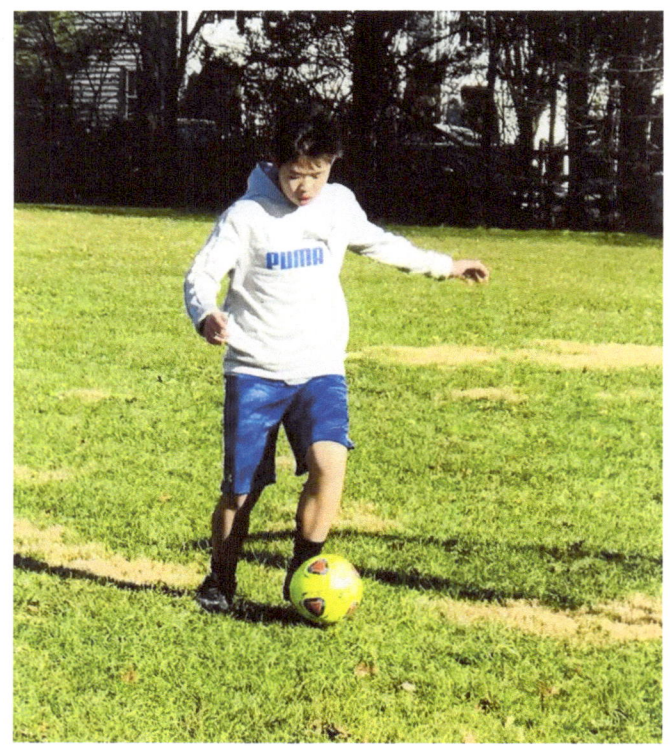

JUNKAI GONG
Princeton High School, USA

Double Octofinalist, Princeton Classic Novice Lincoln Douglas Debate, 2019
Outstanding Academic Excellence, President's Education Awards Program, 2019
Bronze Award for Art, 2nd Liberty Awards, International Society of Young Artists, 2019
Rising Star Award, 1st Liberty Awards, International Society of Young Artists, 2018
2nd Prize, 13th "For Study" Cup Elementary and Secondary School Innovative Composition Contest, 2017
Special Gold Prize, Oral English skill, 12th "Star & Torch" National Junior English Talent Competition, 2016
1st Prize, 4th Evening News Union Cup Cross-Strait Junior with-the-Topic Composition Contest, 2016
Election to **Chinese Young Talents Database,** 2016

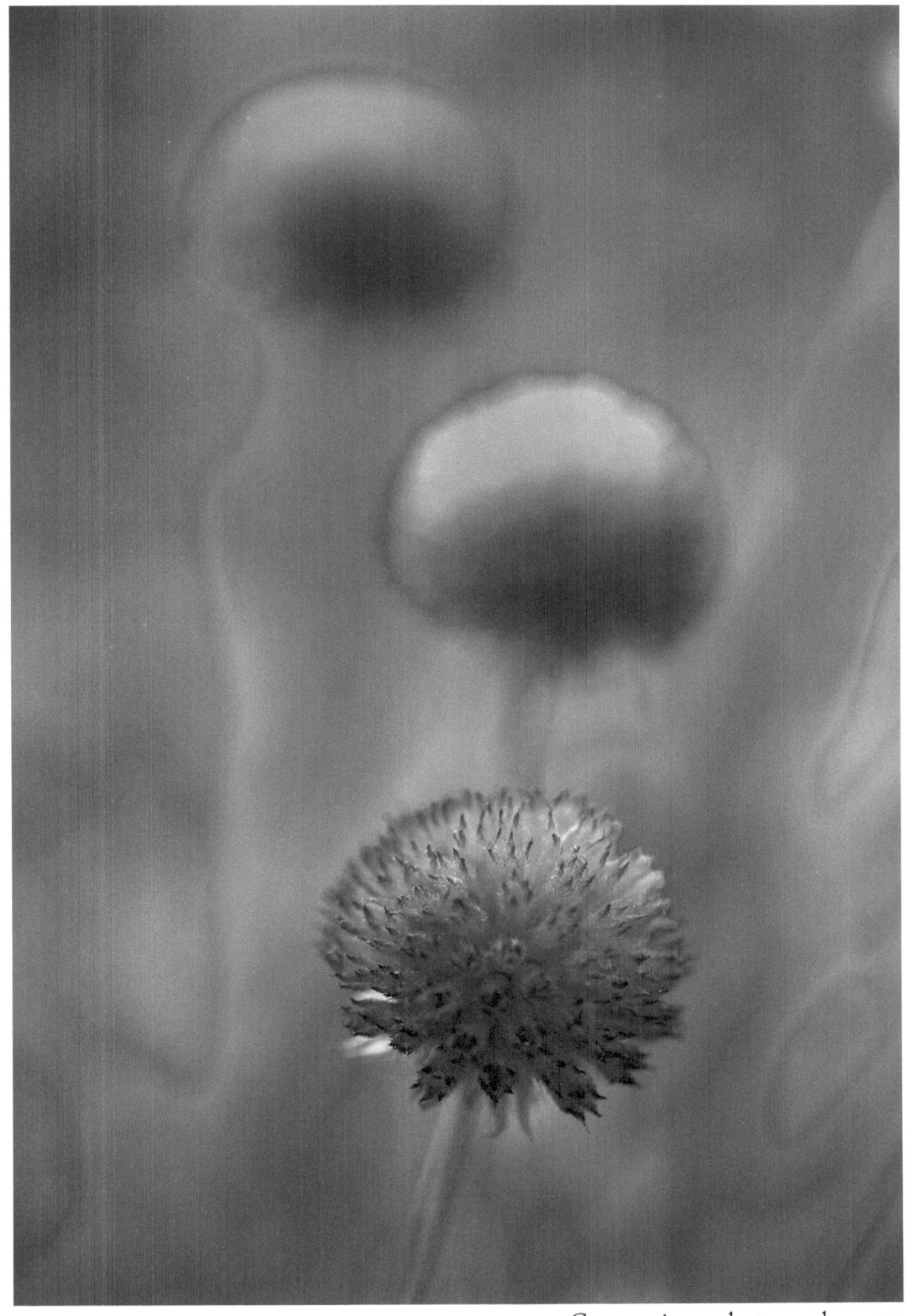

Companions, photography, 2019

JUNKAI GONG

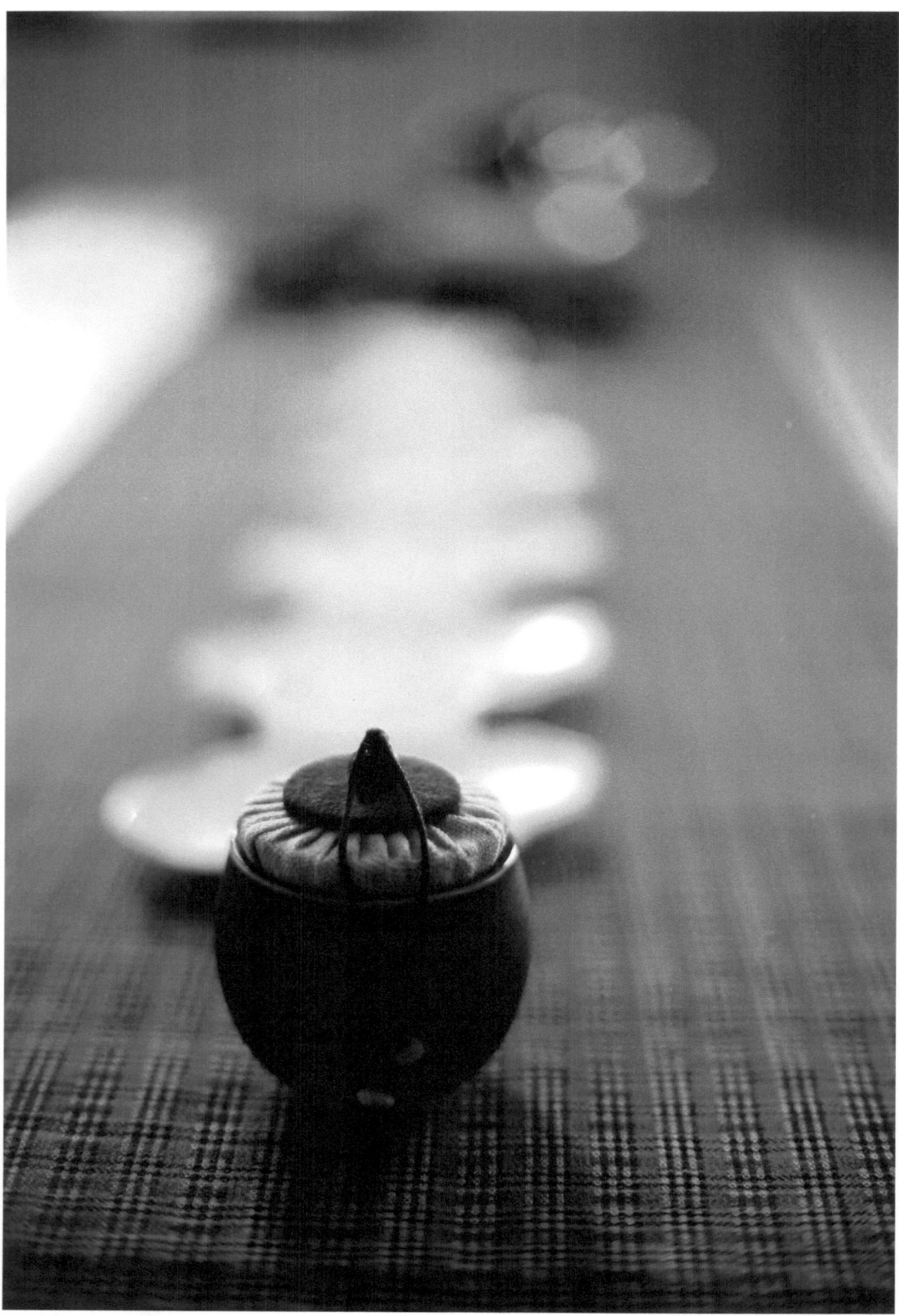

Conversation, photography, 2019

JUNKAI GONG

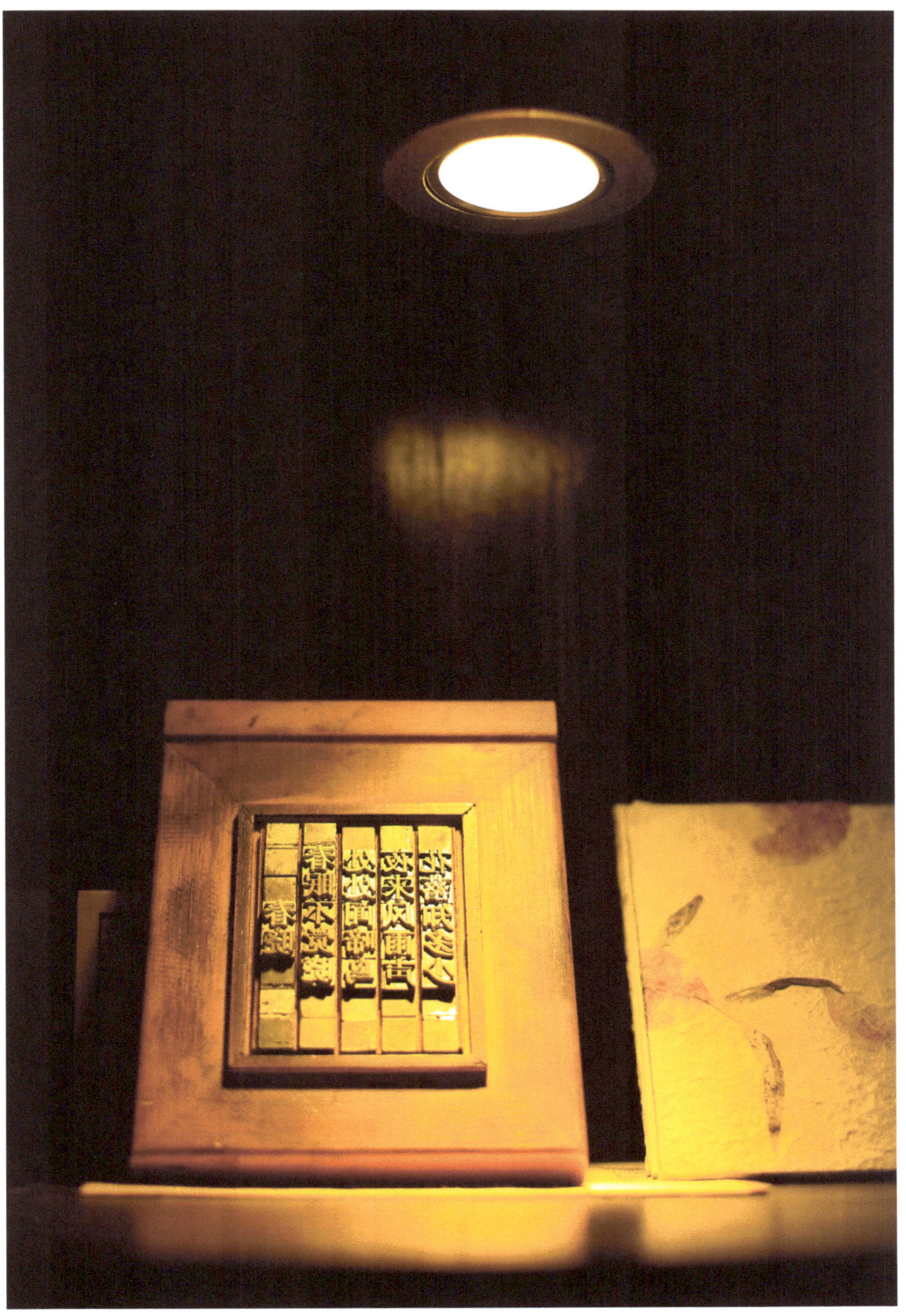

Memory of Time, photography, 2019

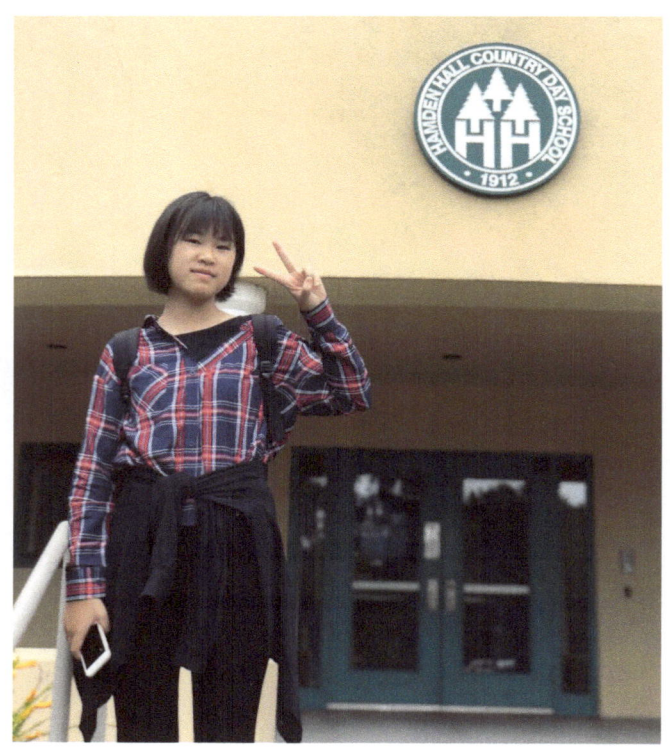

KUN WANG
Hamden Hall Country Day School, USA

Bronze Award for Art, 2nd Liberty Awards, International Society of Young Artists, 2019
Bronze Award for Art, 1st Liberty Awards, International Society of Young Artists, 2018

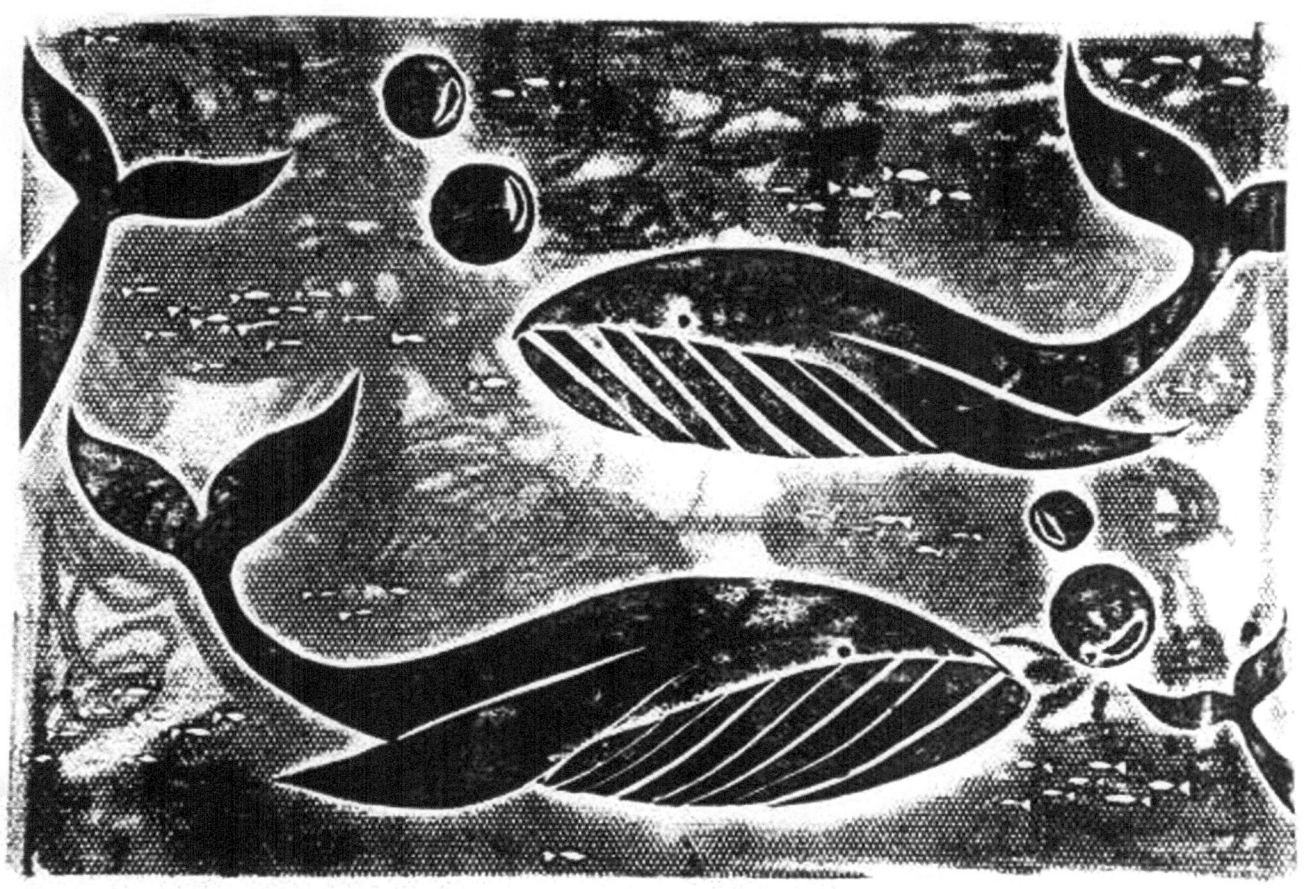

Whales, print, 2018

KUN WANG

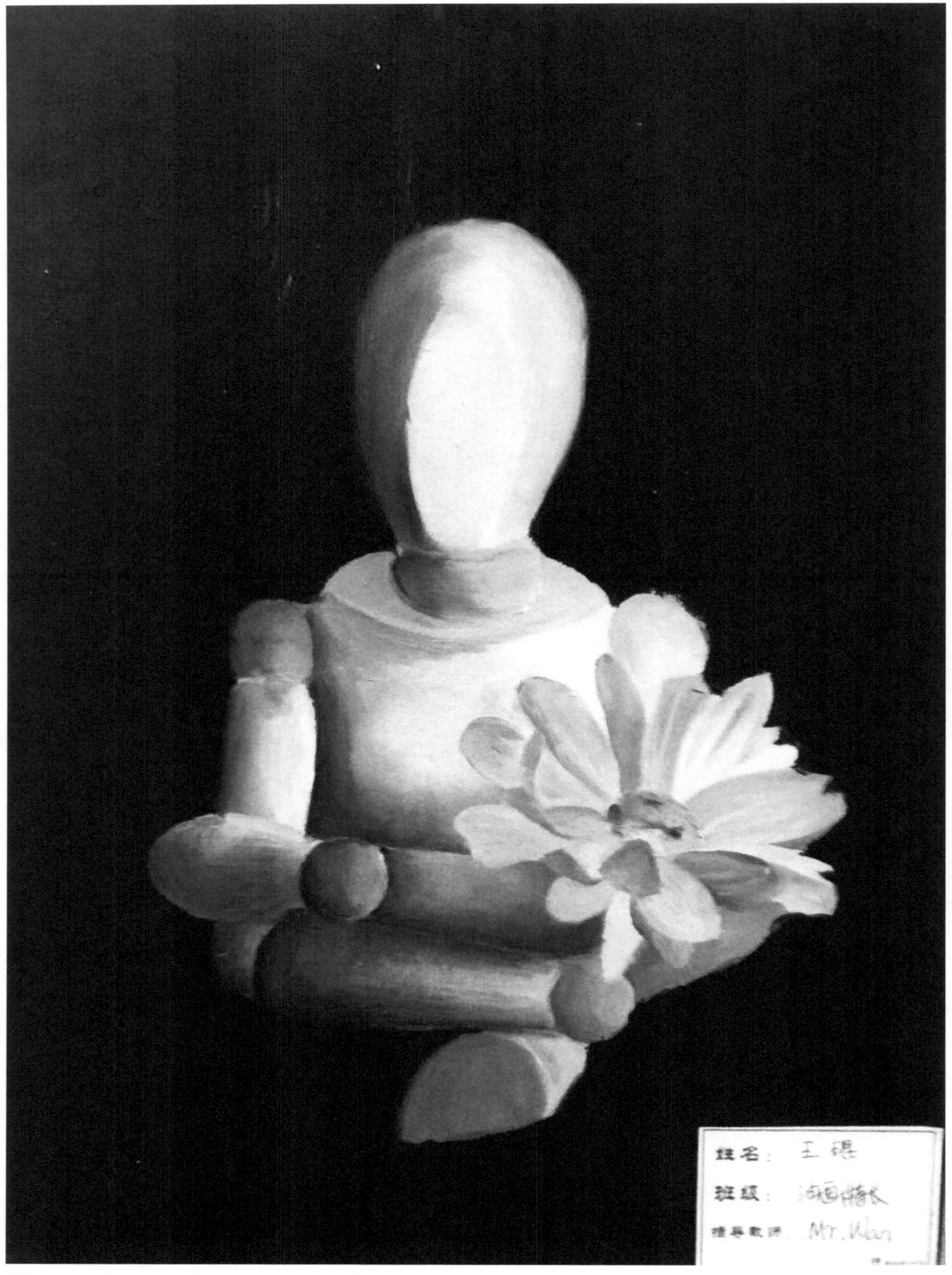

Mannequin, gouache on paper, 2018

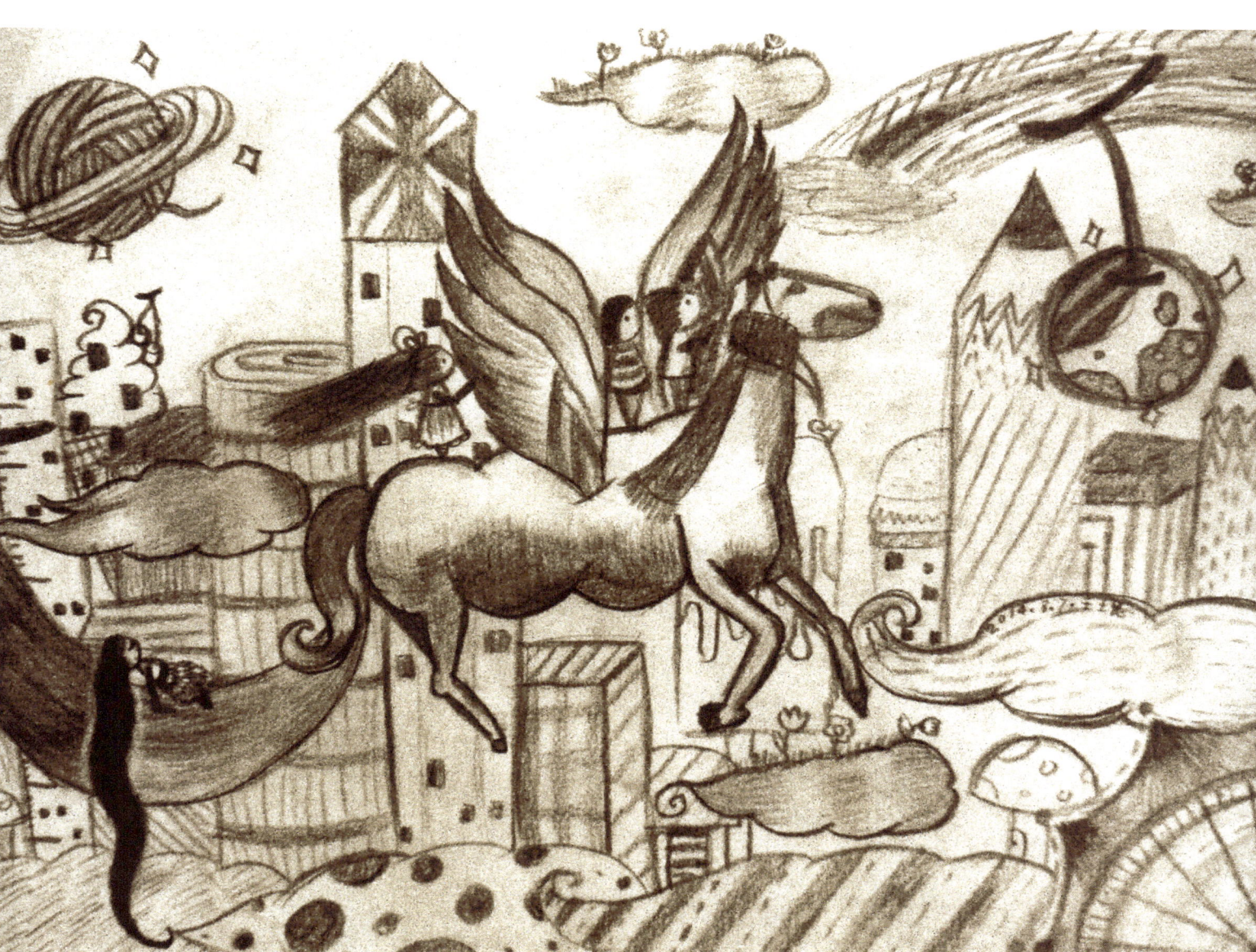

Wandering Up in the Air, pencil on paper, 2014

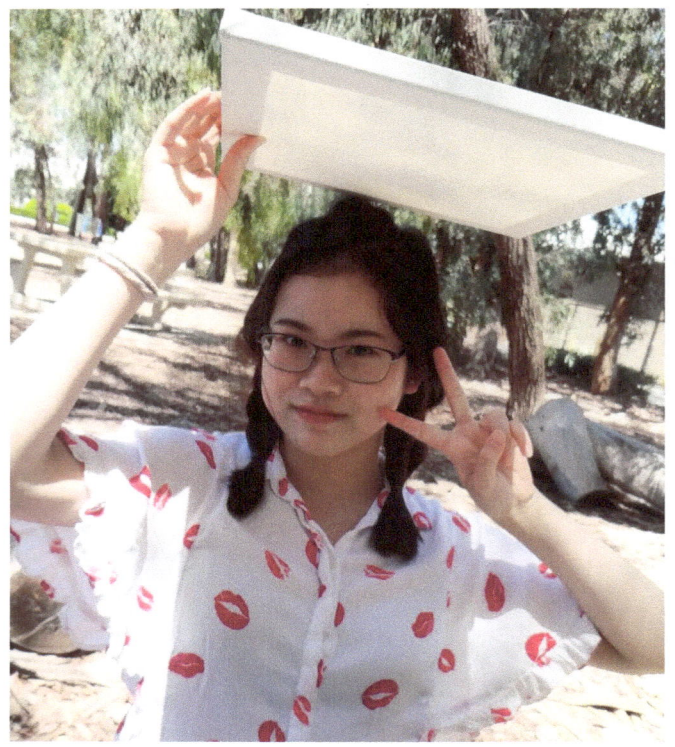

LEYI YANG
Chino Hills High School, USA

Silver Award for Art, 2nd Liberty Awards, International Society of Young Artists, 2019
Bronze Award for Art, 1st Liberty Awards, International Society of Young Artists, 2018

LEYI YANG

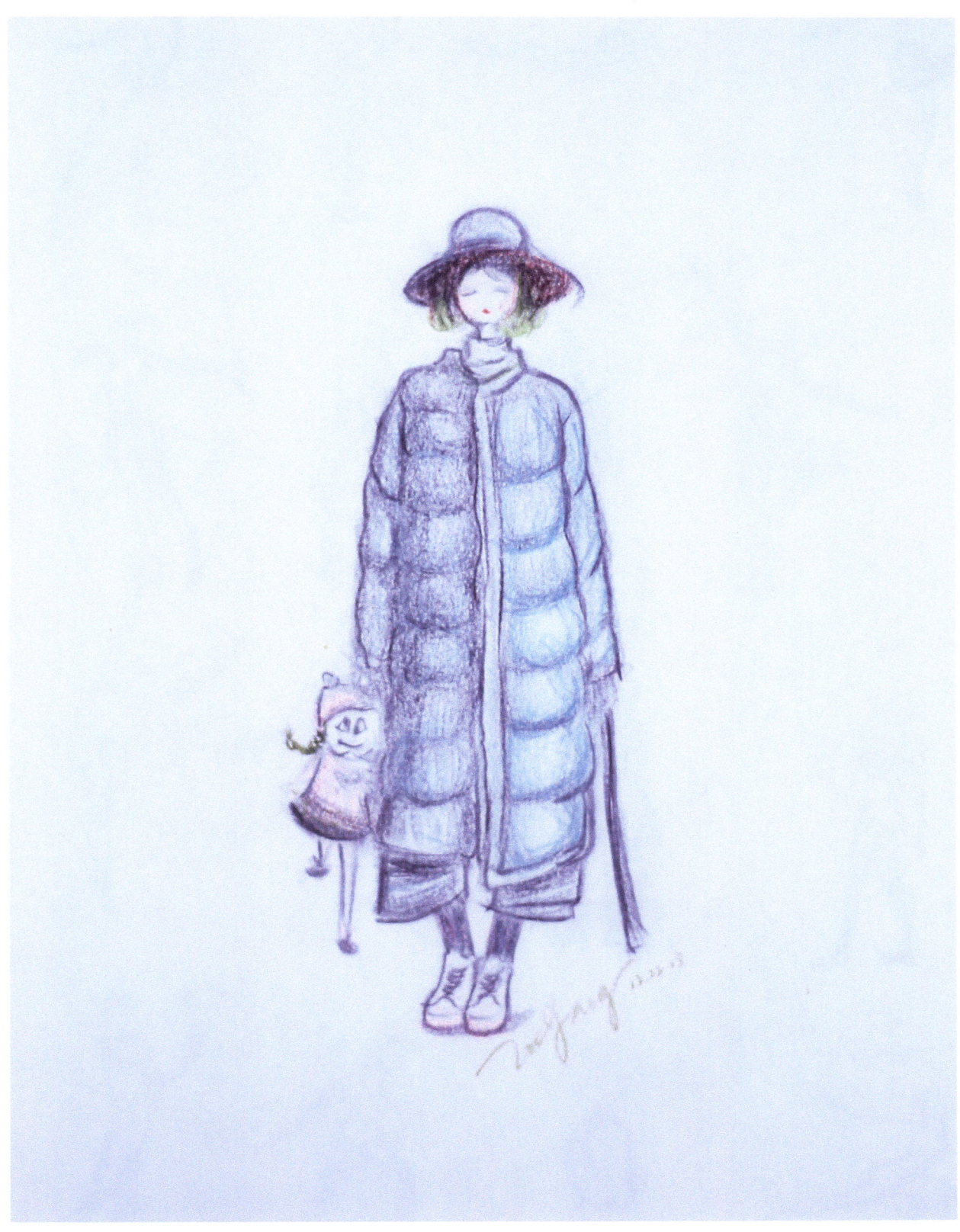

Patience, colored pencil on paper, 2018

LEYI YANG

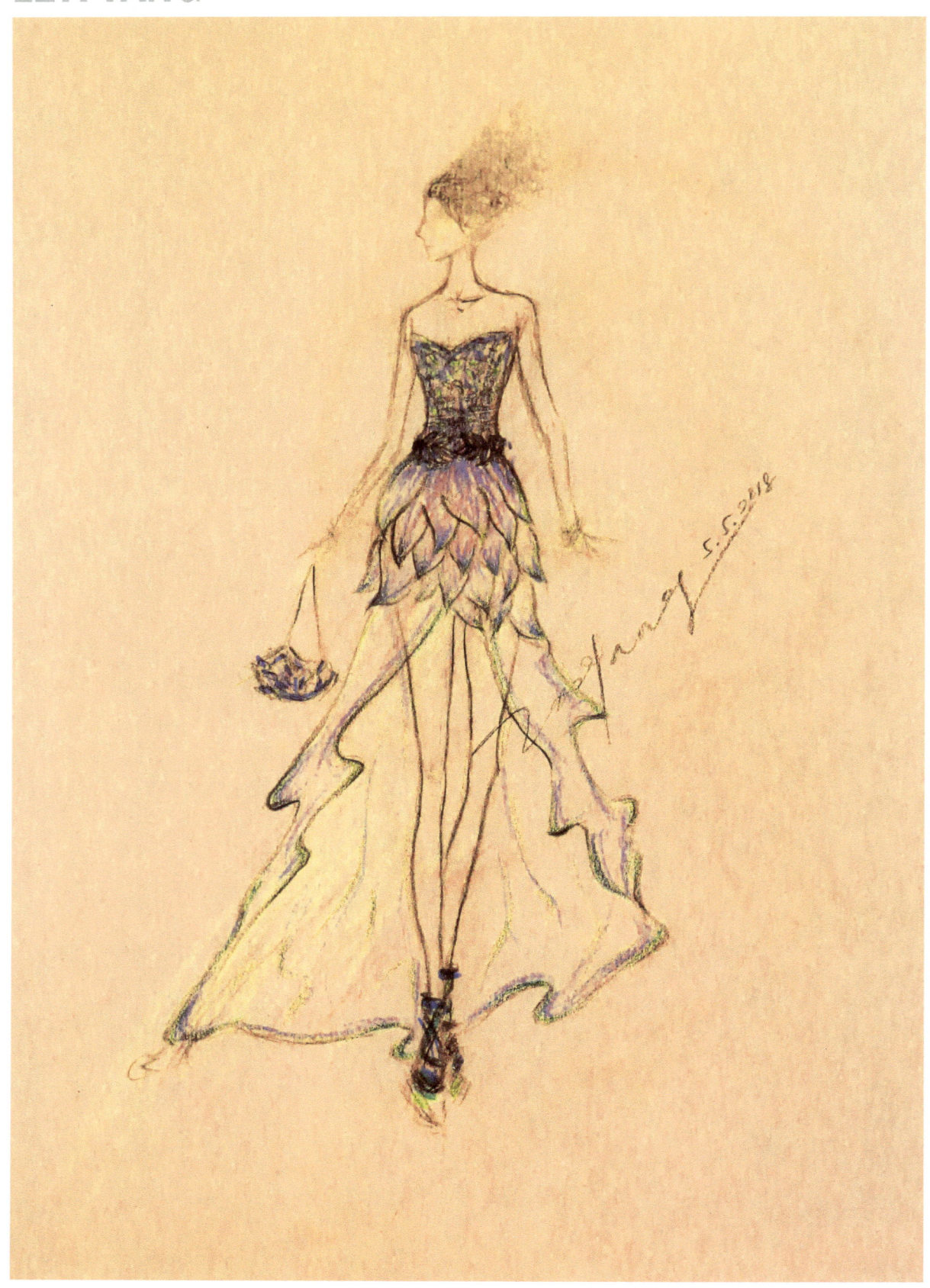

Blooming Louts, colored pencil on paper, 2018

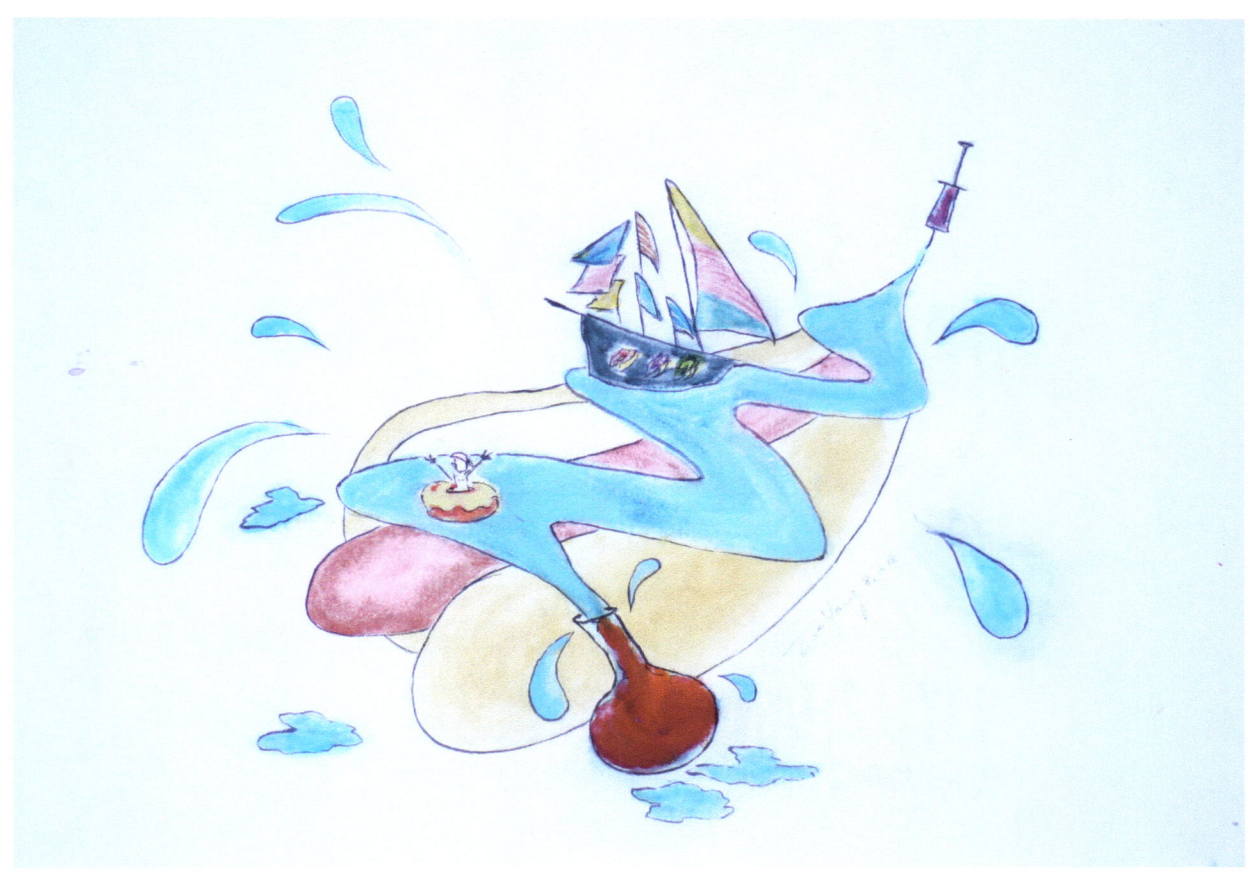

Water Park, acrylic on paper, 2017

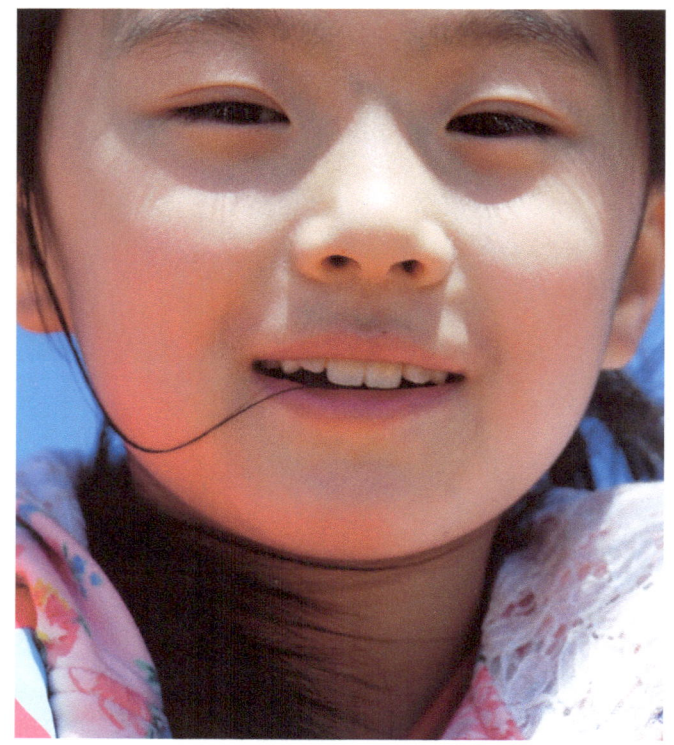

LIYU ZHANG
Qingdao No.2 Experimental Middle School, China

Rising Star Award, 1st Liberty Awards, International Society of Young Artists, 2018

LIYU ZHANG

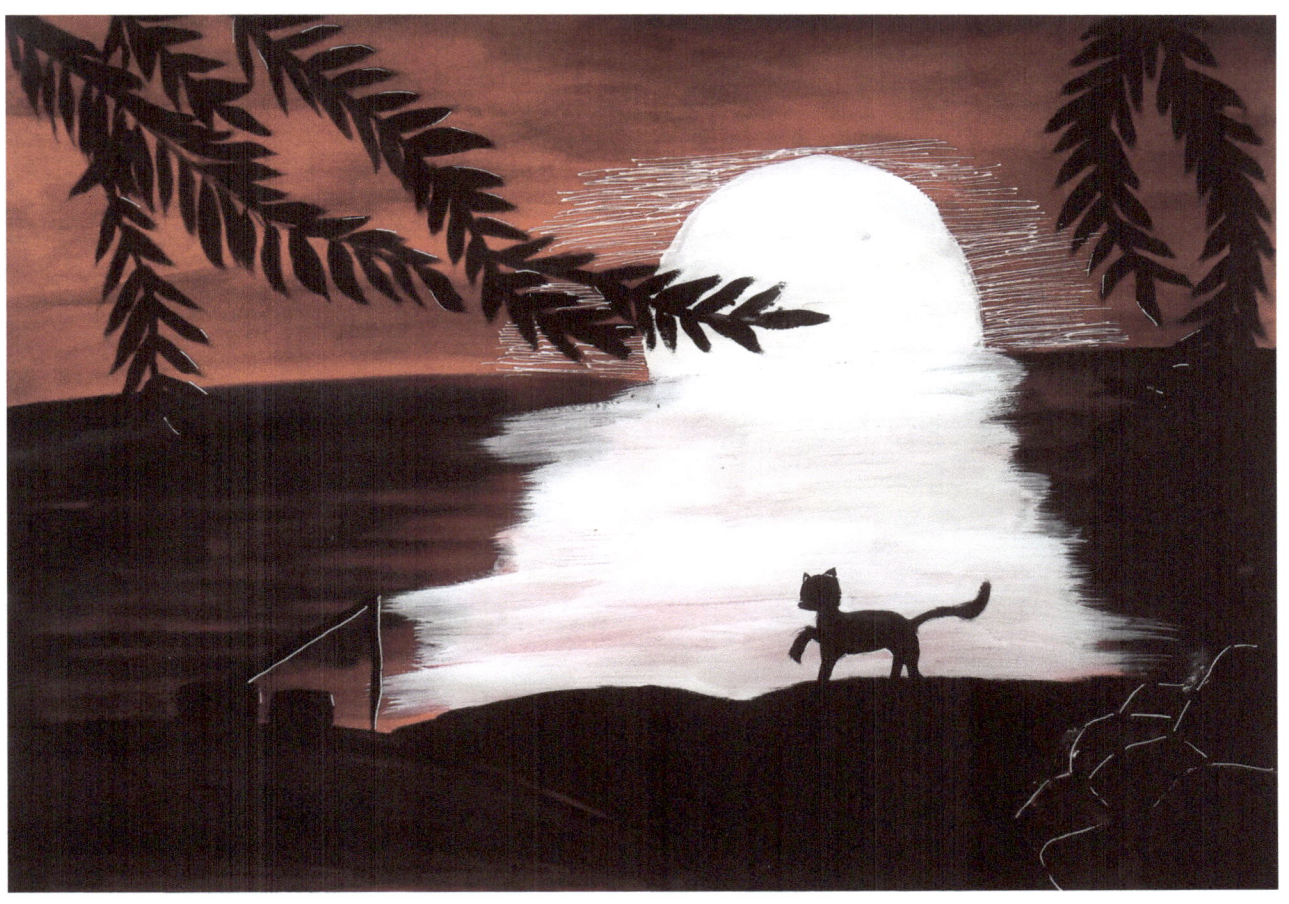

A Cat, gouache on paper, 2018

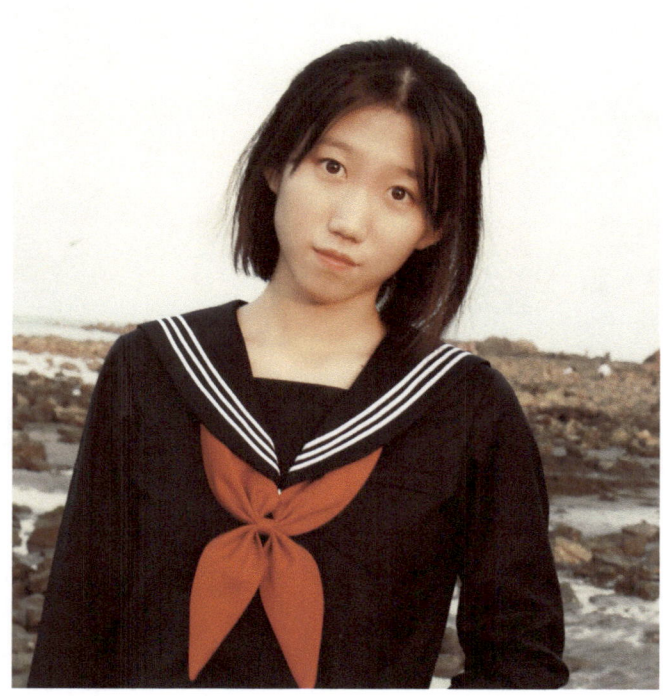

PEIYU WU
Qufu Normal University, China

Gold Award for Art, 2nd Liberty Awards, International Society of Young Artists, 2019
Rising Star Award, 1st Liberty Awards, International Society of Young Artists, 2018
Bronze Medal, 6th National University & Middle School Student Marine Culture Design Contest, 2017
2nd Prize, International Space Settlement Design Competition (China), 2016

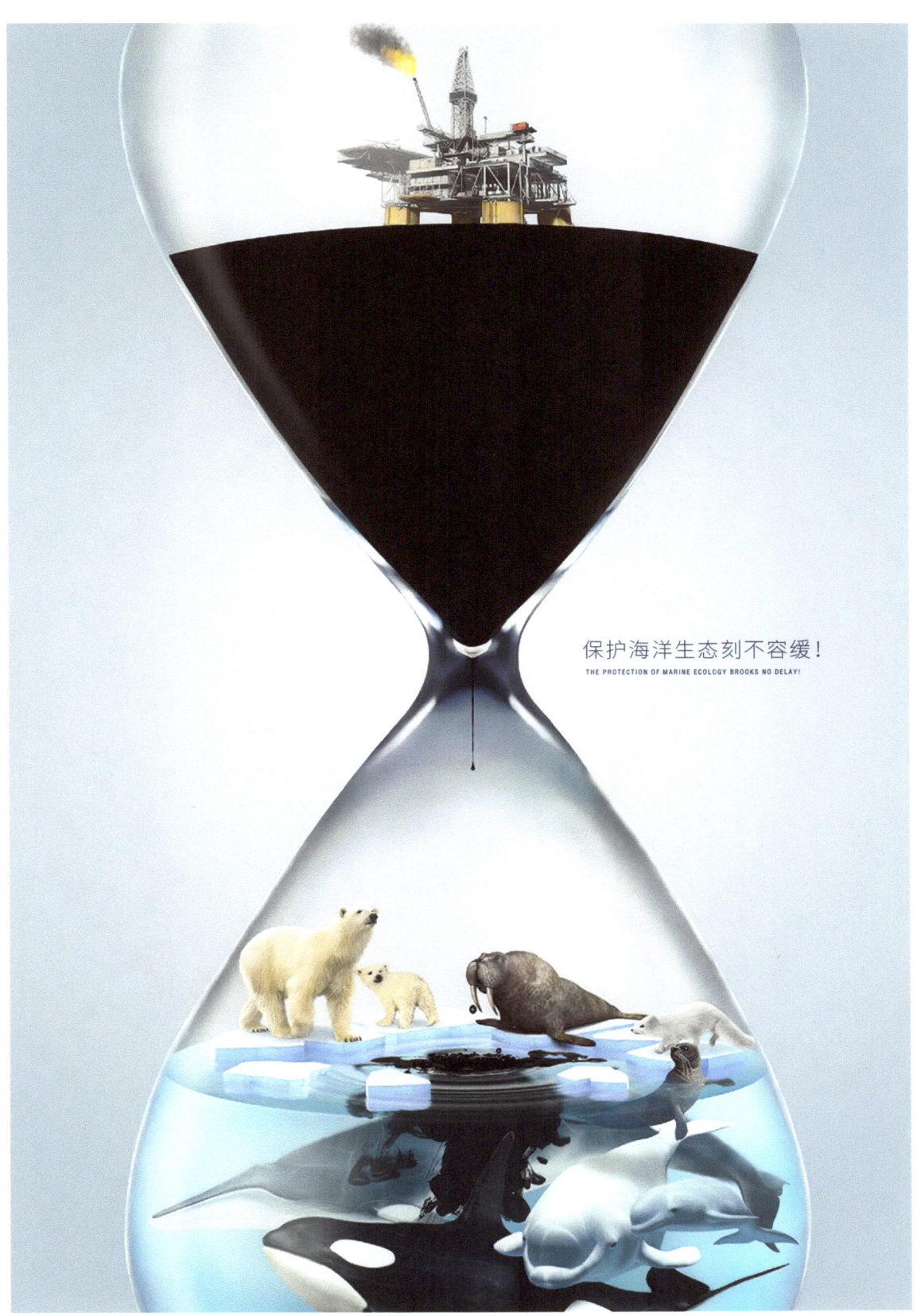

Public Service Advertising 1, digital, 2017

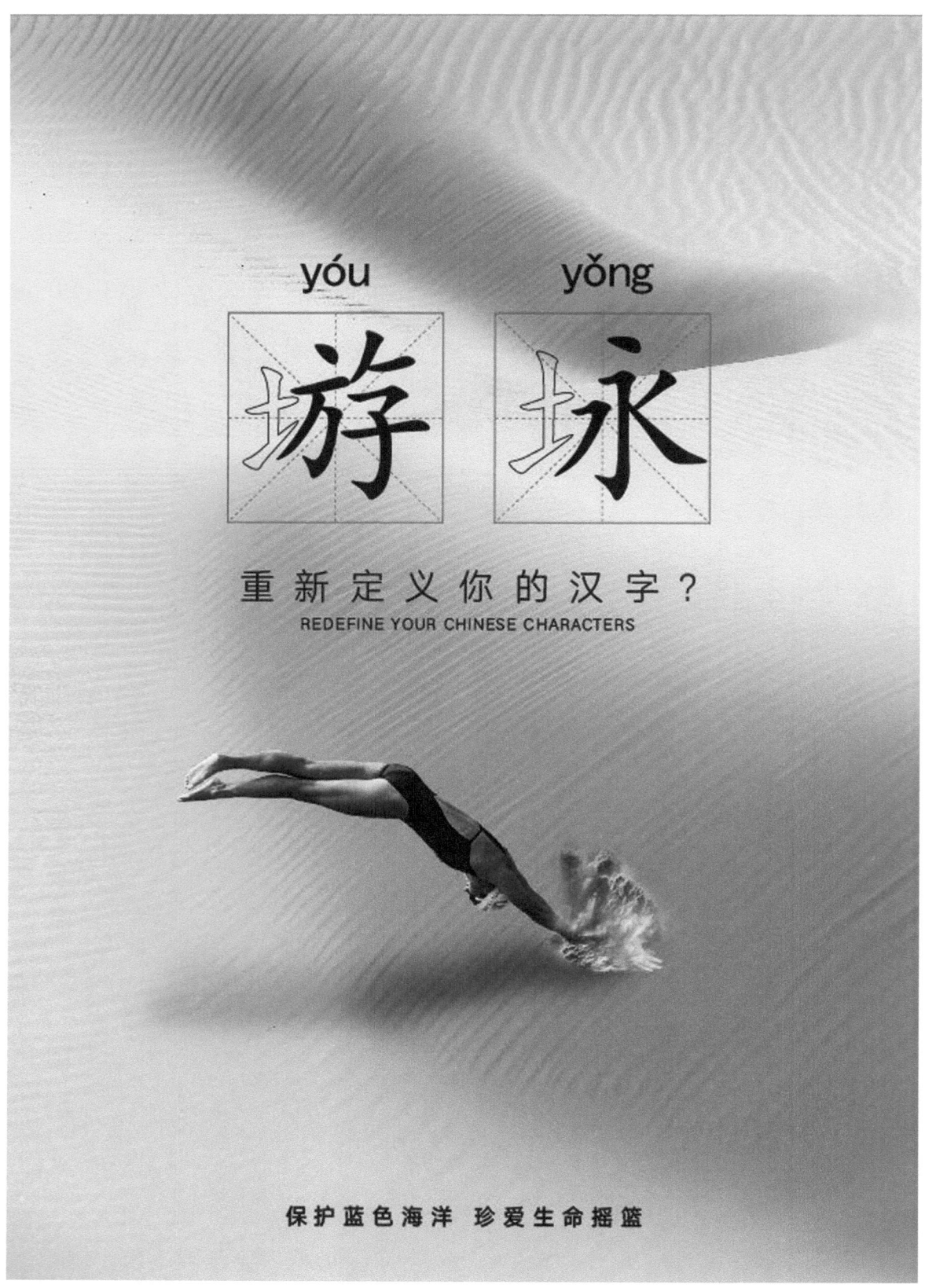

Public Service Advertising 2, digital, 2017

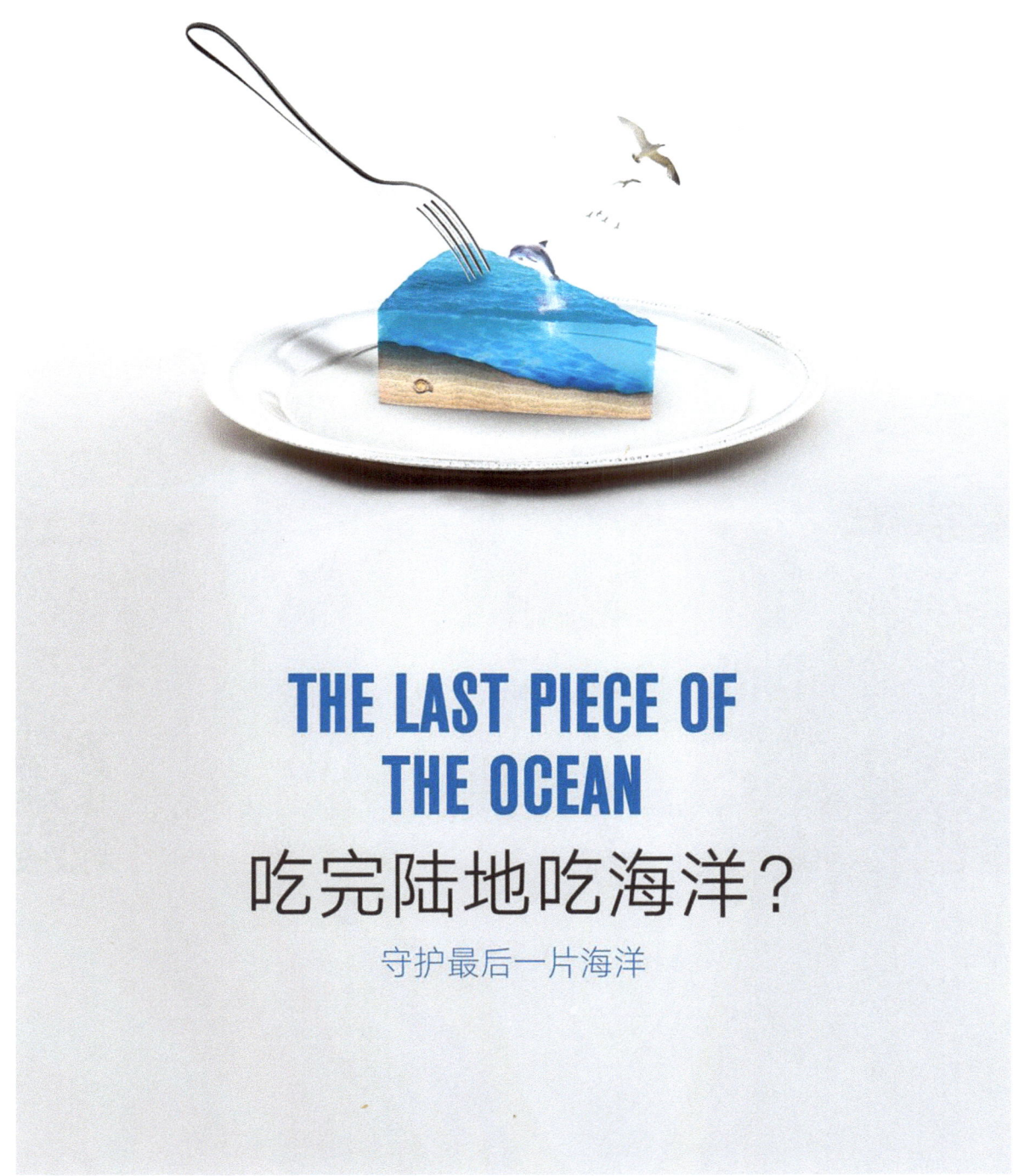

Public Service Advertising 3, digital, 2017

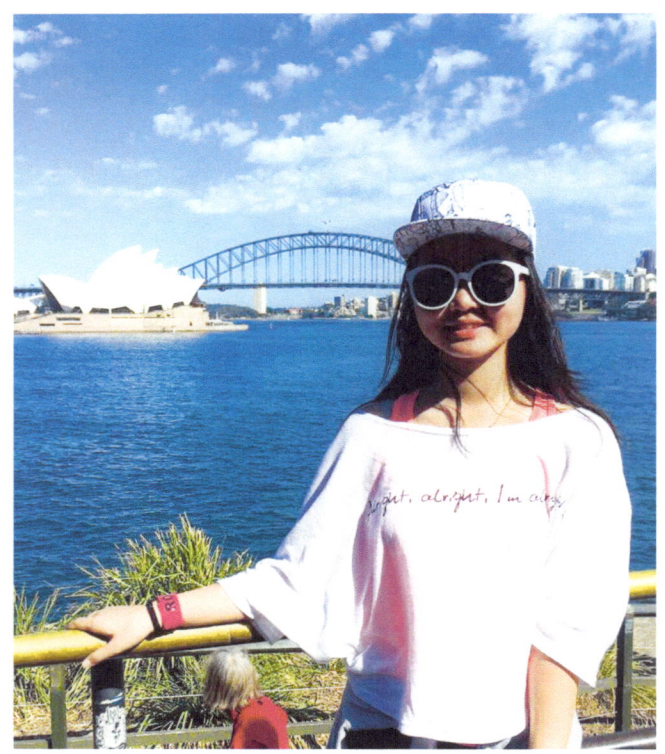

QINGXIA SONG
Qingdao No.58 High School, China

Silver Award for Art, 2nd Liberty Awards, International Society of Young Artists, 2019
Silver Award for Art, 1st Liberty Awards, International Society of Young Artists, 2018
Silver Award, "The Colorful Peace" Art Project Honoring the 100th Anniversary of the WWI Armistice, International Society of Young Artists, 2018
3rd Prize, ACT National Youth English Proficiency Demonstration and Communication Show, 2016
2nd Prize, ACT National Youth English Proficiency Demonstration and Communication Show of Qingdao, 2016

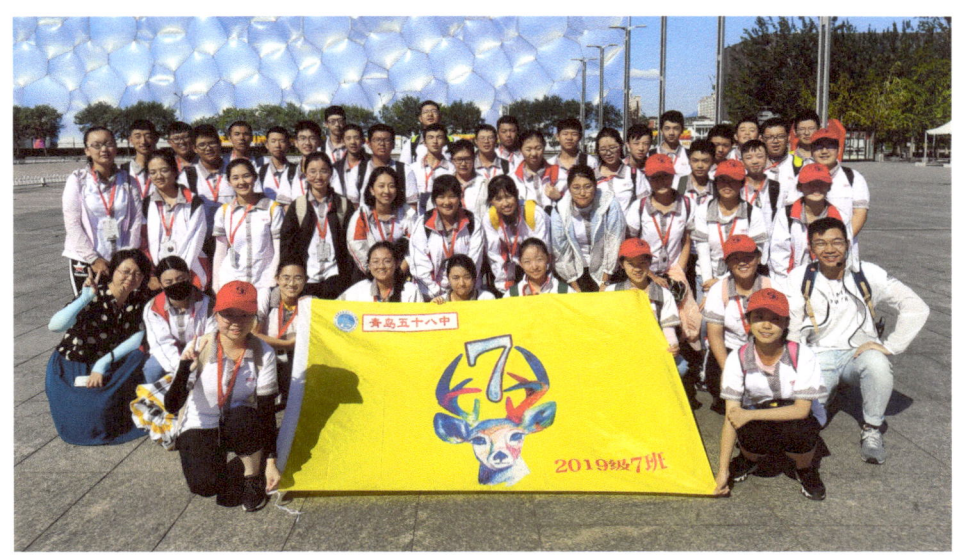

Logo on the Flag

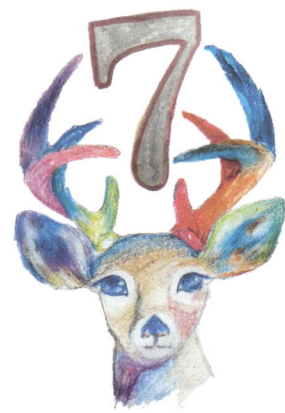

The Logo

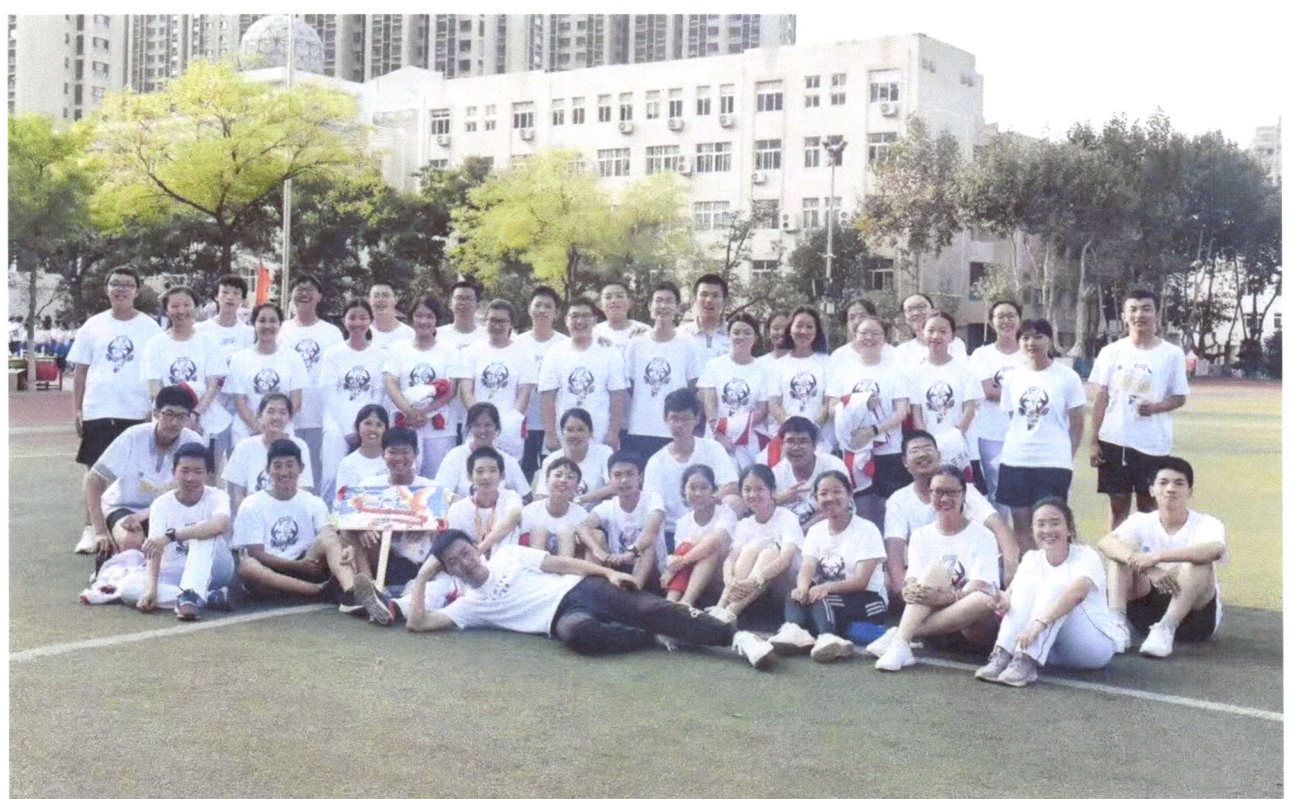

Logo on the Class Uniform

#1 Logo for Class 2022, Qingdao No.58 High School, 2019

QINGXIA SONG

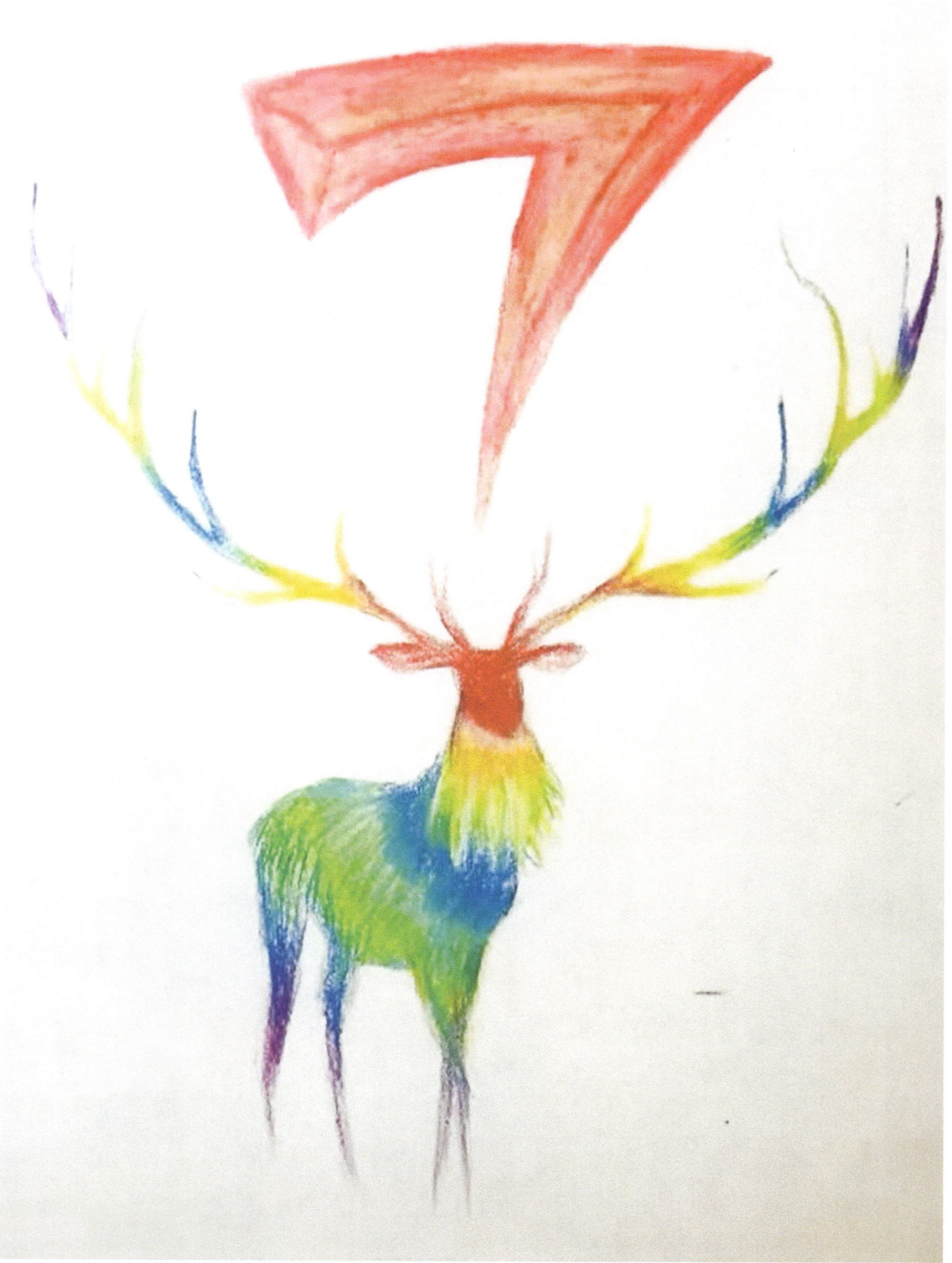

#2 Logo for Class 2022, Qingdao No.58 High School
Oil pastel and colored pencil on paper, 2019

QINGXIA SONG

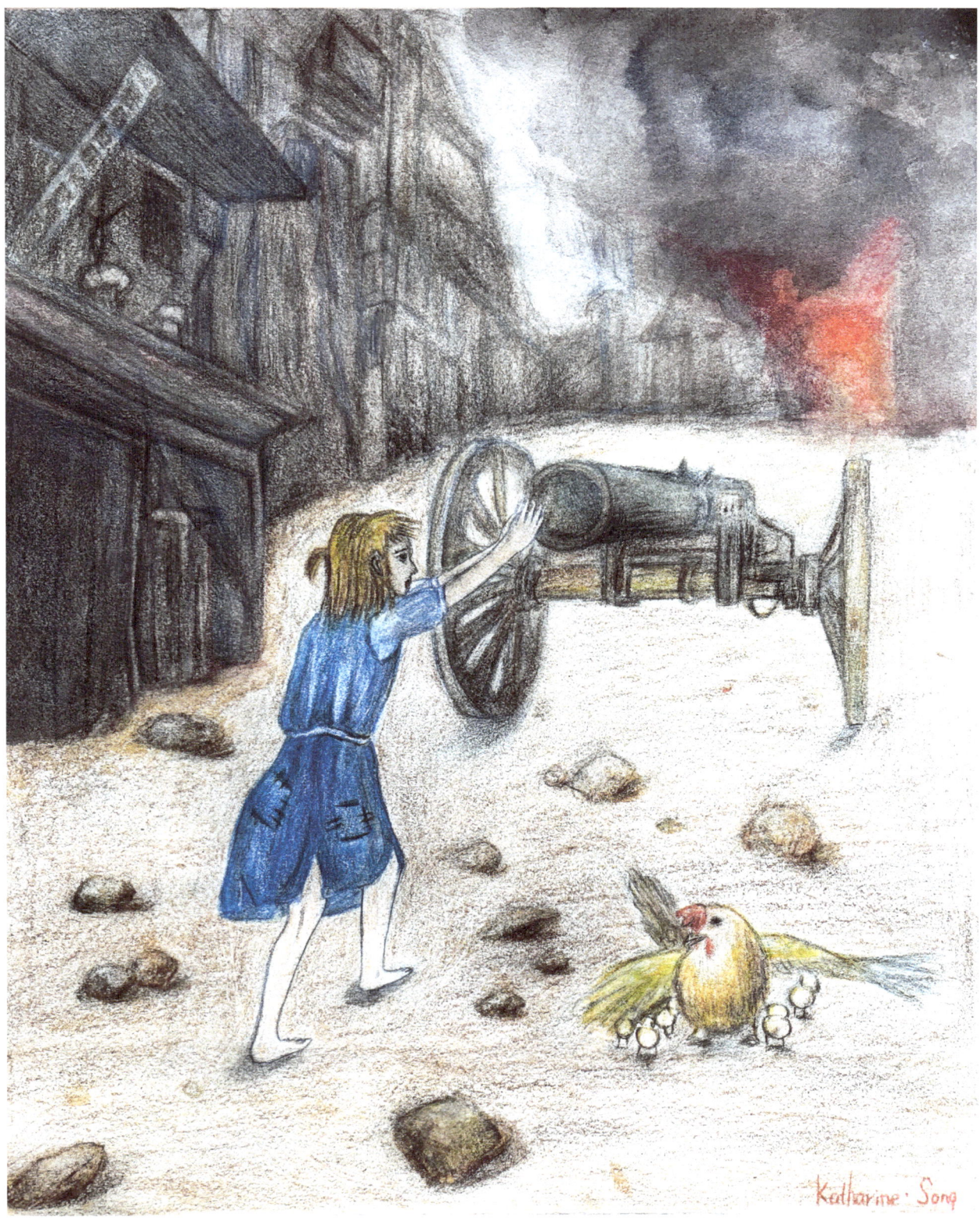

Do Not Intrude Our Village: in Honor of the 100th Anniversary of the WWI Armistice
Colored pencil on paper, 2018

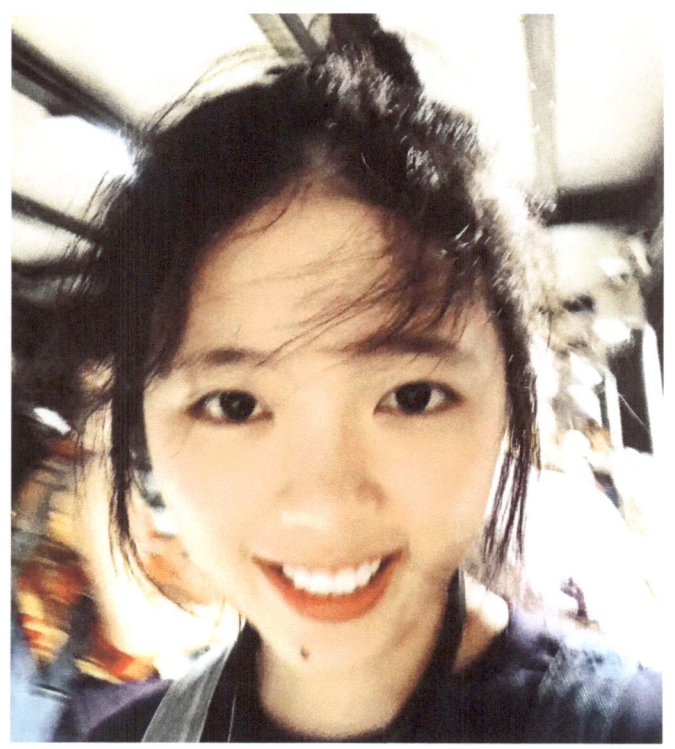

RONG HONG
Qingdao No. 1 High School, China

Gold Award for Art, 2nd Liberty Awards, International Society of Young Artists, 2019
Rising Star Award, 1st Liberty Awards, International Society of Young Artists, 2018

RONG HONG

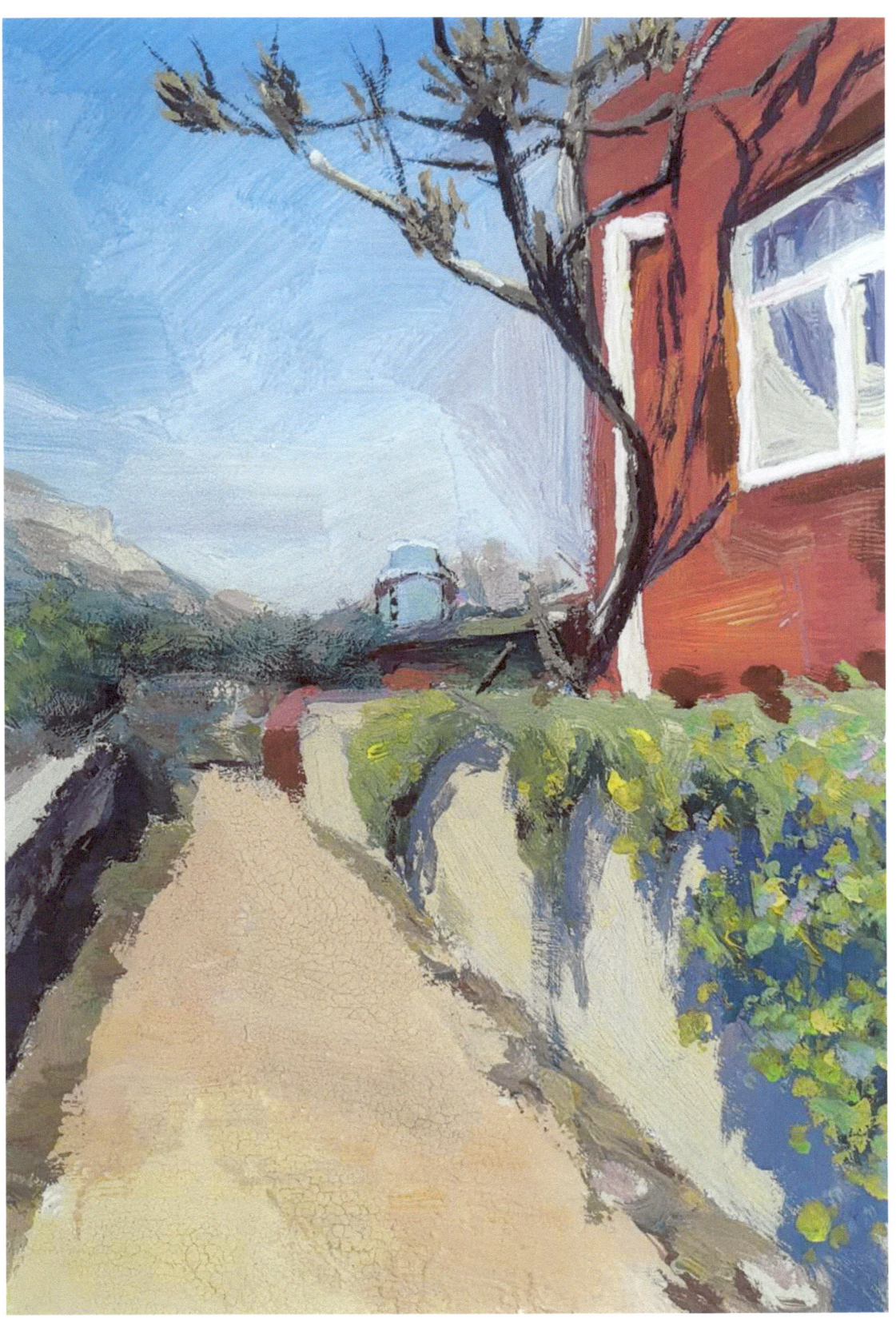

A Sight of Yangkou, gouache on paper, 2019

RONG HONG

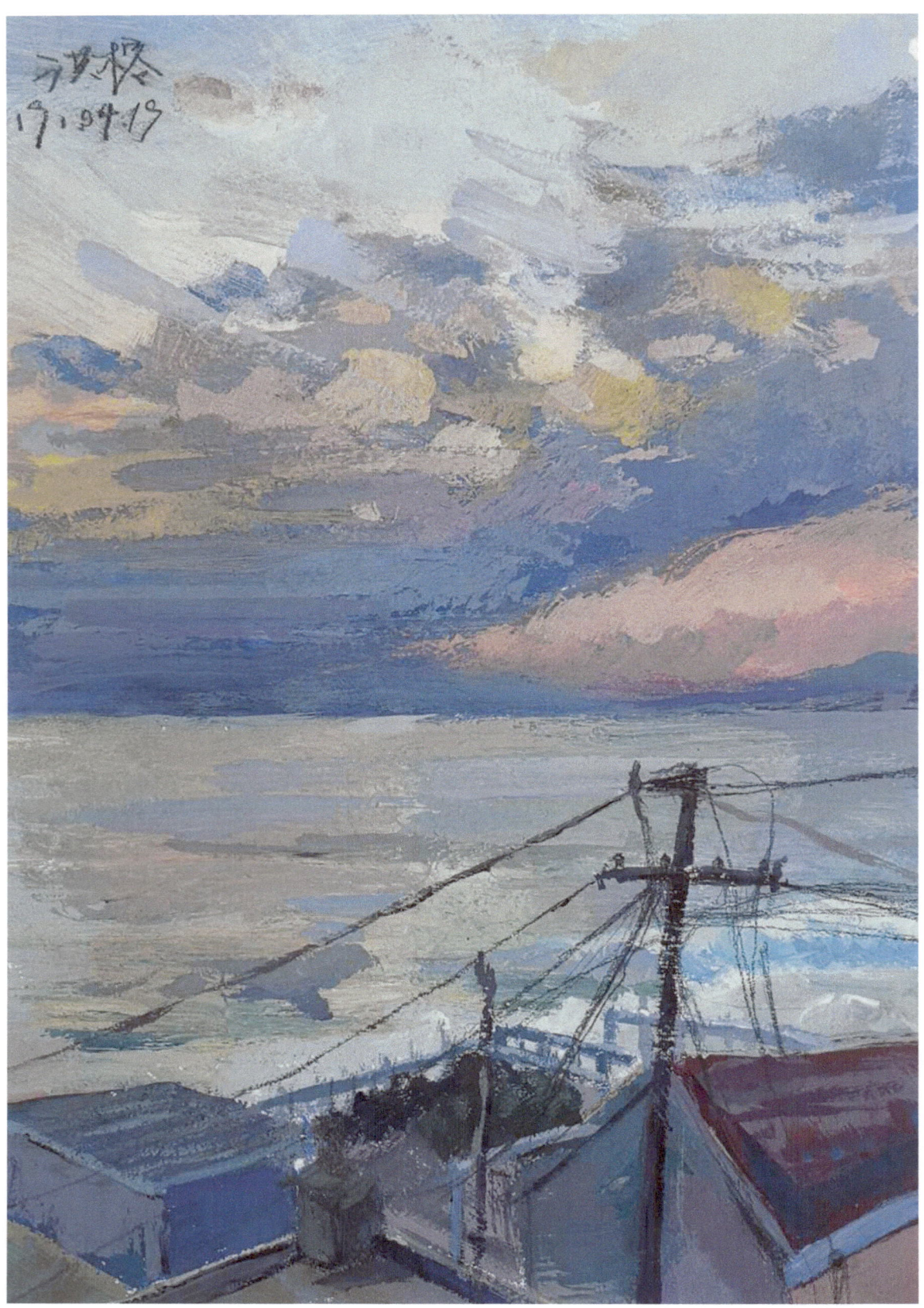

Archaic Fishing Port at Yangkou, gouache on paper, 2019

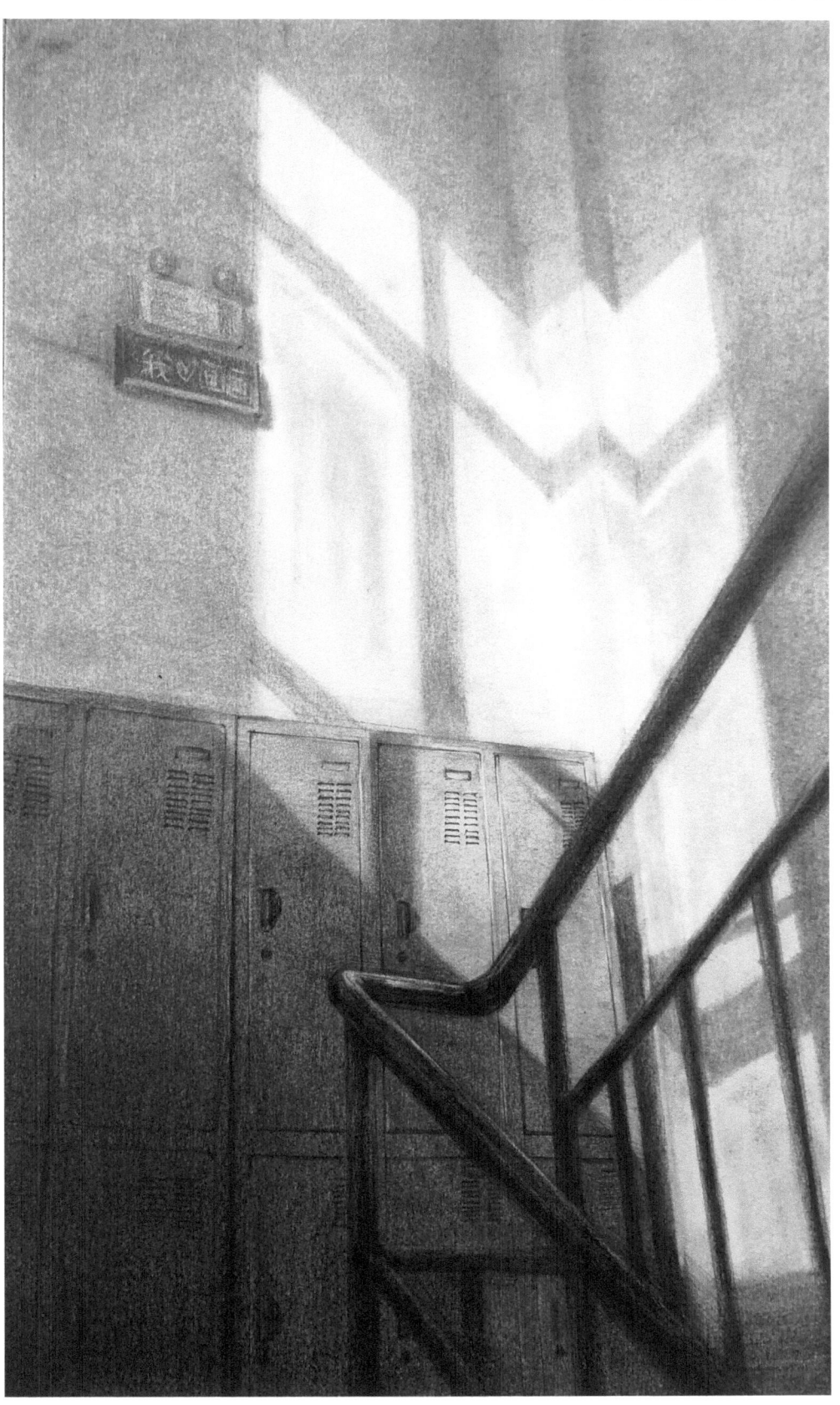

Afternoon, pencil on paper, 2019

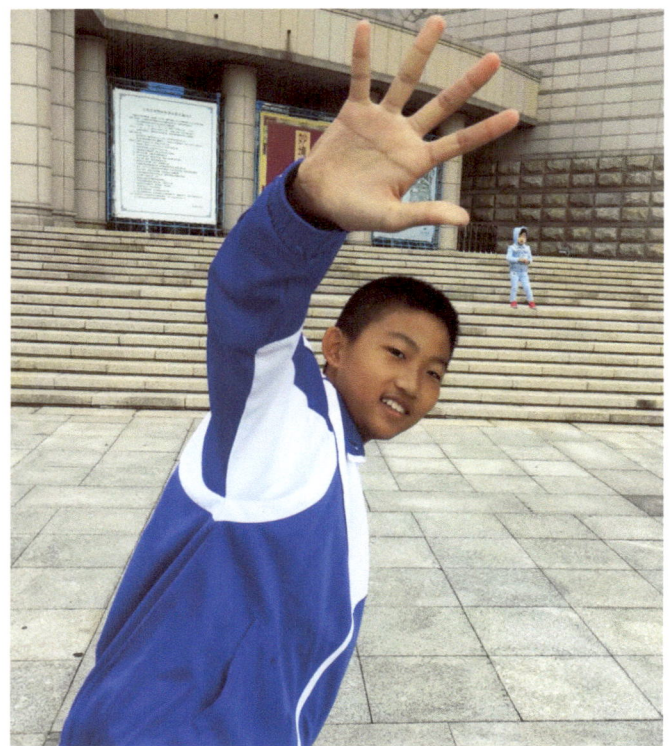

RUI LI
Qingdao University Affiliated Middle School, China

Bronze Award for Art, 2nd Liberty Awards, International Society of Young Artists, 2019
Rising Star Award, 1st Liberty Awards, International Society of Young Artists, 2018
3rd Prize, Painting, 5th Annual Qiluqing Shandong Province Campus Student Talent Show Contest, 2016

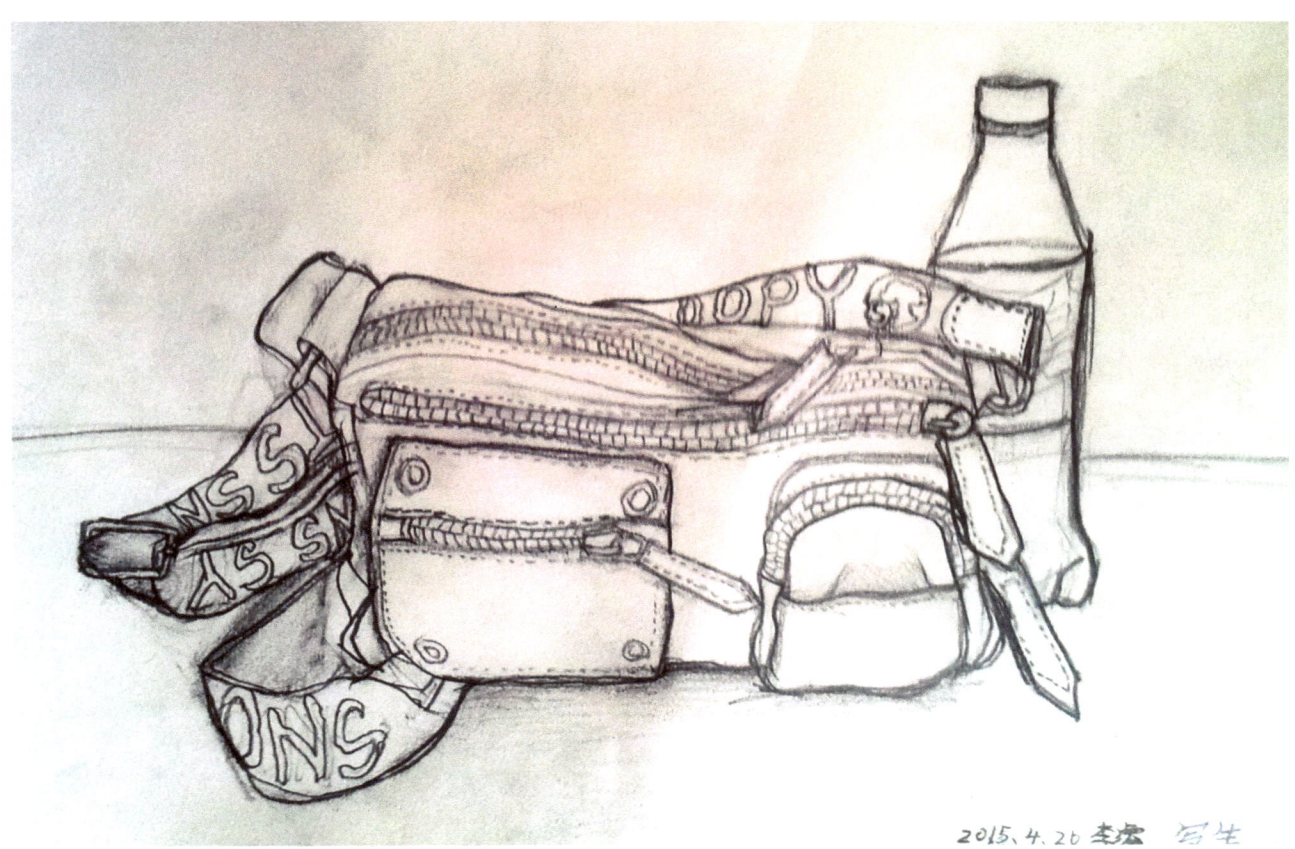

Crossbody Bag, pencil on paper, 2015

RUI LI

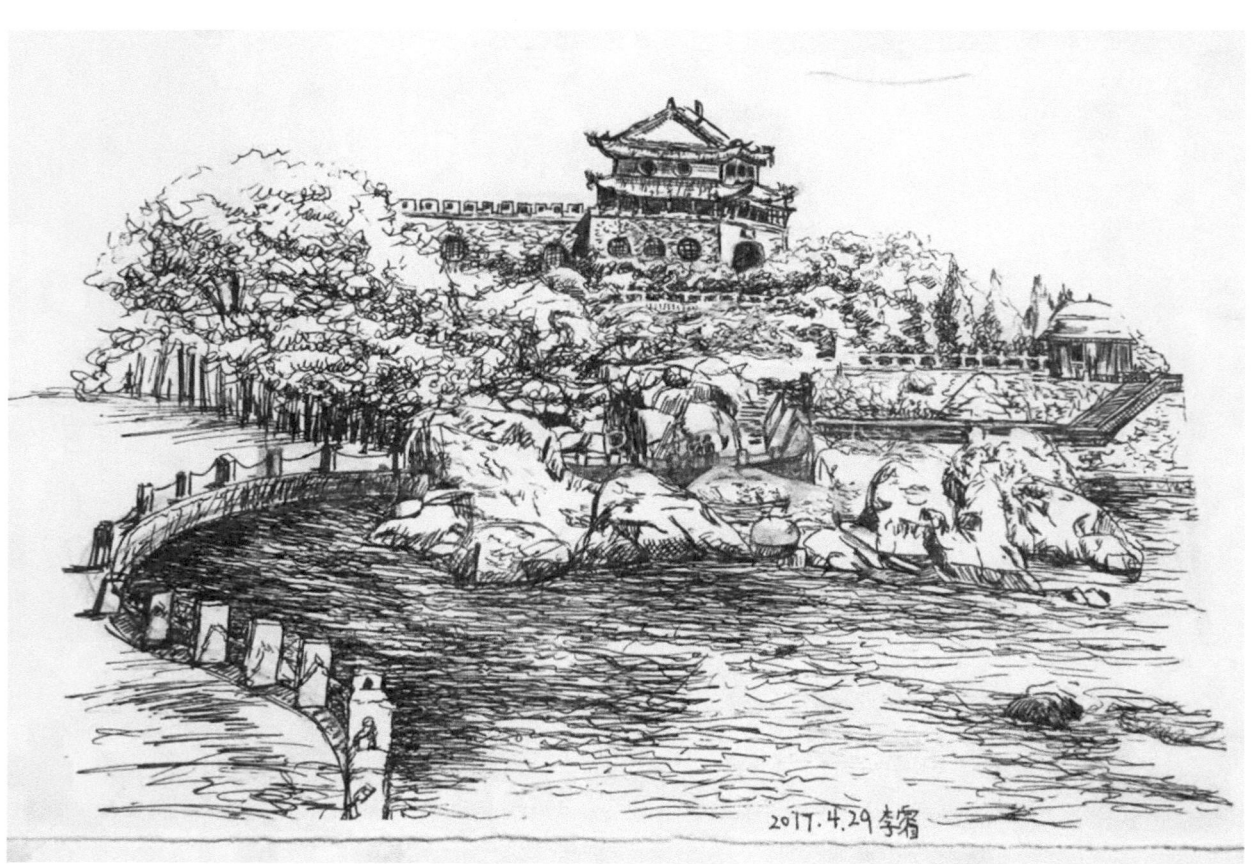

Qingdao Aquarium, pencil on paper, 2017

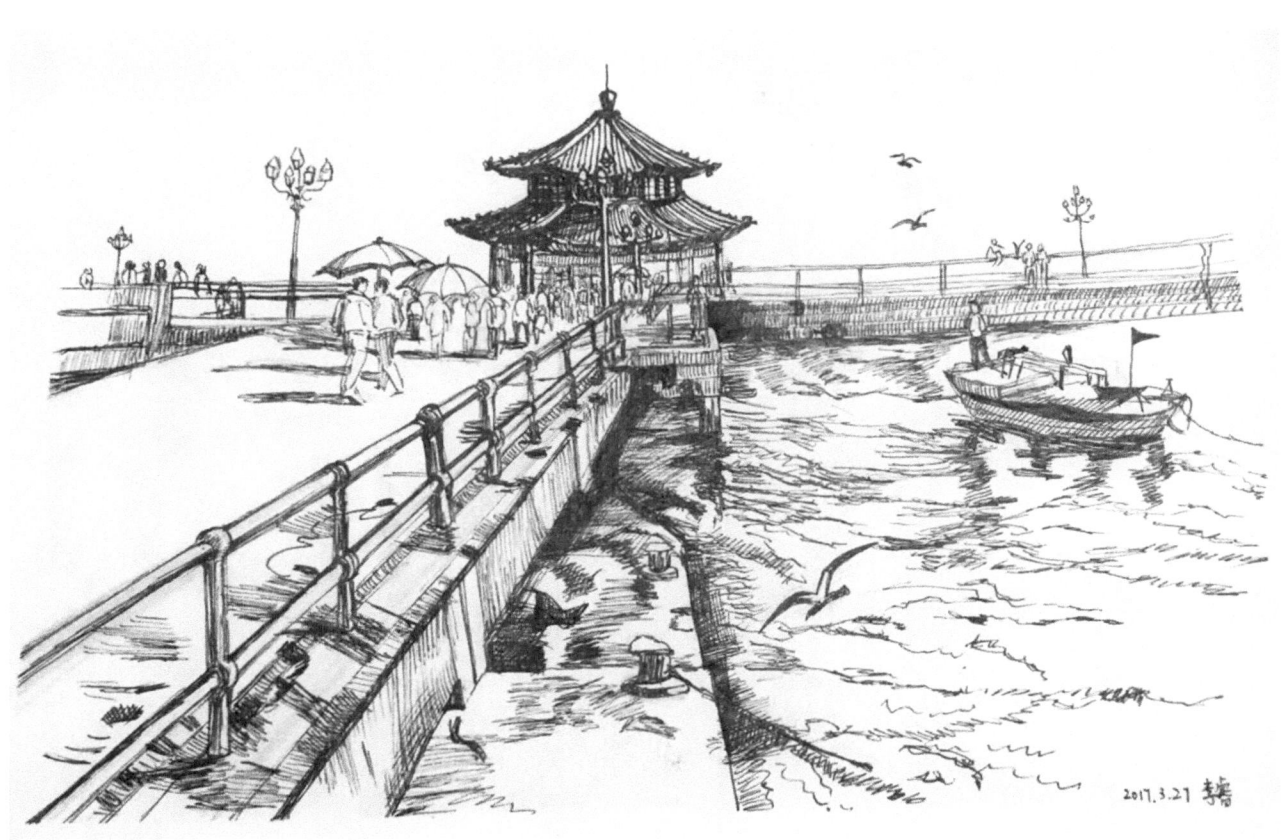

Zhanqiao Pier, pencil on paper, 2017

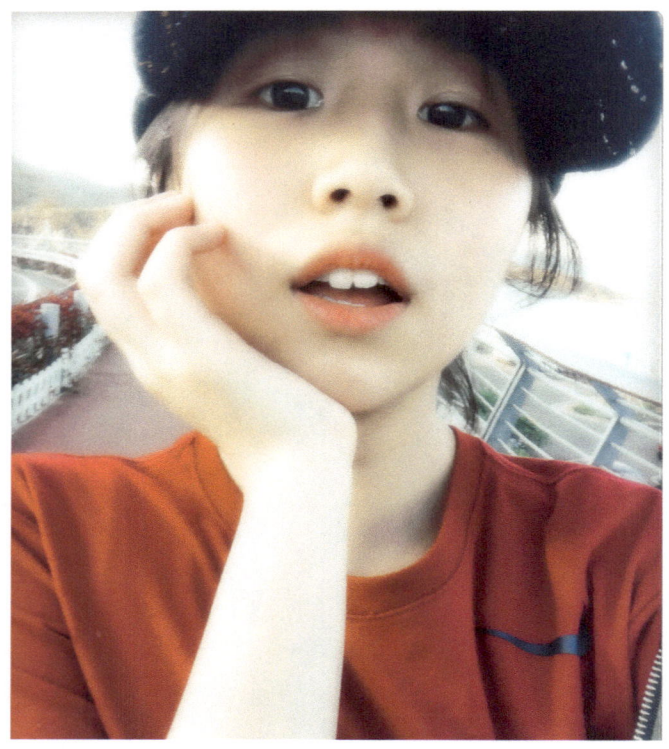

SHUO PANG
Jiaonan No.1 Middle School, China

Rising Star Award, 2nd Liberty Awards, International Society of Young Artists, 2019
Rising Star Award, 1st Liberty Awards, International Society of Young Artists, 2018
Honor Student of Qingdao, Qingdao Bureau of Education, 2017
Excellent Student Leader of Qingdao, Qingdao Bureau of Education, 2017
1st Prize, Exploratory Learning Achievement Selection, Qingdao Education Scientific Research Institute, 2016
1st Prize, Qingdao Oral English Competition, 2016

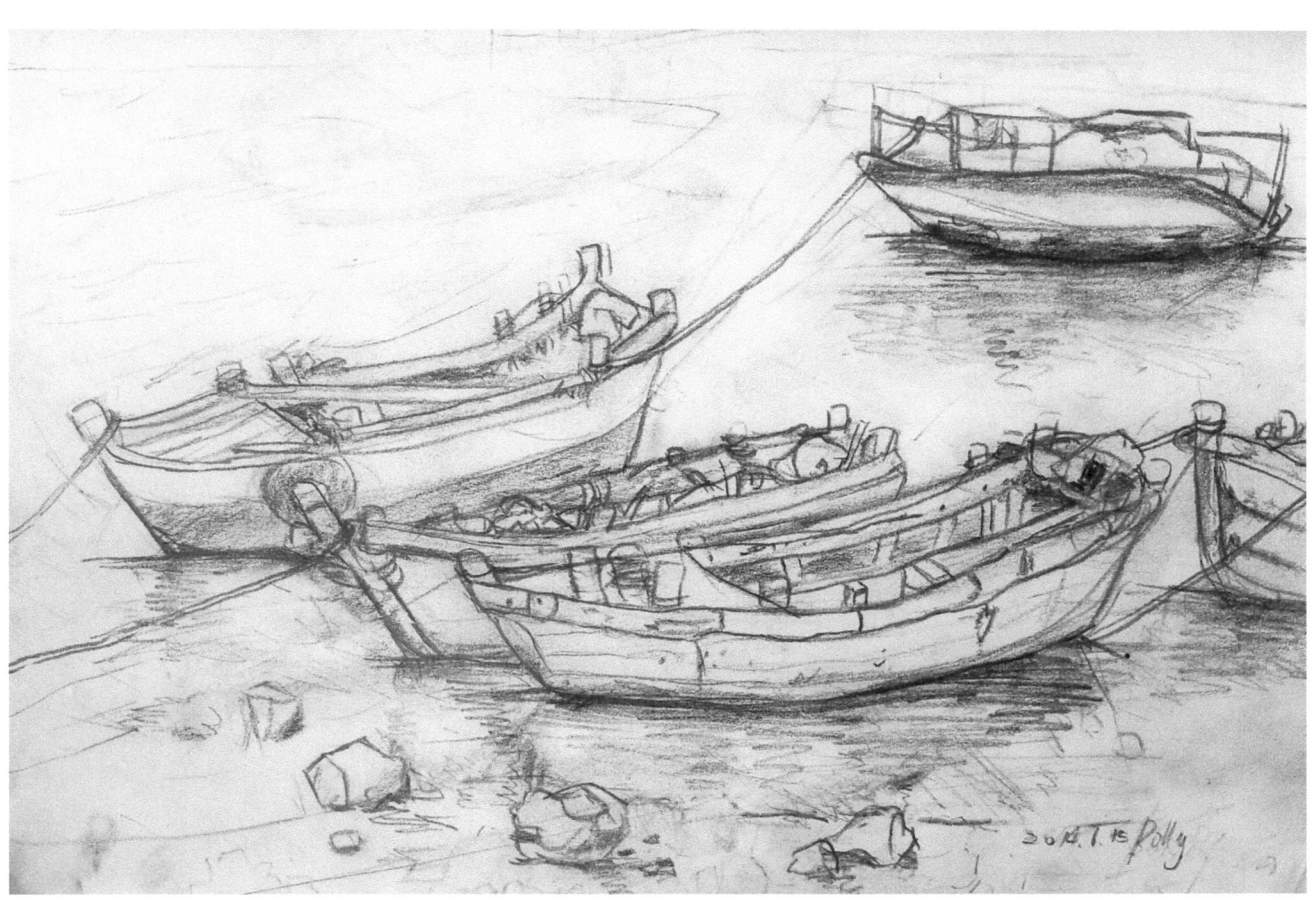

Fishing Boats, pencil on paper, 2014

SHUO PANG

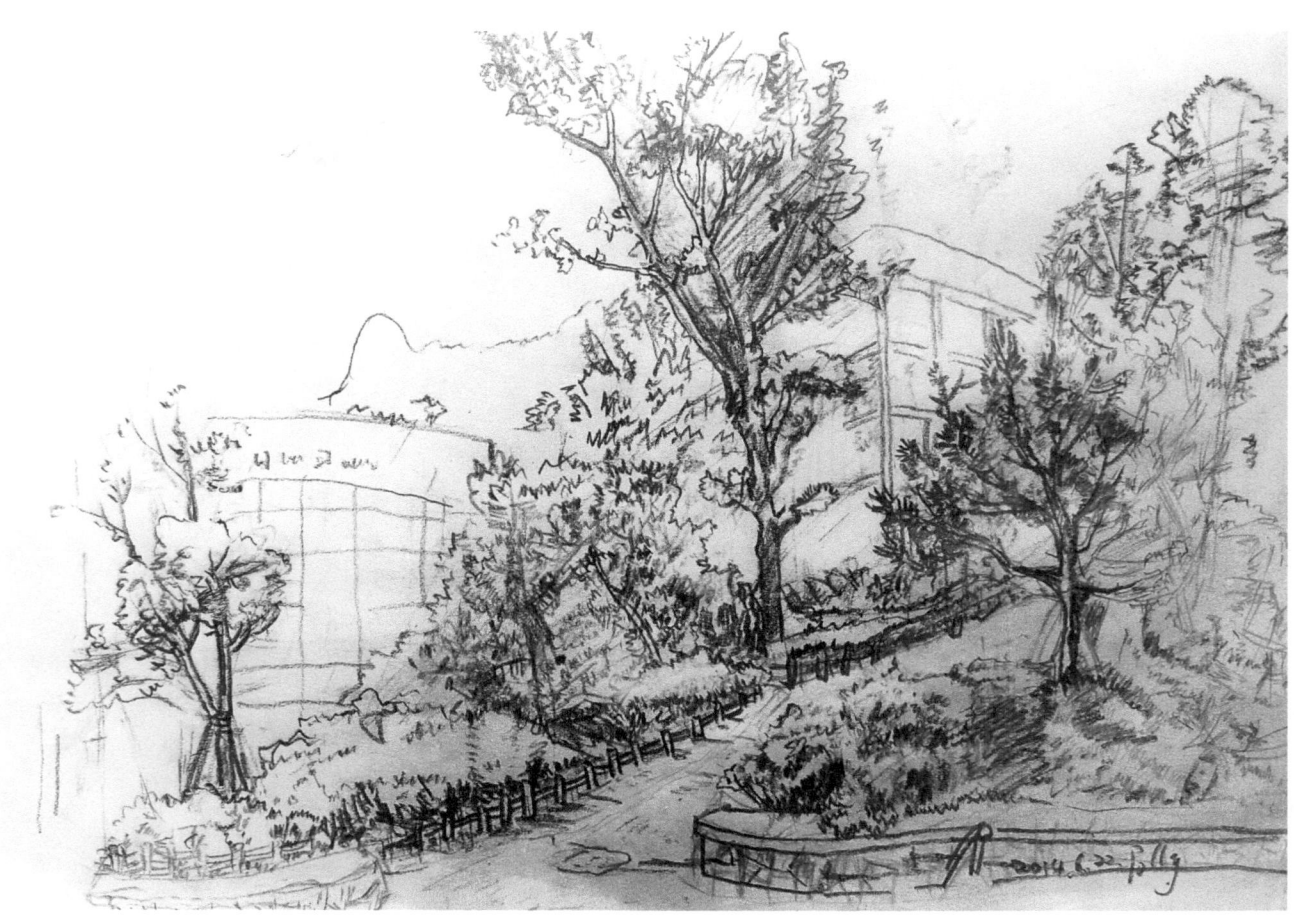

Qingdao Sculpture Park, pencil on paper, 2014

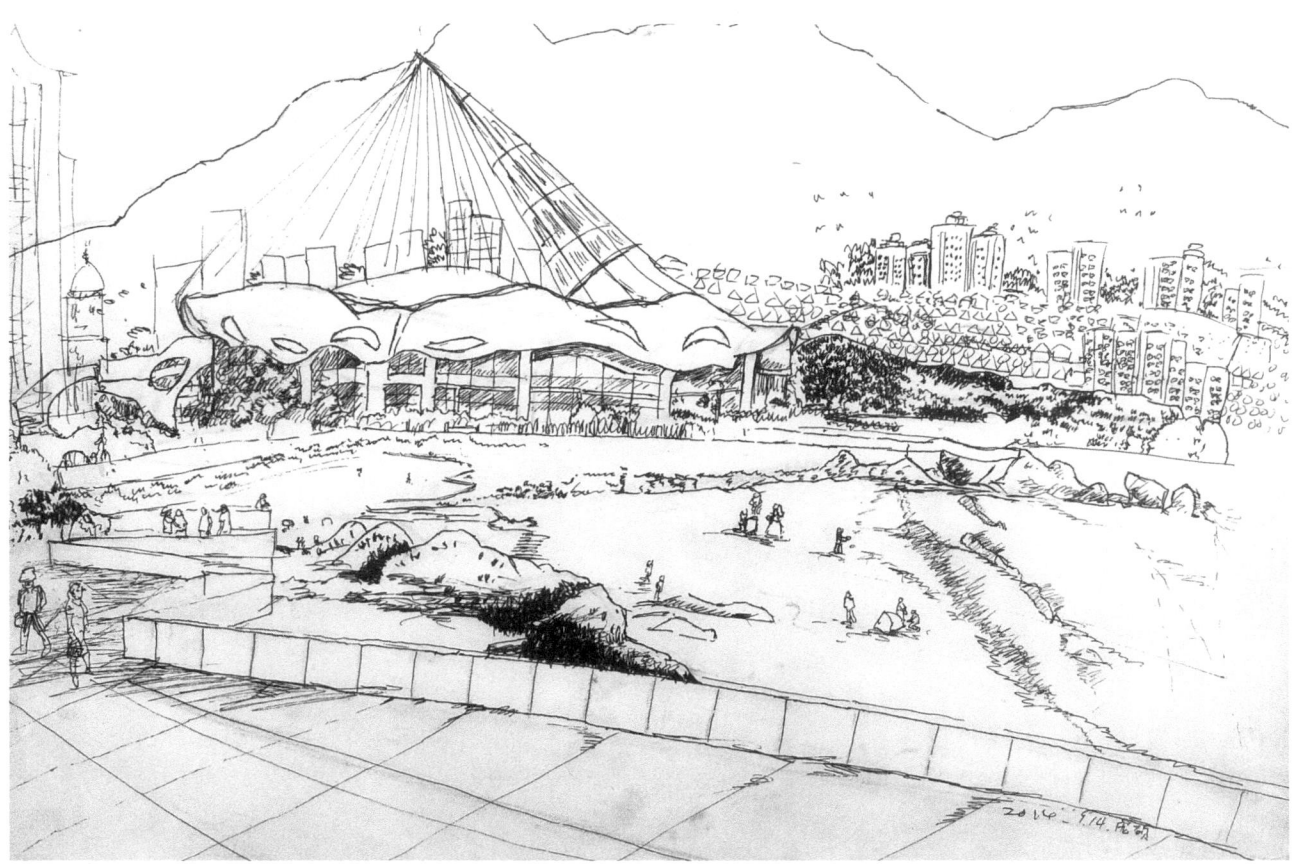

Qingdao Planning Exhibition Center, pen on paper, 2014

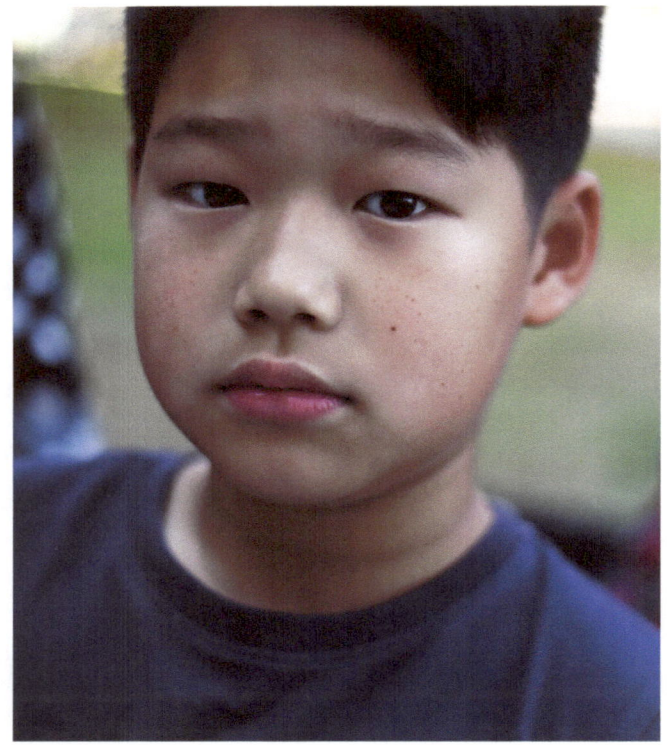

TIMOTHY X. WU
Chaparral Elementary School, USA

Bronze Award for Art, 2nd Liberty Awards, International Society of Young Artists, 2019
Bronze Award for Art, 1st Liberty Awards, International Society of Young Artists, 2018

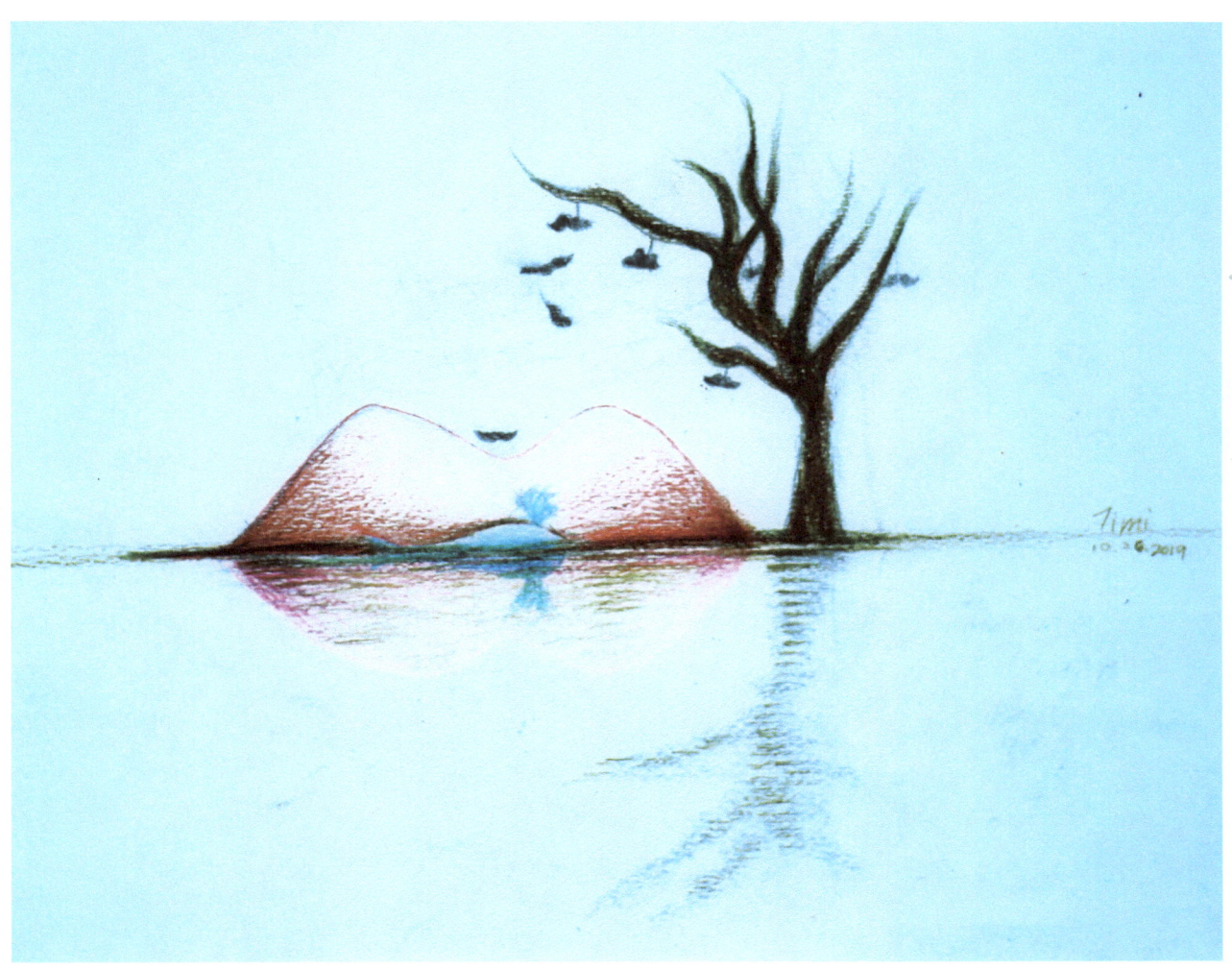

Island, colored pencil on paper, 2019

TIMOTHY X. WU

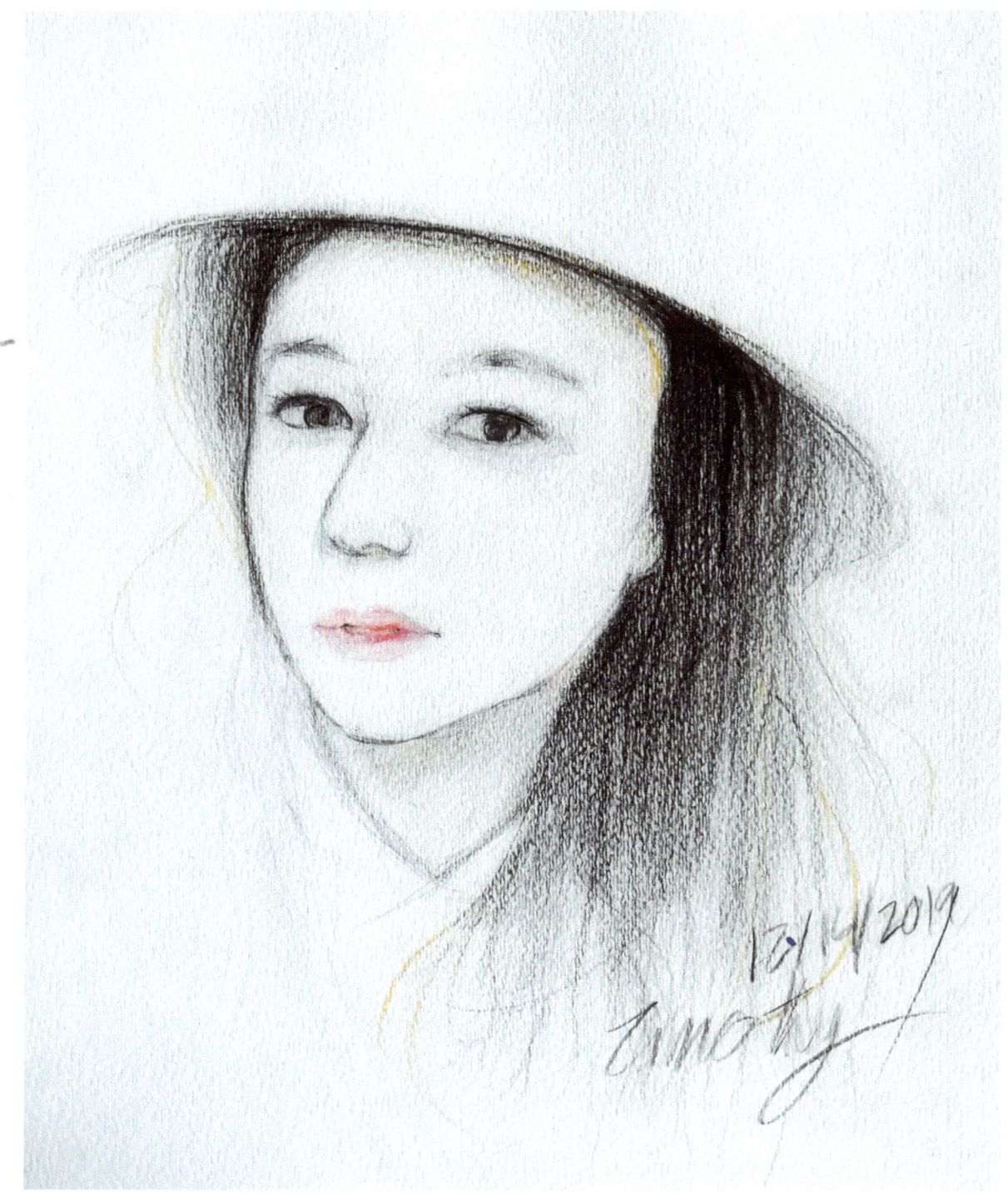

My Mom, pencil and colored pencil on paper, 2019

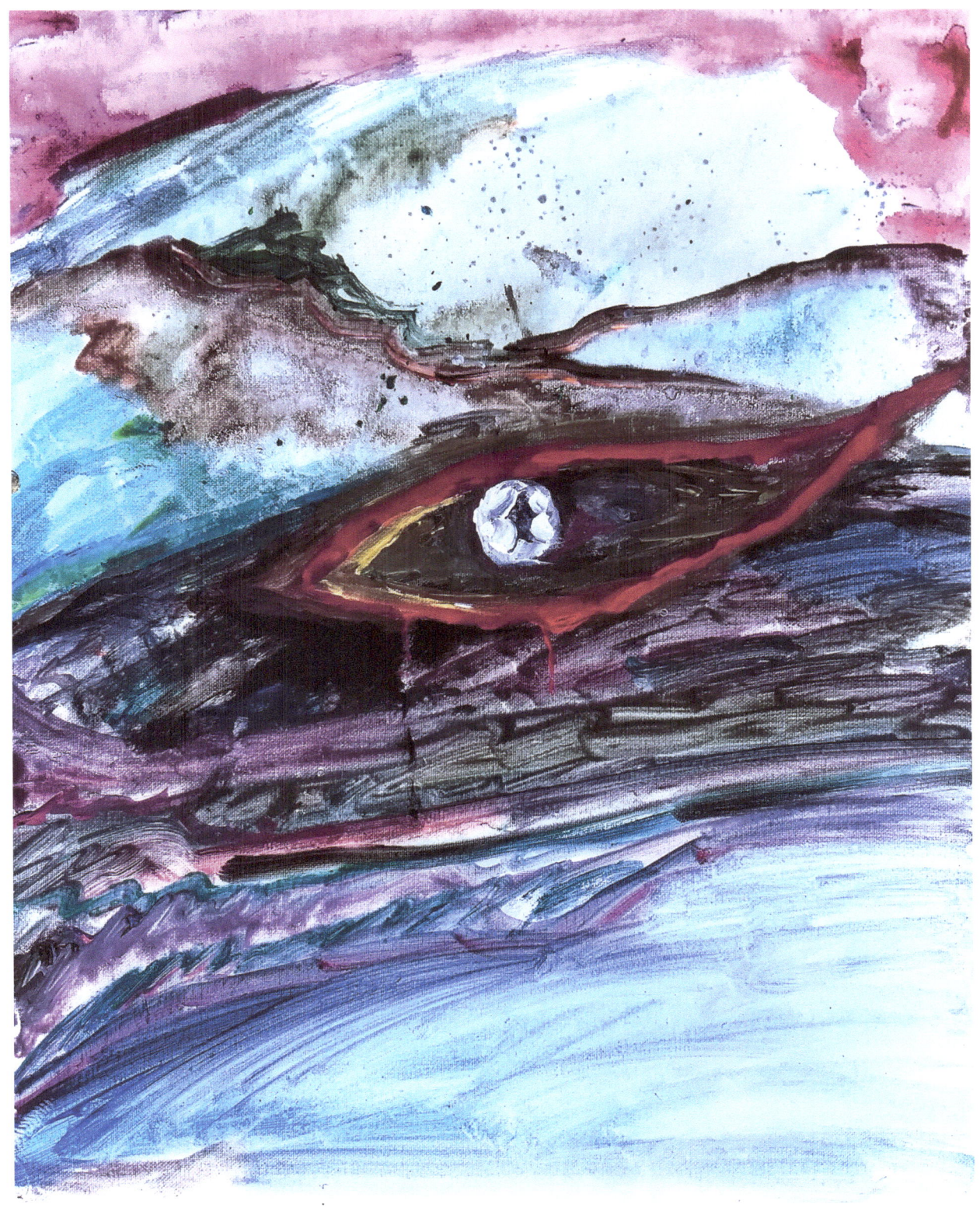

The Eye in the Chaos, acrylic on canvas, 2018

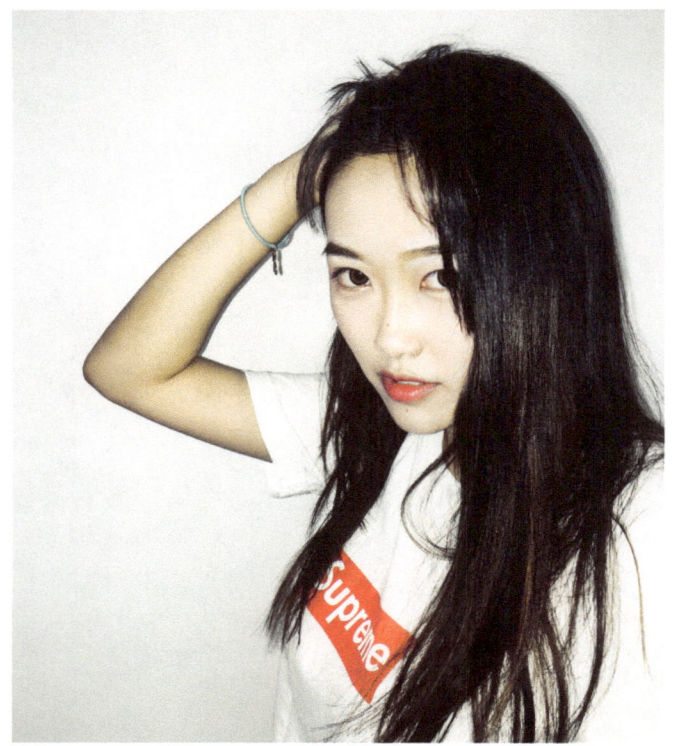

WANCHEN ZHANG
University of Göttingen, Germany

Bronze Award for Art, 1st Liberty Awards, International Society of Young Artists, 2018

WANCHEN ZHANG

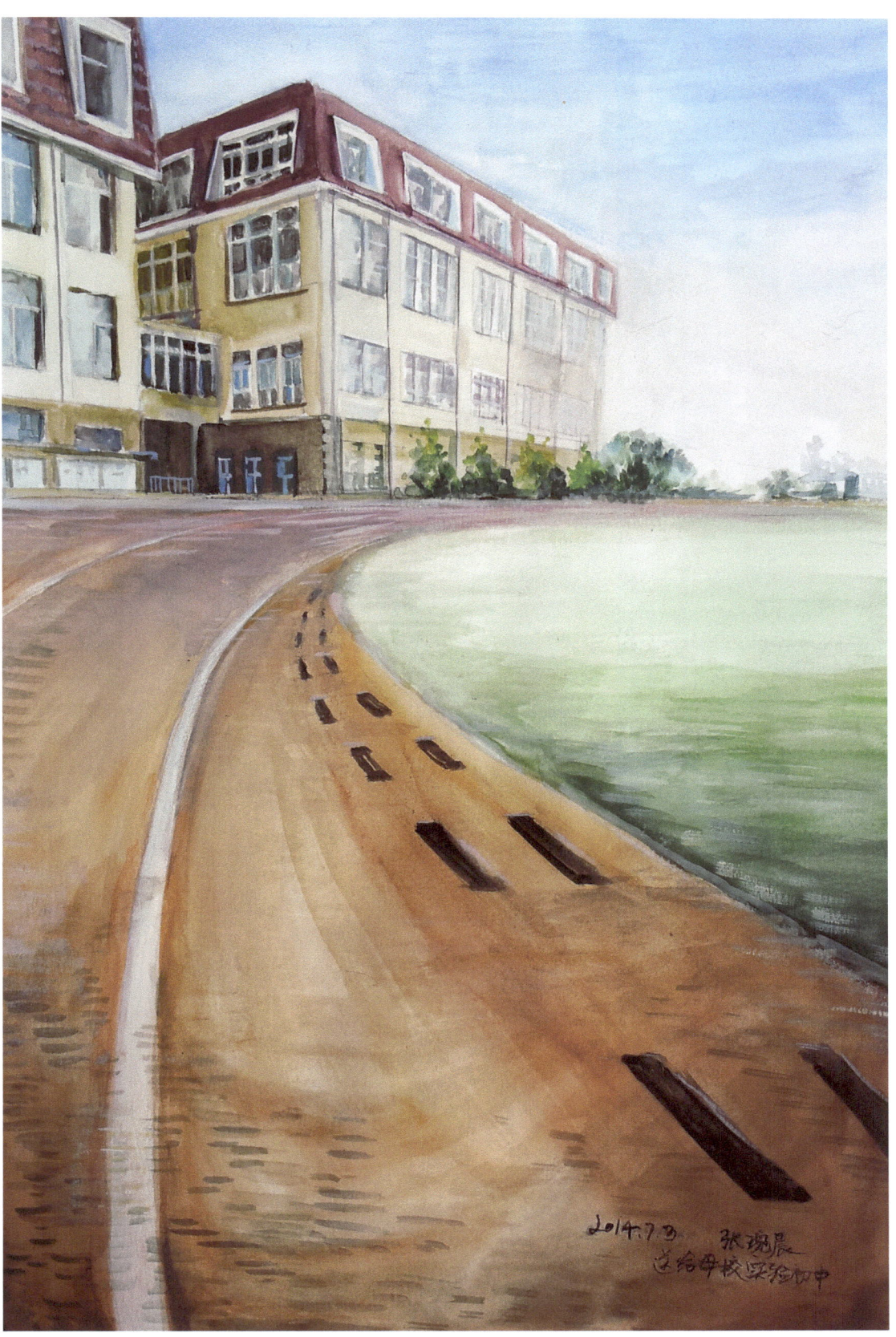

Qingdao Experimental Junior High school, gouache on paper, 2014

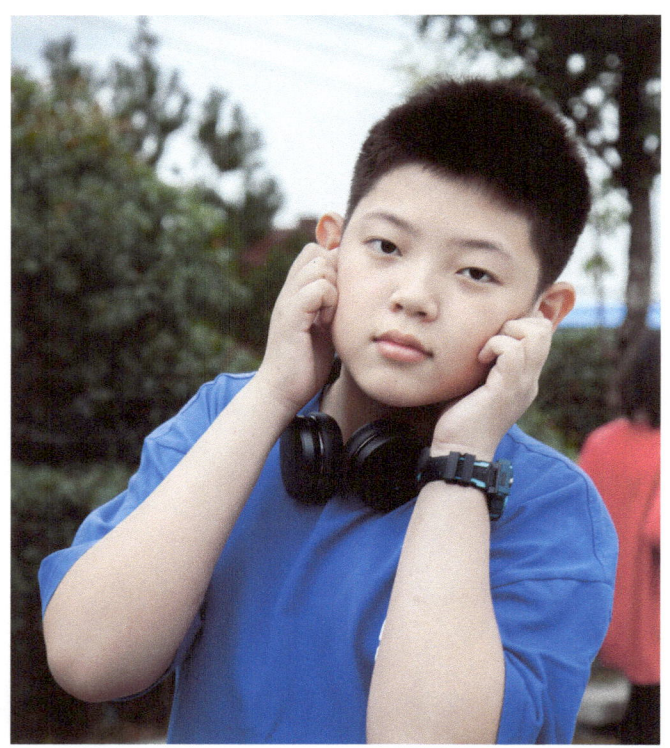

XIKAI XU
Qingdao University Affiliated Middle School, China

Bronze Award for Art, 2nd Liberty Awards, International Society of Young Artists, 2019
Bronze Award for Art, 1st Liberty Awards, International Society of Young Artists, 2018
Bronze Award, "The Colorful Peace" Art Project Honoring the 100th Anniversary of the WWI Armistice, International Society of Young Artists, 2018

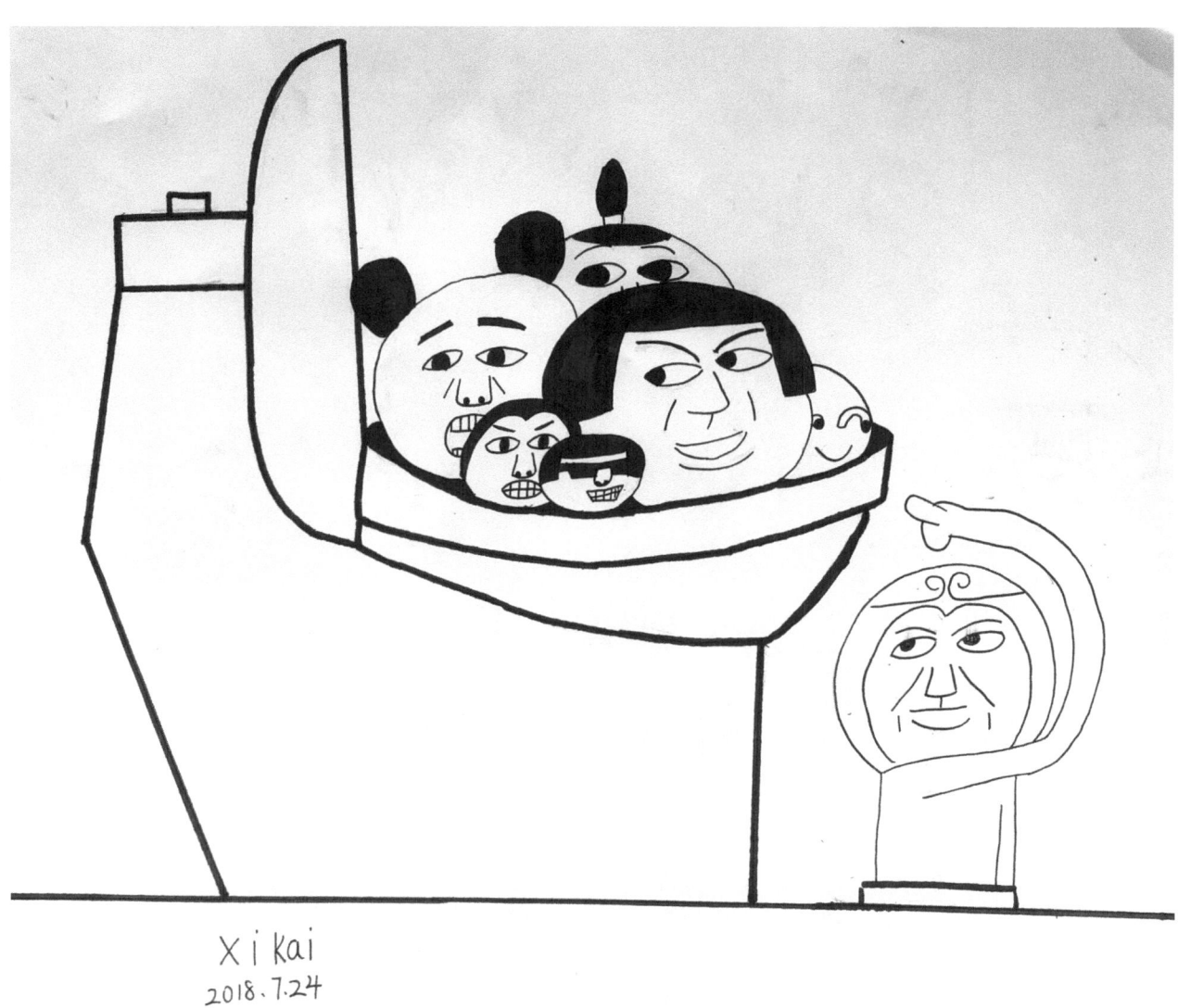

Toilet Guys, pen and marker on paper, 2018

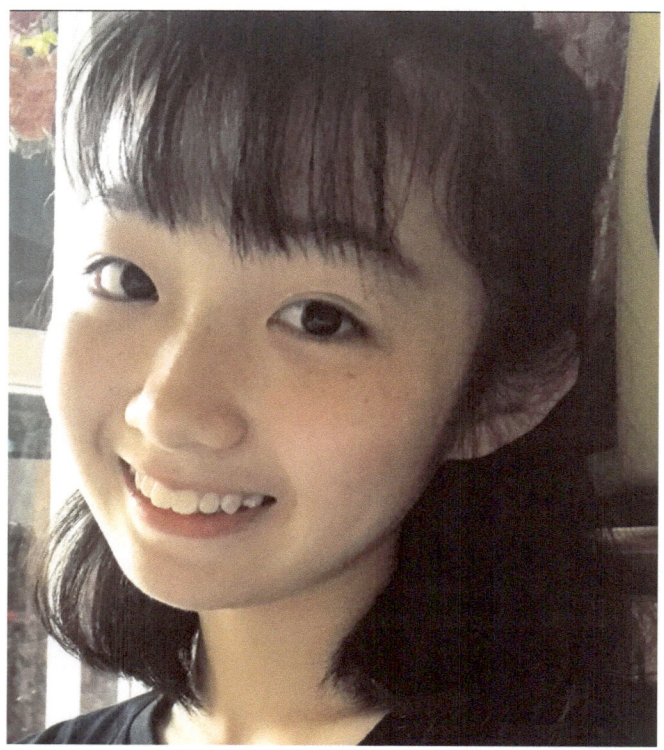

XIN WEN
Qingdao University Affiliated Middle School, China

Bronze Award for Art, 1st Liberty Awards, International Society of Young Artists, 2018
Excellent Performance, 8th "China Meets Europe" Art Festival in 2018
1st Prize, Simulated Remote-Controlled Helicopter Crossing Contest, Qingdao Junior Aeromodelling Competition, 2018
1st Prize, Guzheng, 6th Annual Qiluqing Shandong Province Campus Student Talent Show Contest, 2017
1st Prize, Guzheng, 5th Annual Qiluqing Shandong Province Campus Student Talent Show Contest, 2016
Gold Medal, Guzheng, 8th "the Same Sky" National Campus Culture Art Festival in Shanghai, 2016

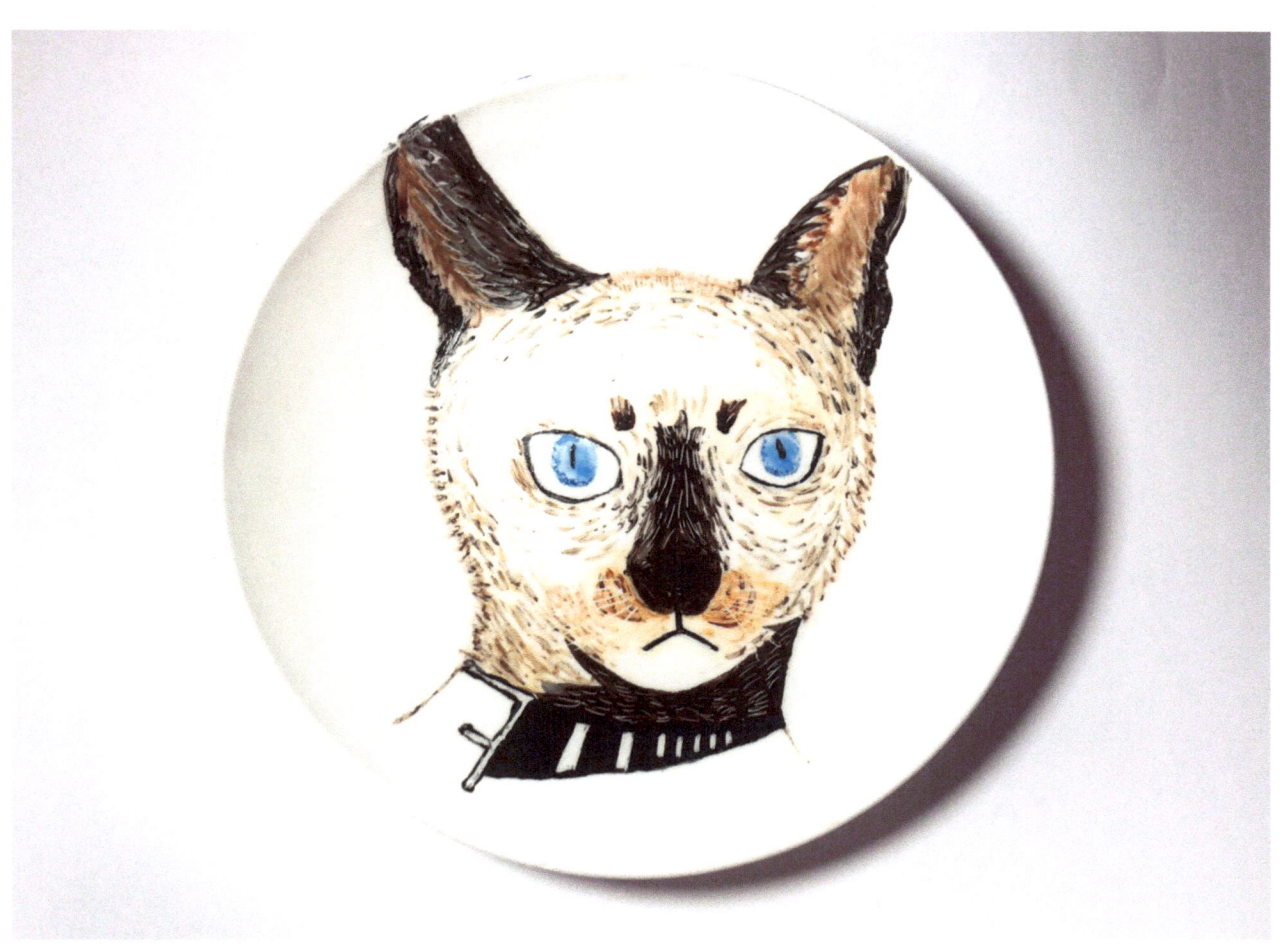

Akashi, Color Glaze on Ceramic, 2019

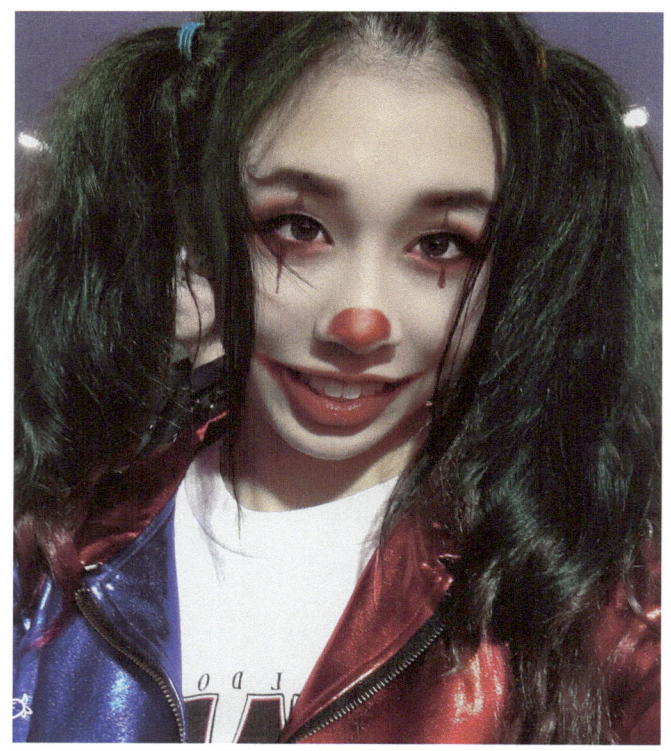

XUNYAN KUANG
Ruben S. Ayala High School, USA

Person of 2019, International Society of Young Artists, 2019
Gold Award for Art, 2nd Liberty Awards, International Society of Young Artists, 2019
Bronze Award for Art, 1st Liberty Awards, International Society of Young Artists, 2018

XUNYAN KUANG

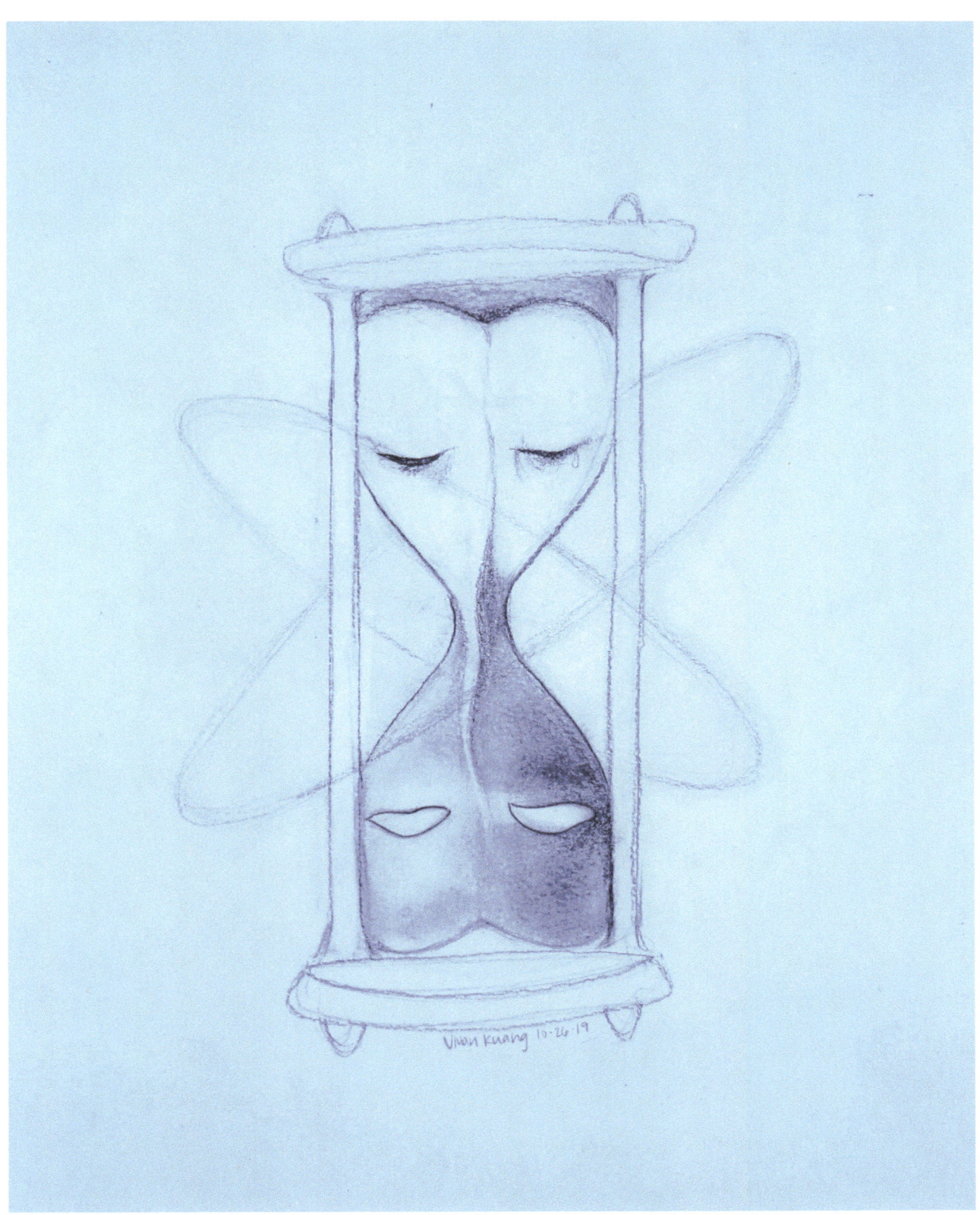

Society, pencil on paper, 2019

XUNYAN KUANG

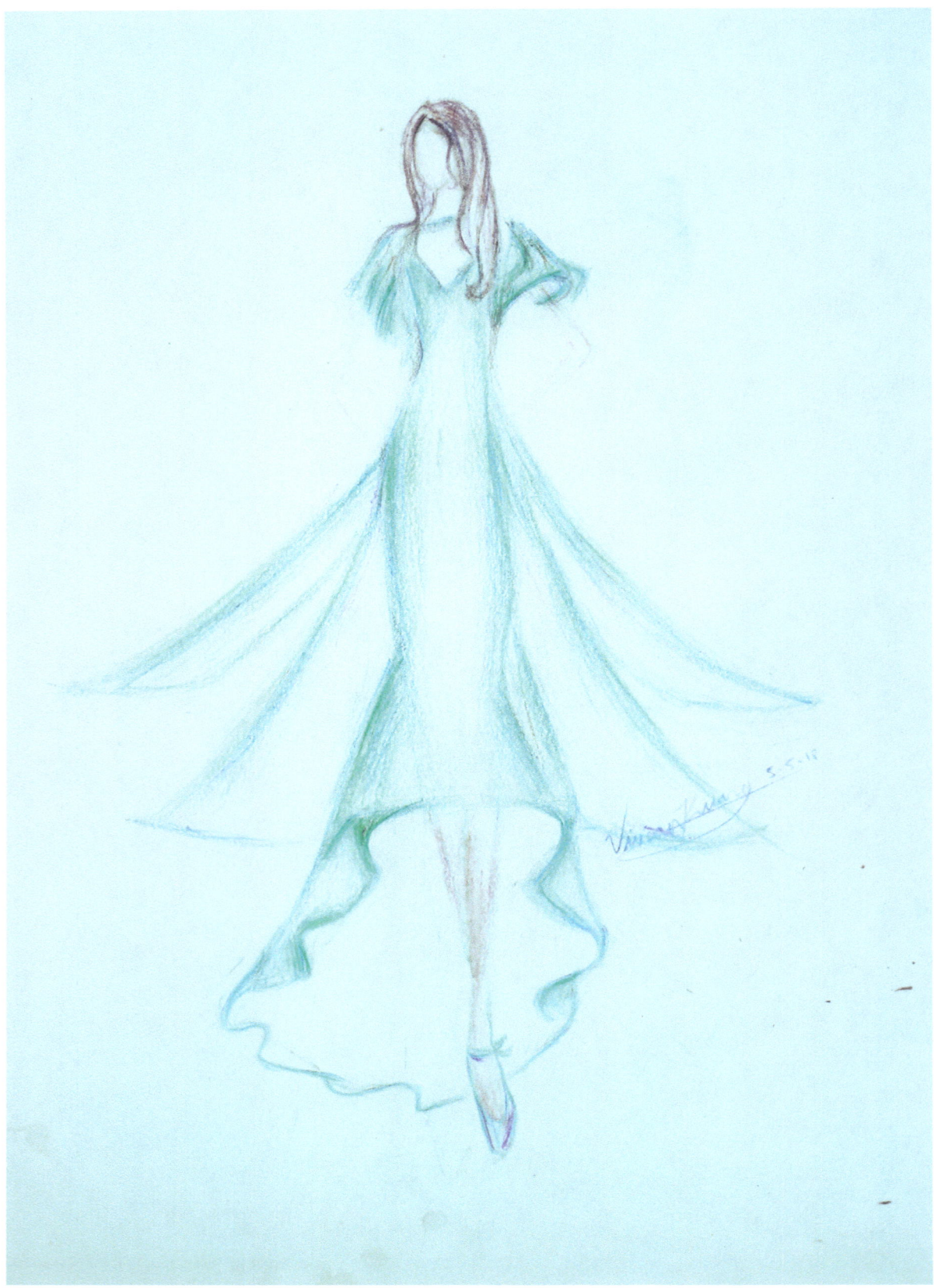

Cucumber, colored pencil on paper, 2018

XUNYAN KUANG

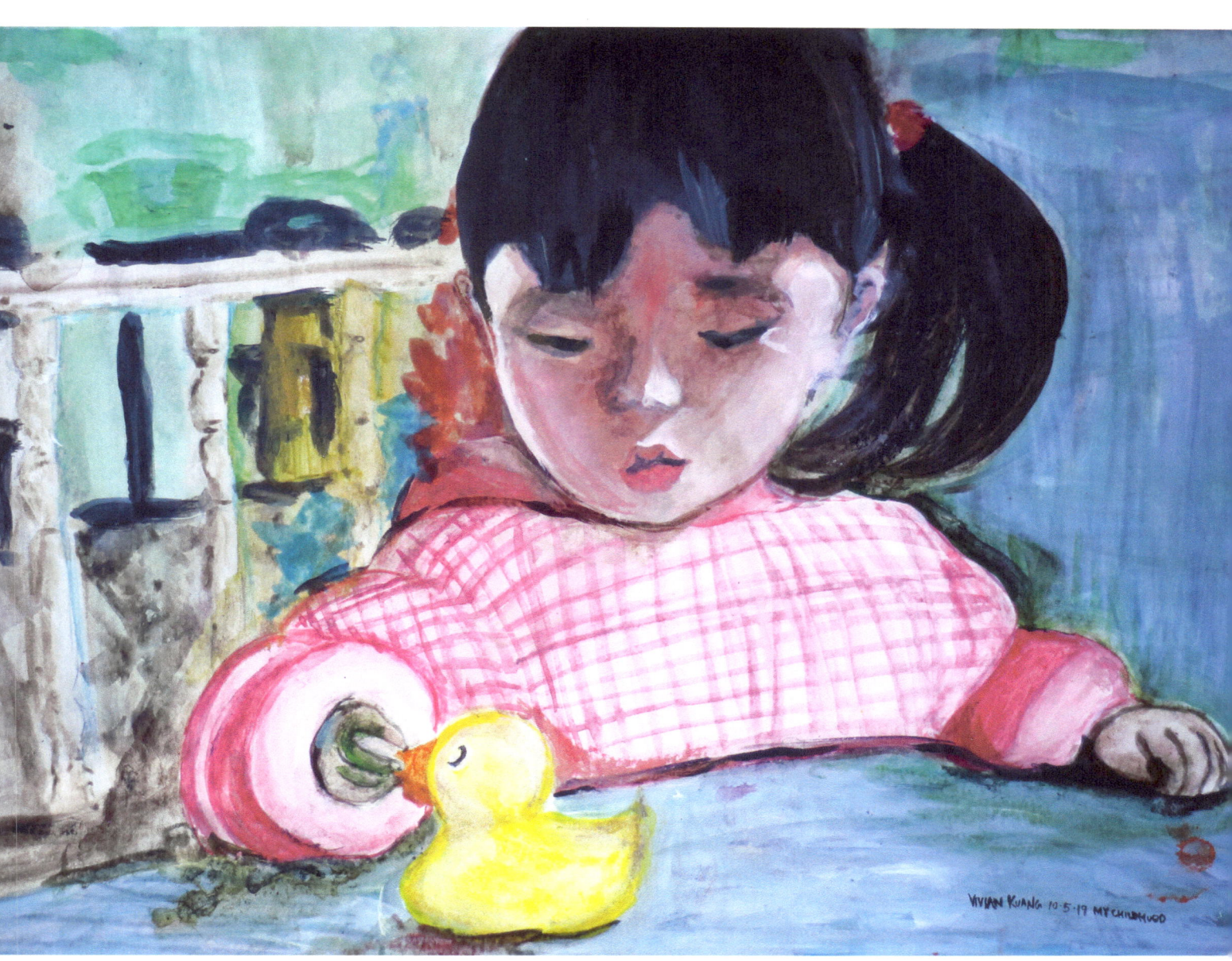

Childhood, acrylic on paper, 2019

XUNYAN KUANG

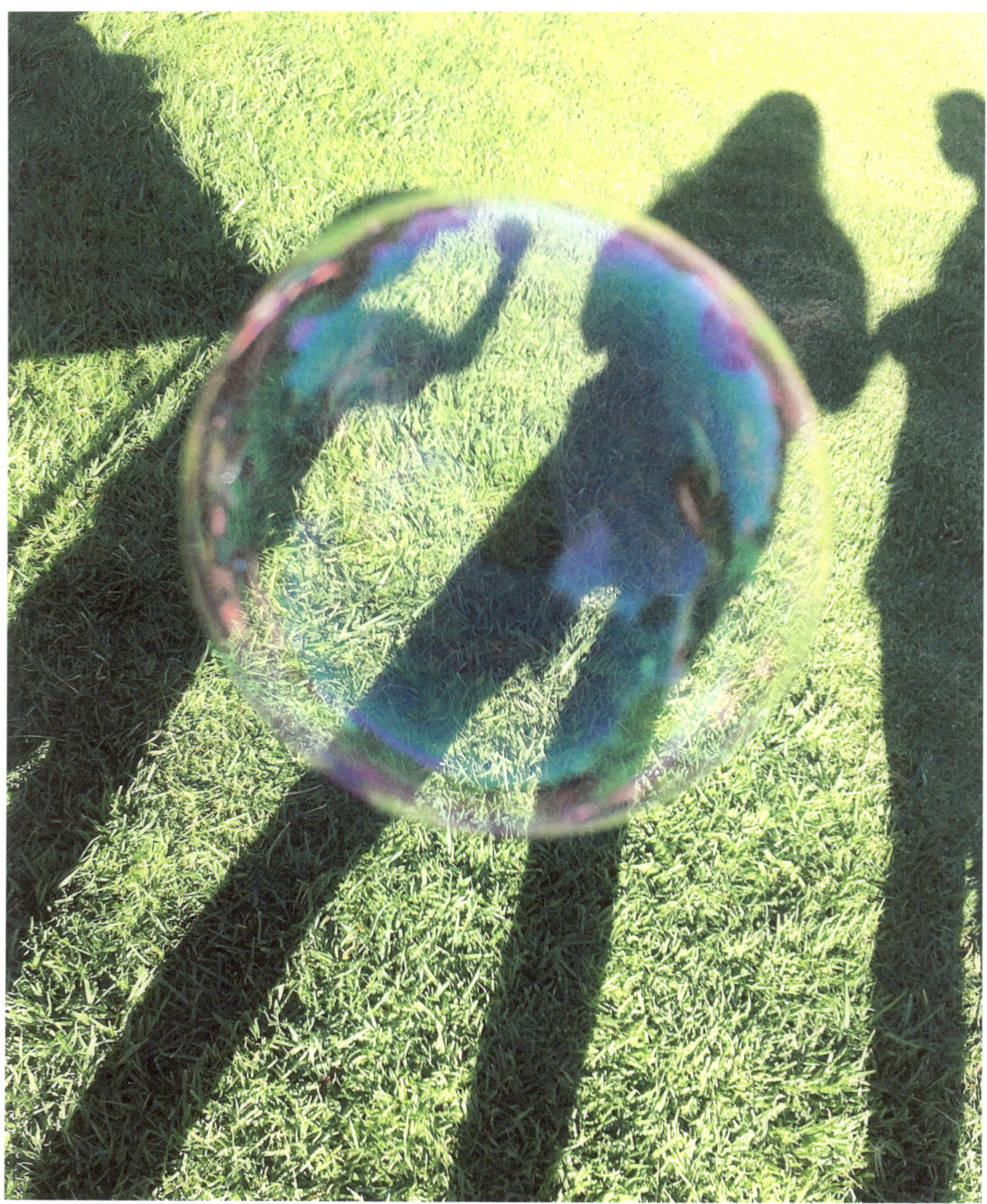

Bubble, photography, 2019

XUNYAN KUANG

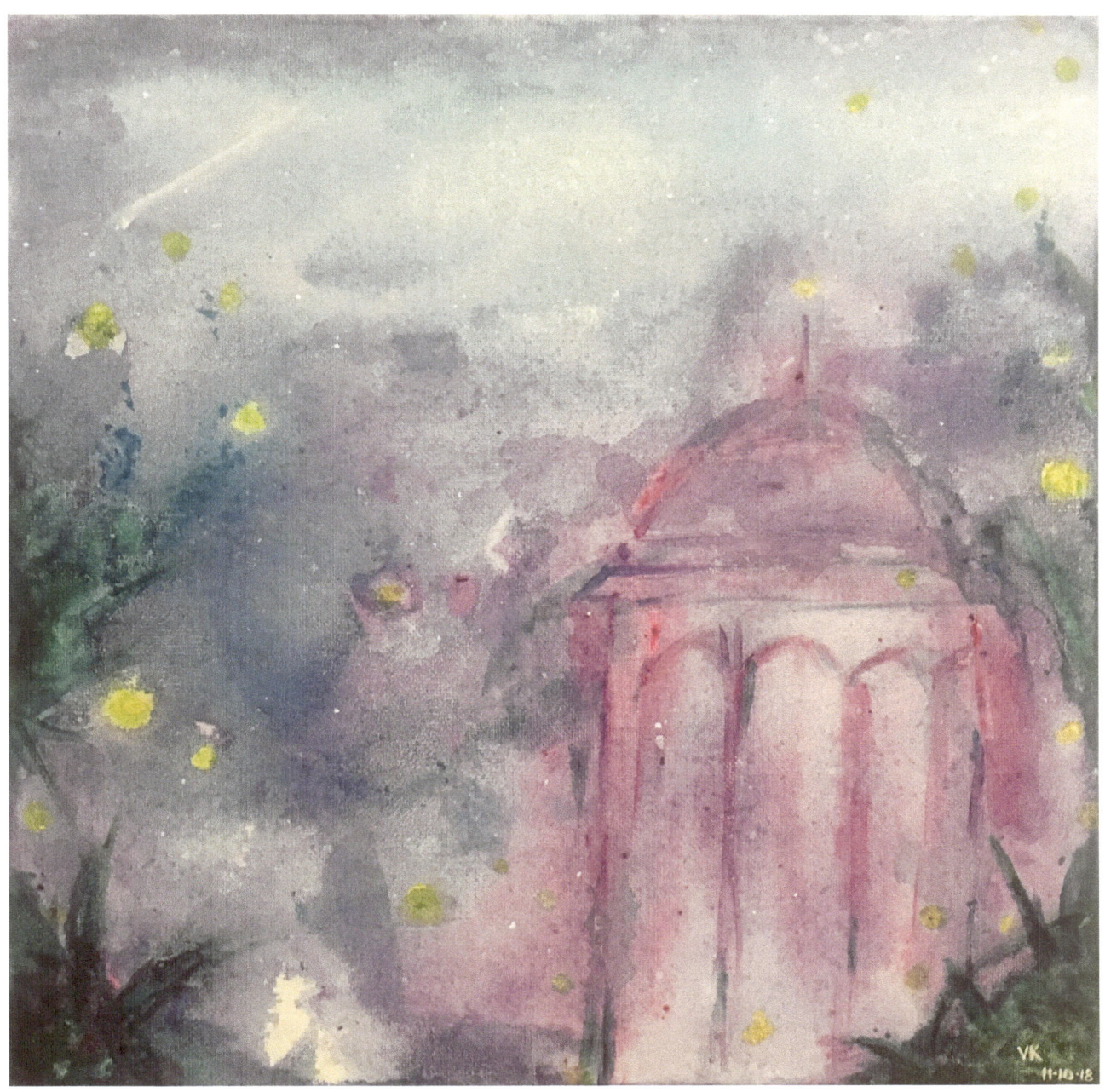

Firefly, acrylic on canvas, 2018

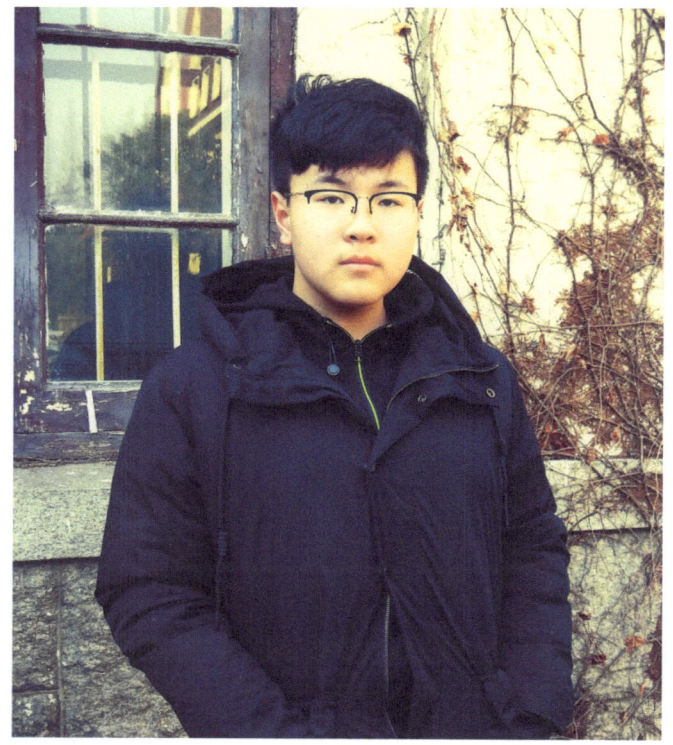

YIFEI WANG
Qingdao No. 1 High School, China

Bronze Award for Art, 2nd Liberty Awards, International Society of Young Artists, 2019
Bronze Award for Art, 1st Liberty Awards, International Society of Young Artists, 2018

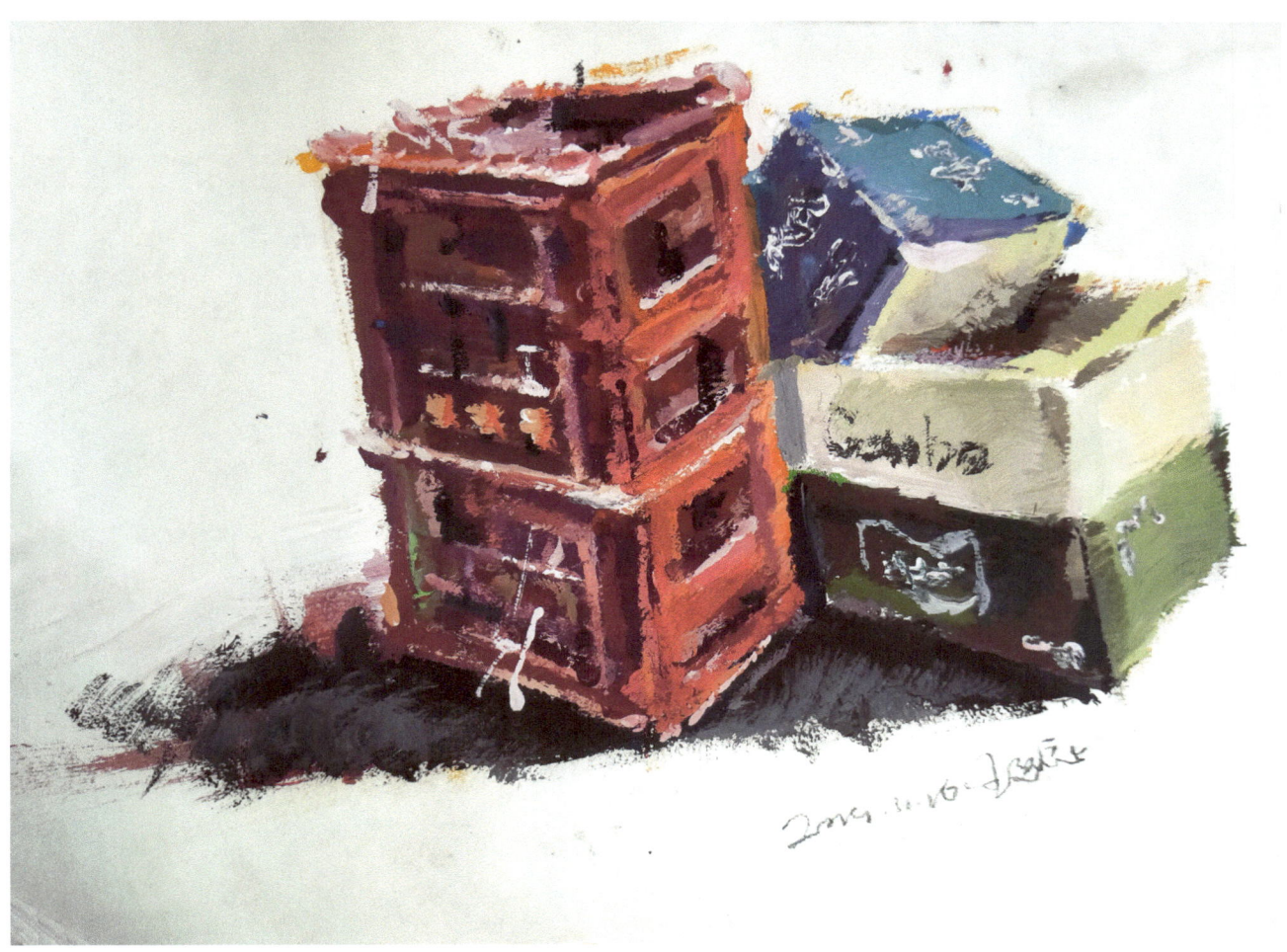

Boxes, gouache on paper, 2019

YIFEI WANG

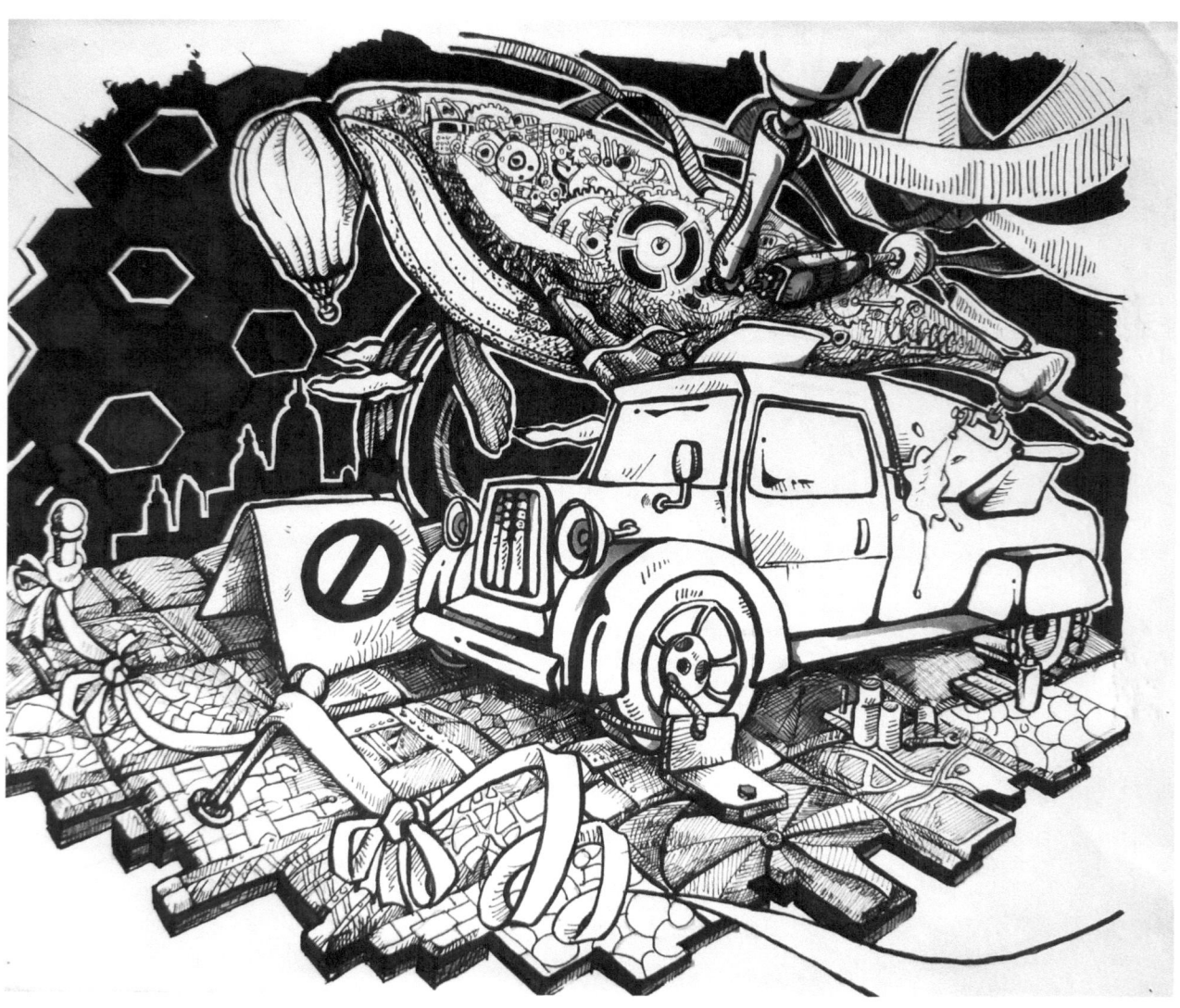

Chaos, pen on paper, 2019

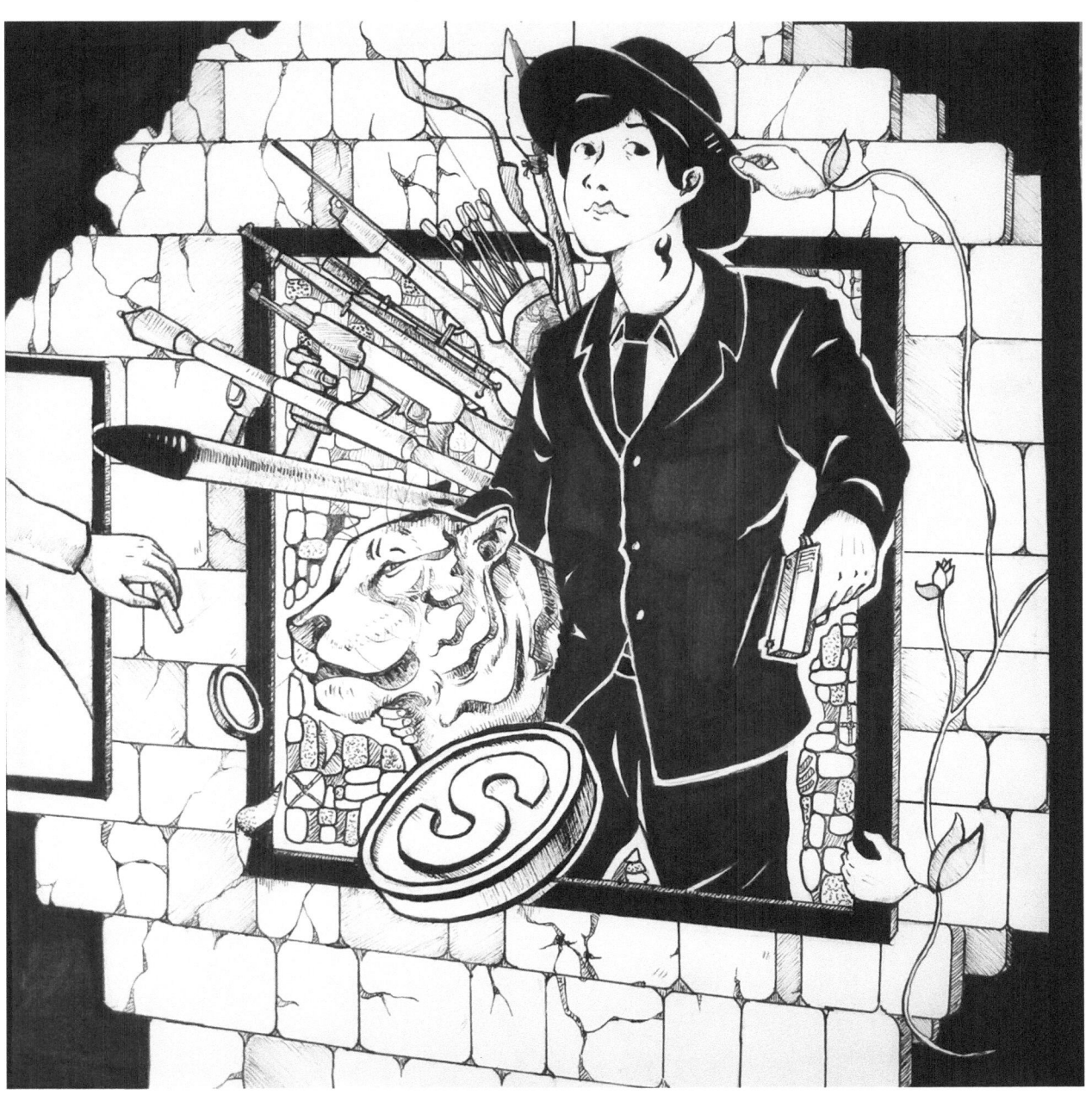

Guns N' Tiger, pen on paper, 2018

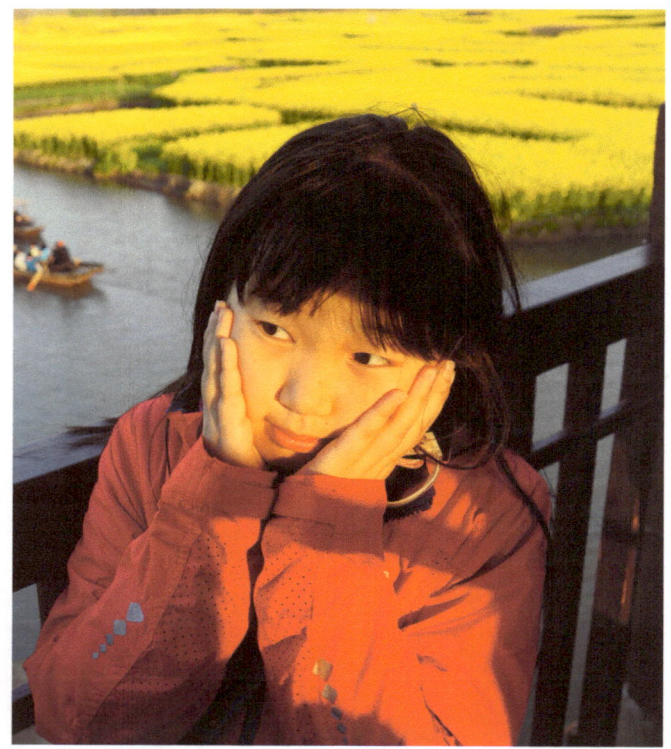

YIFEI XIAO
Qingdao No. 66 High School, China

Gold Award for Art, 1st Liberty Awards, International Society of Young Artists, 2018
Gold Award, "The Colorful Peace" Art Project Honoring the 100th Anniversary of the WWI Armistice, International Society of Young Artists, 2018

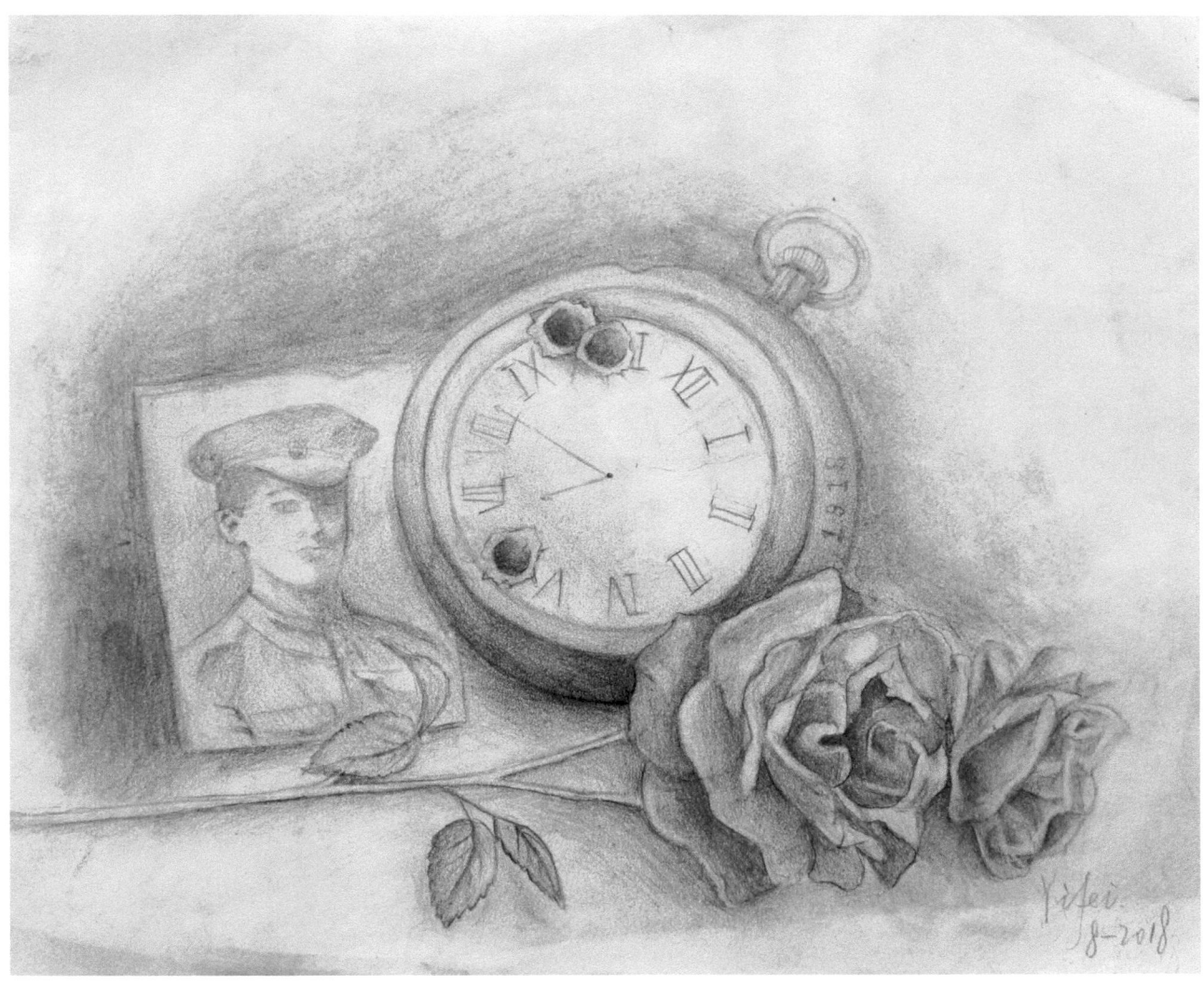

The Scarred Pocket Watch: in Honor of the 100th Anniversary of the WWI Armistice
Pencil on paper, 2018

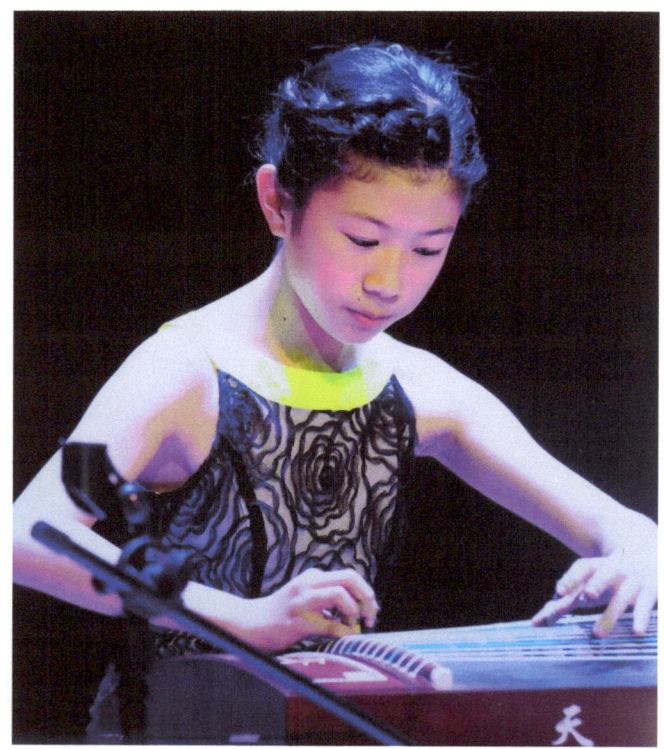

YIHAN ZHANG
Ocean University of China Affiliated Middle School, China

Gold Award for Art, 2nd Liberty Awards, International Society of Young Artists, 2019
Rising Star Award, 1st Liberty Awards, International Society of Young Artists, 2018
National 2nd Prize, Guzheng, 2nd Music Creates Future International Youth Talent Plan, 2018
1st Prize, Guzheng, 2nd Music Creates Future International Youth Talent Plan of Shandong, 2018
Gold Medal, Guzheng, National Juvenile Art Show by Central Conservatory of Music, 2017
2nd Prize, Guzheng, 5th Annual Qiluqing Shandong Province Campus Student Talent Show Contest, 2016

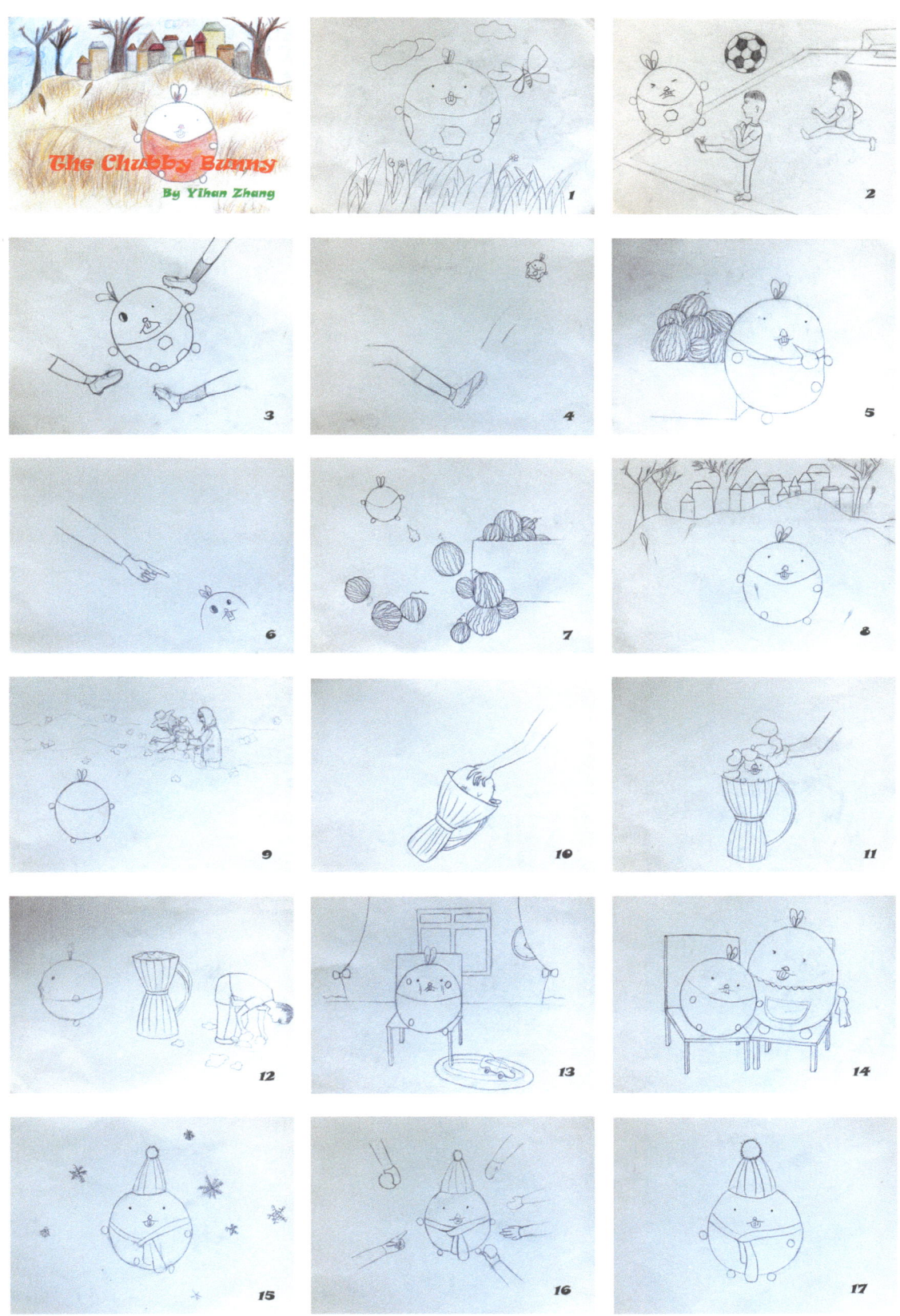

The Chubby Bunny, picture book, 2015-18

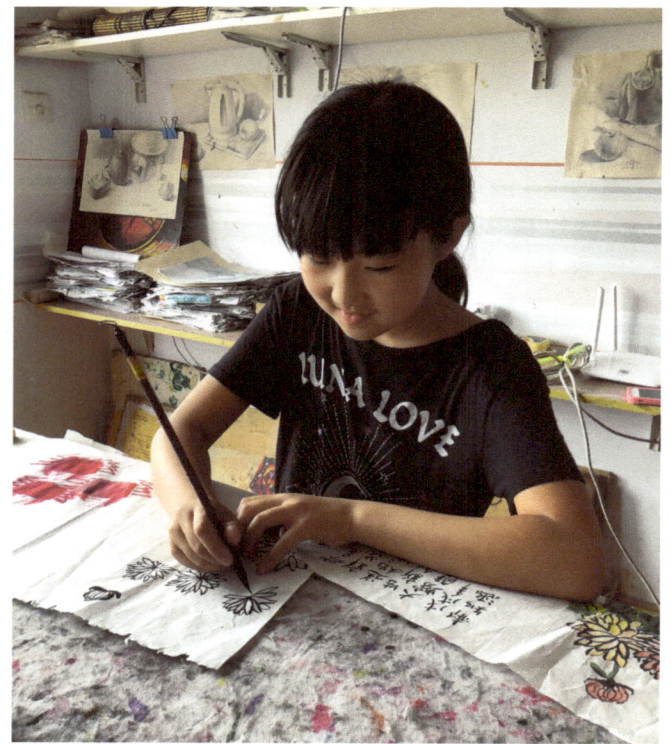

YUE WANG
Qingdao Cornerstone Bilingual School, China

Rising Star Award, 2nd Liberty Awards, International Society of Young Artists, 2019
Rising Star Award, 1st Liberty Awards, International Society of Young Artists, 2018

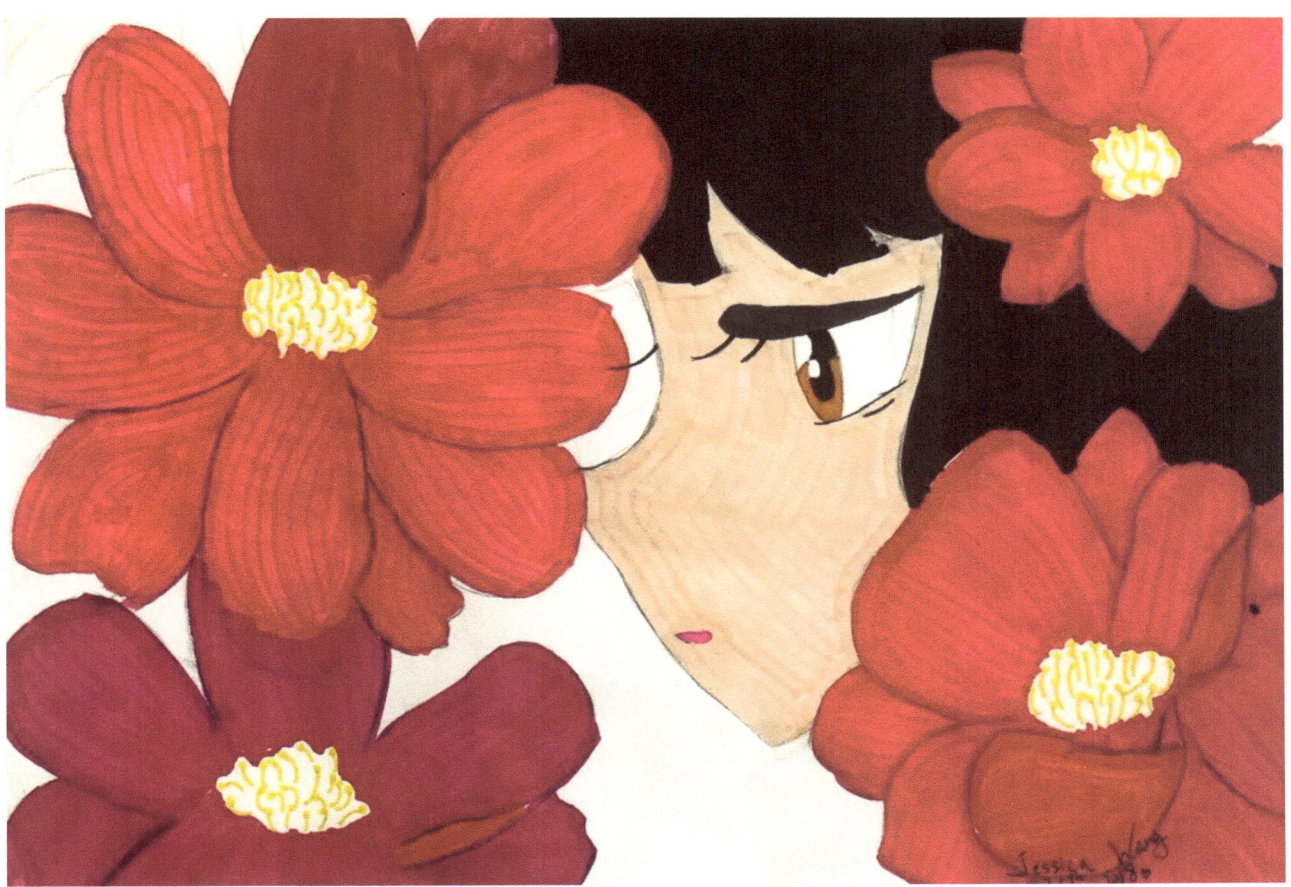

Red, coloring marker on paper, 2018

YUE WANG

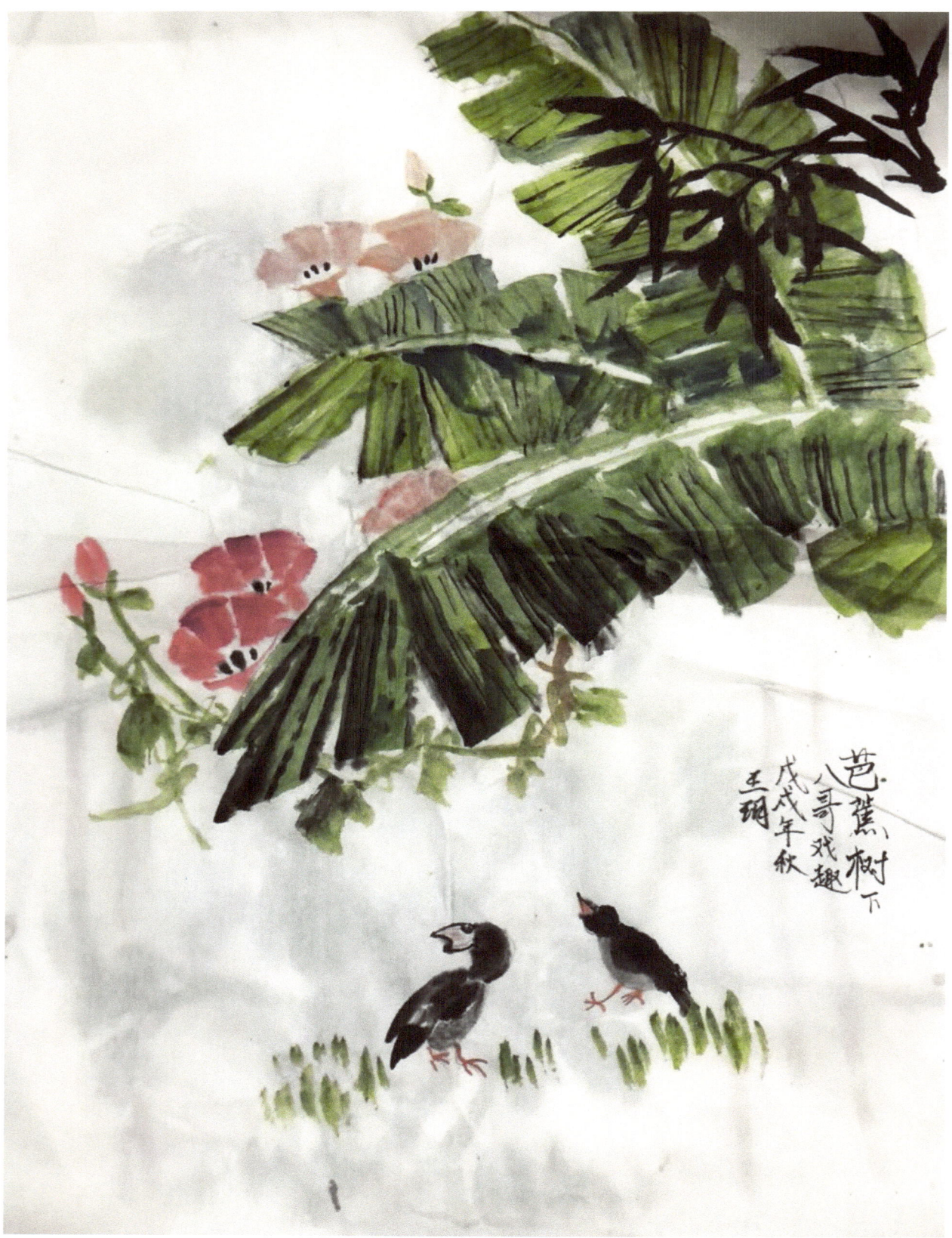

Under the Banana Tree, Chinese painting pigment on rice paper, 2018

YUE WANG

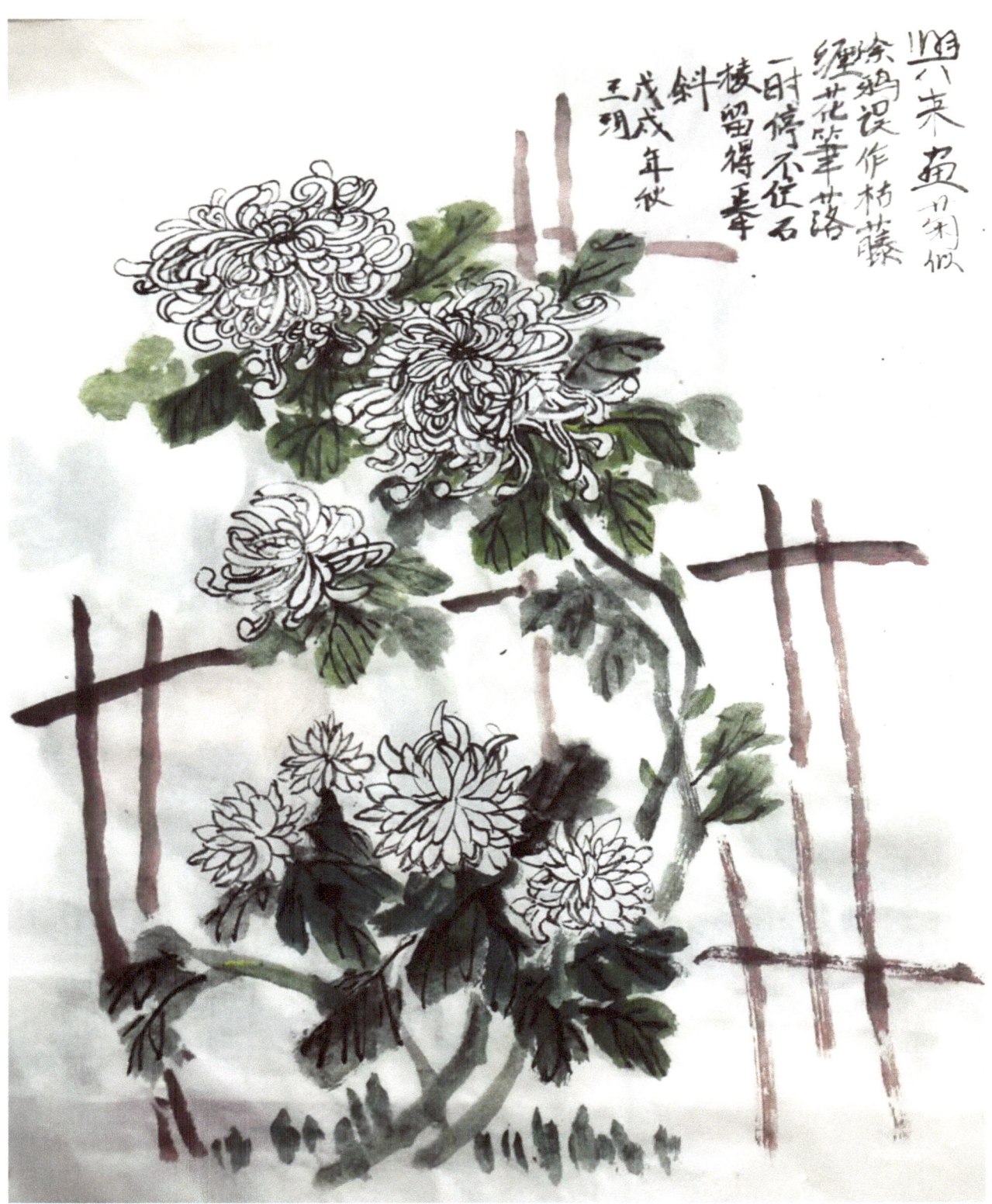

Chrysanthemum, Chinese painting pigment on rice paper, 2018

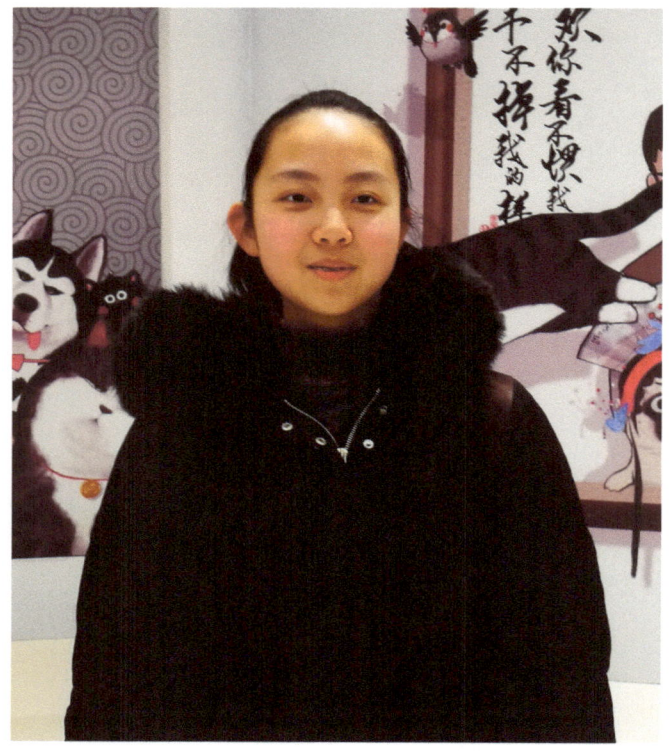

YU JIANG
Qingdao No.58 High School, China

Bronze Award for Art, 2nd Liberty Awards, International Society of Young Artists, 2019
Gold Award for Art, 1st Liberty Awards, International Society of Young Artists, 2018

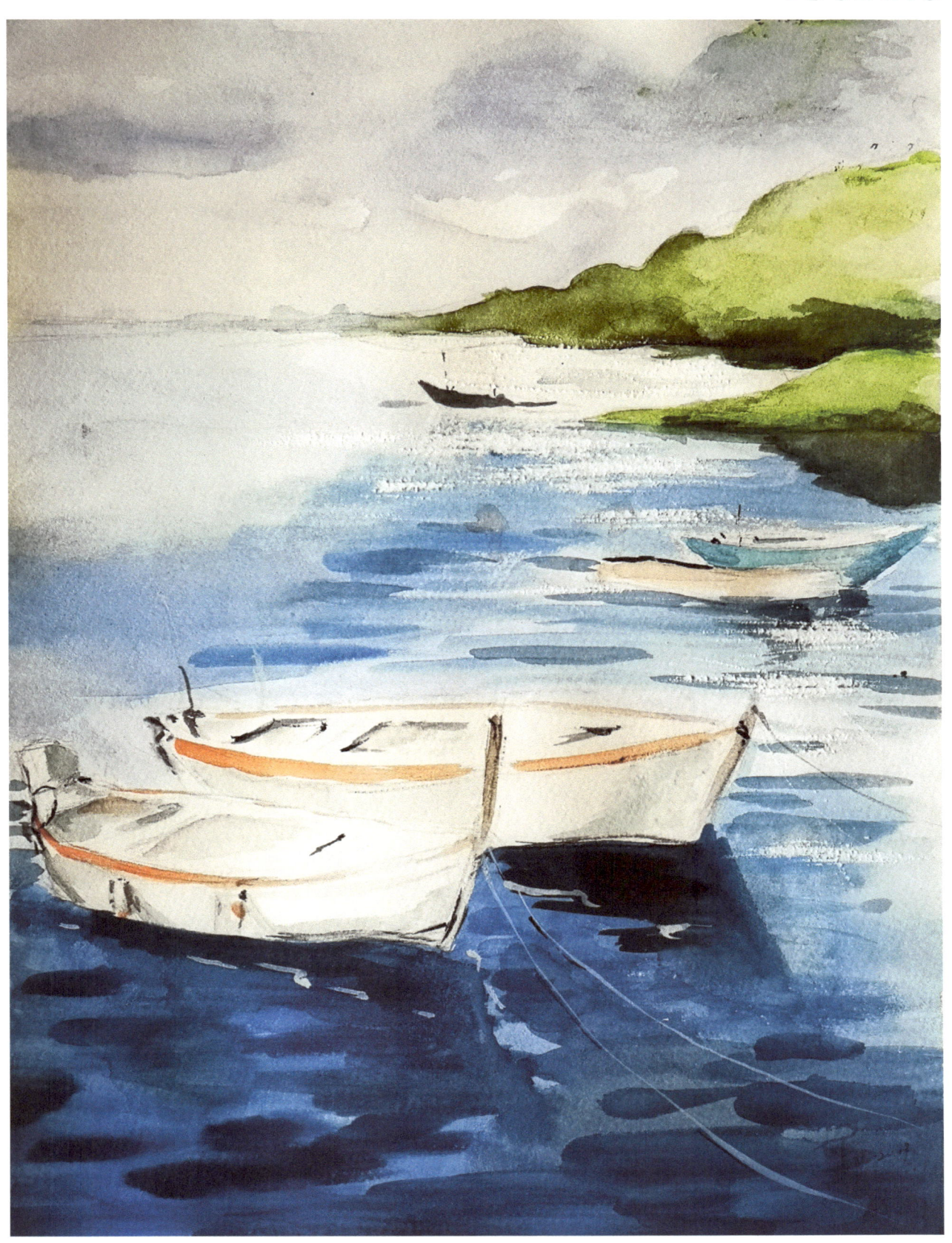

Leisure, watercolor on paper, 2019

YU JIANG

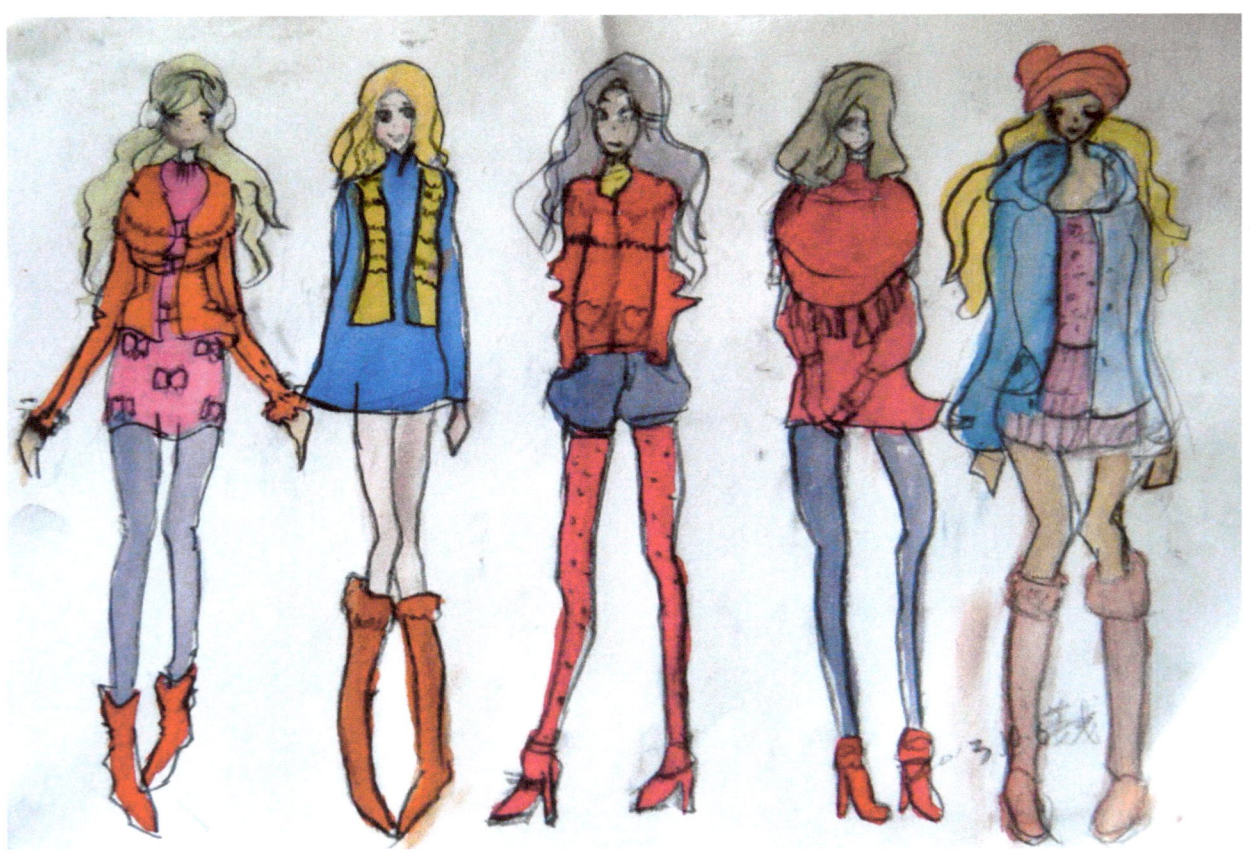

Fashion, gouache on paper, 2013

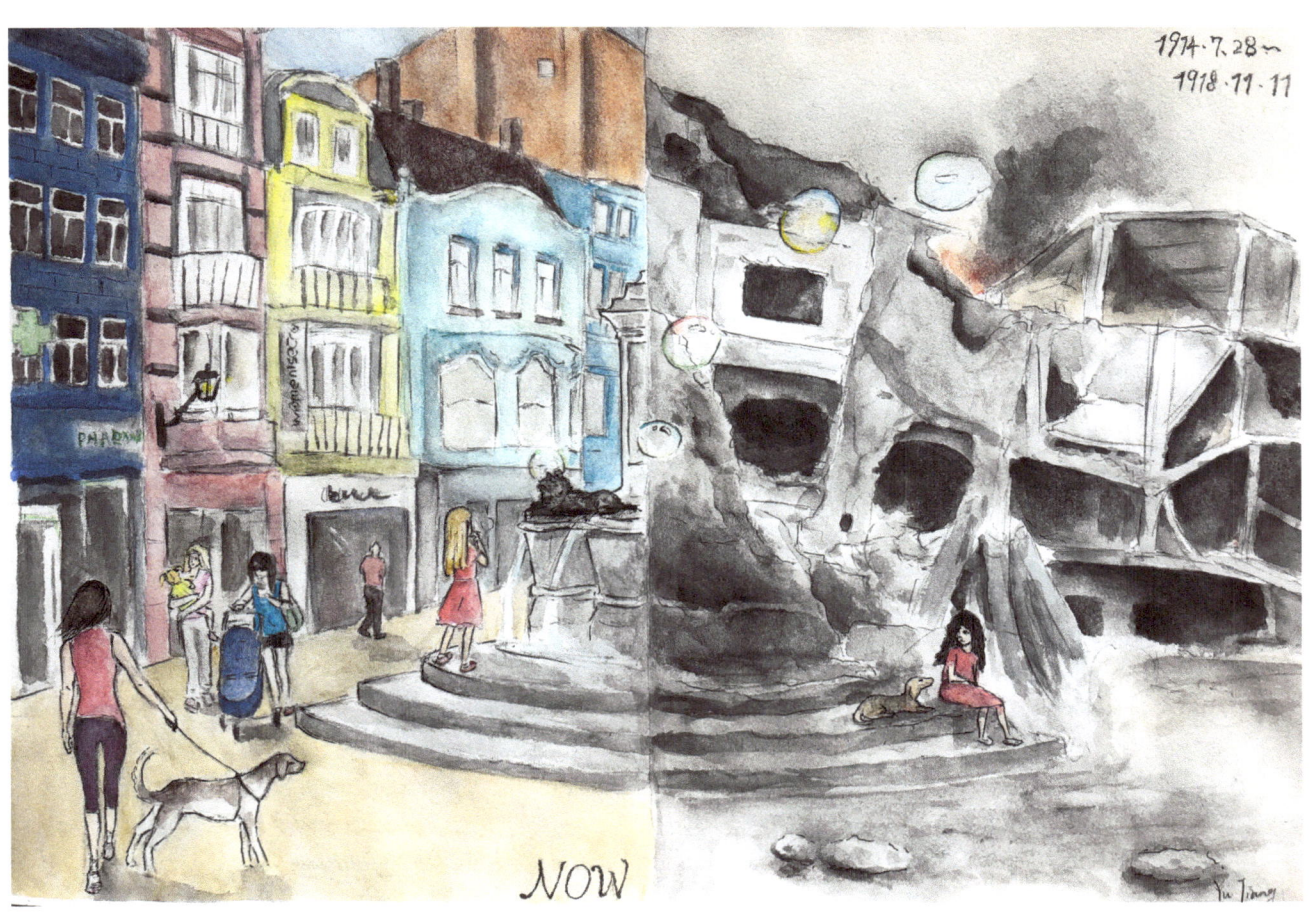

War and Peace: in Honor of the 100th Anniversary of the WWI Armistice
Acrylic on paper, 2018

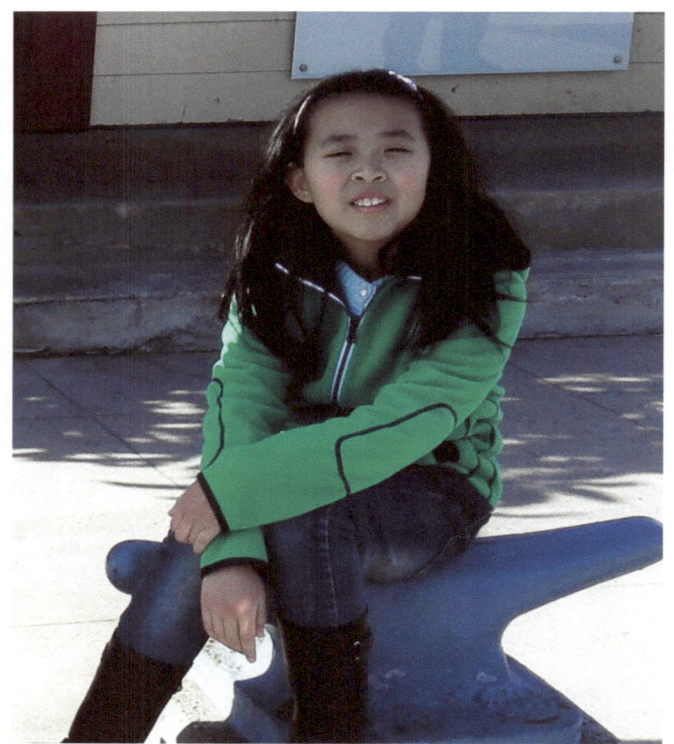

YUNING YANG
Qingdao University Affiliated Middle School, China

Bronze Award for Art, 2nd Liberty Awards, International Society of Young Artists, 2019
Bronze Award for Art, 1st Liberty Awards, International Society of Young Artists, 2018
3rd Prize, Painting, 22nd National Elementary and Secondary School Painting and Calligraphy Competition, 2017
3rd Prize, Painting, 6th Annual Qiluqing Shandong Province Campus Student Talent Show Contest, 2017

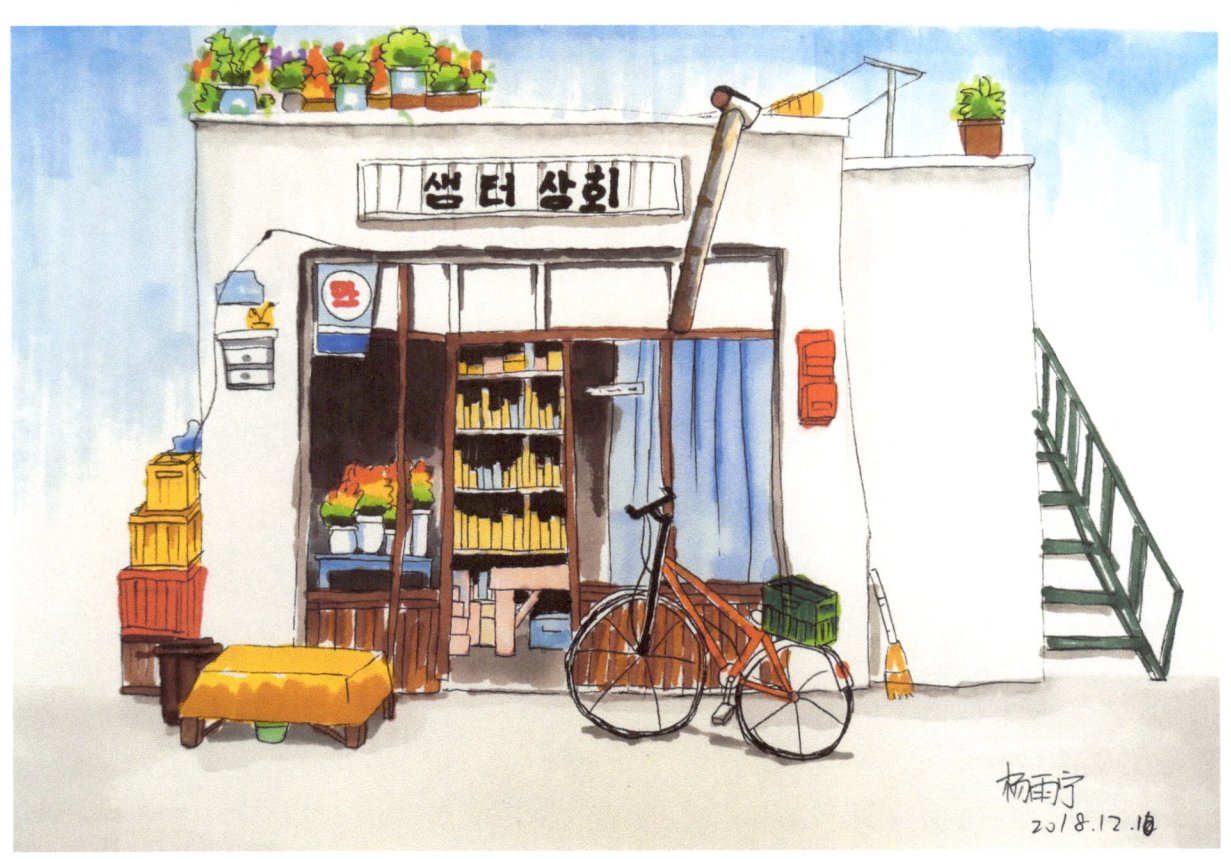

Grocery, coloring marker on paper, 2018

YUNING YANG

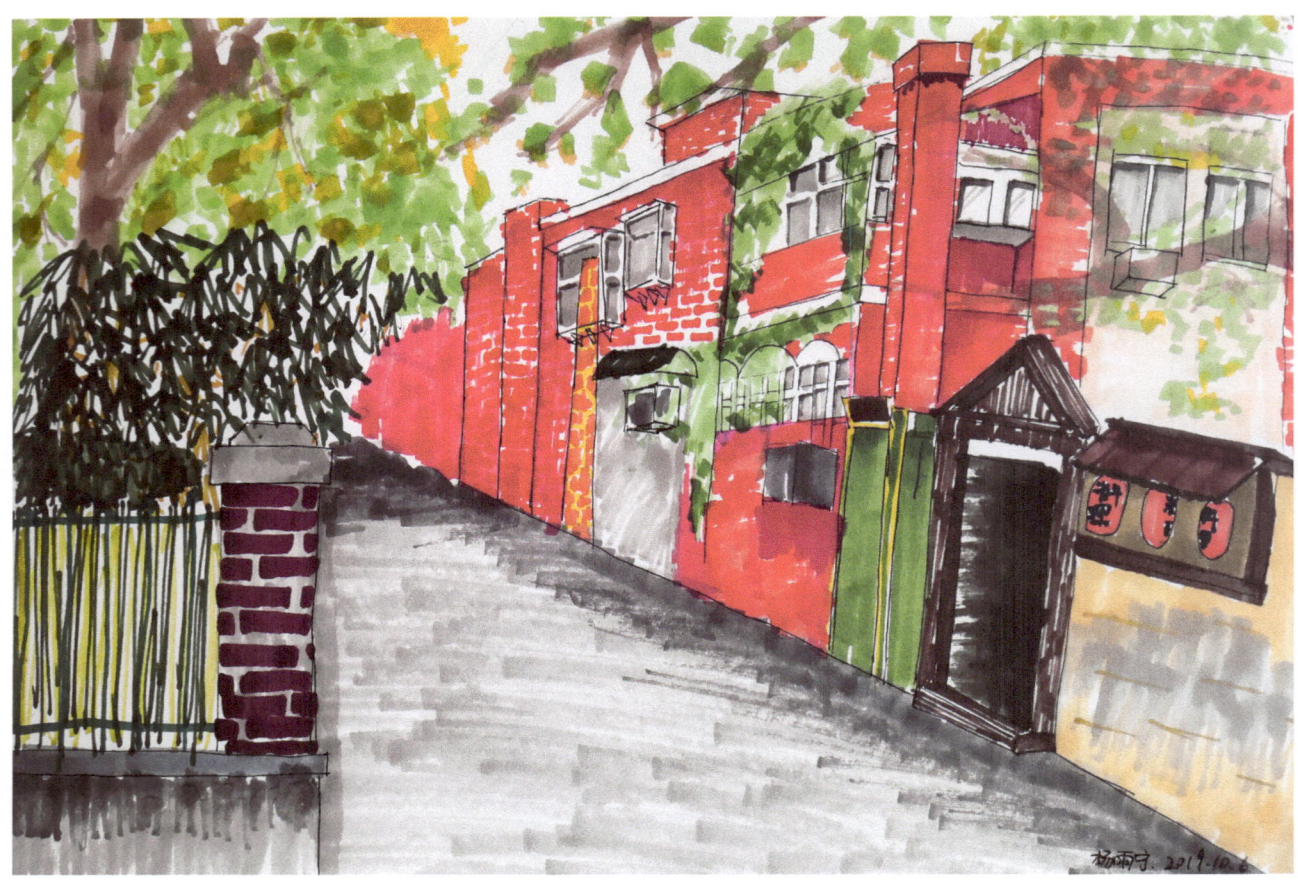

Huangxian Road, coloring marker on paper, 2019

YUNING YANG

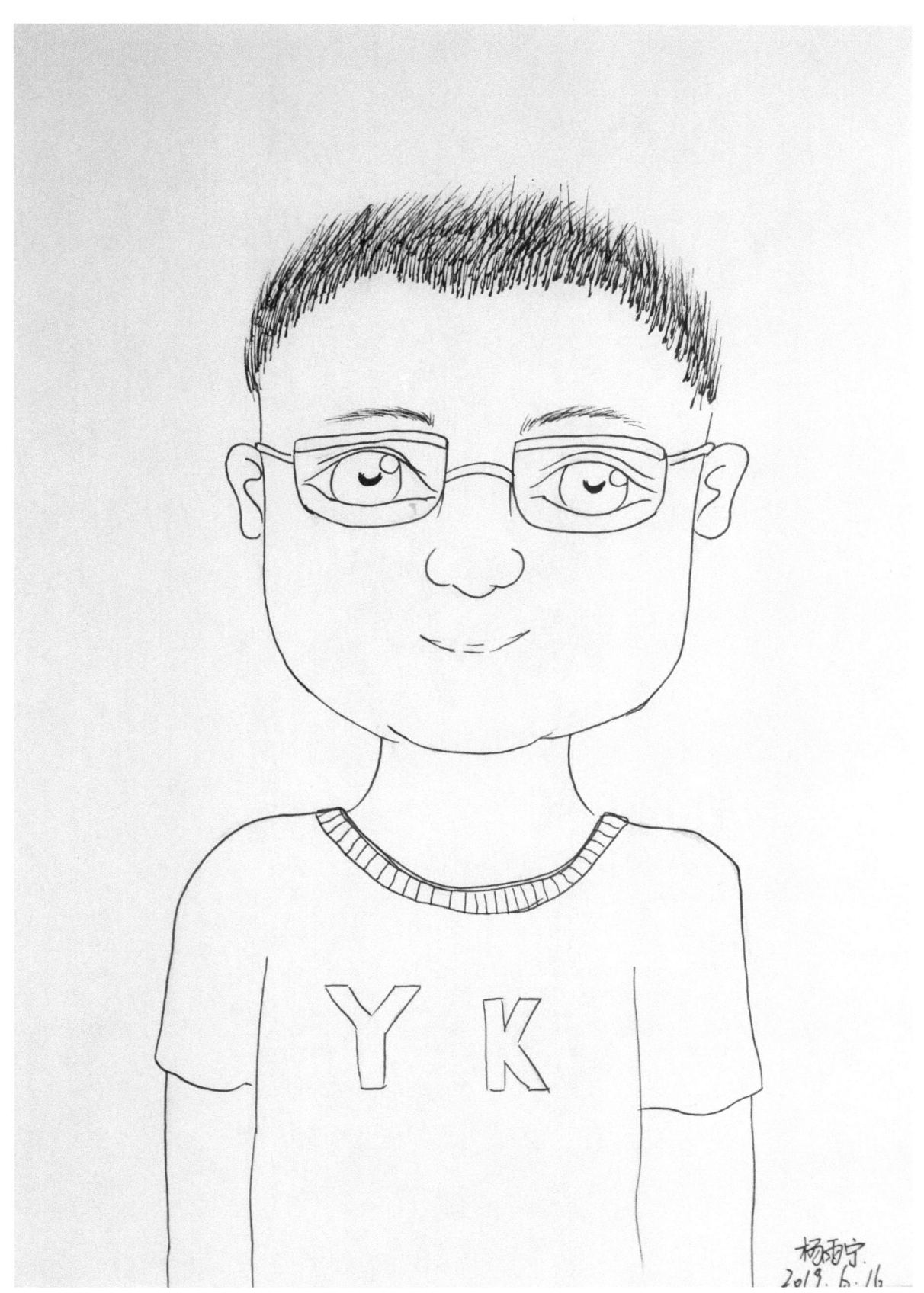

My Daddy, pen on paper, 2019

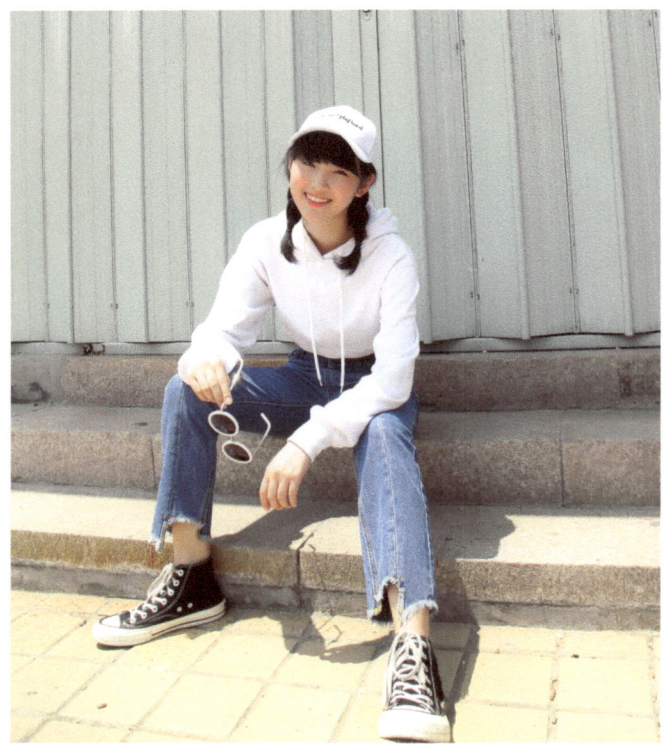

YUTING HE
Qingdao No.17 High School, China

Gold Award for Art, 2nd Liberty Awards, International Society of Young Artists, 2019
Silver Award for Art, 1st Liberty Awards, International Society of Young Artists, 2018
2nd Prize, National Middle School Students Mathematics Proficiency Contest of Qingdao, 2018
2nd Prize, National Middle School Students English Proficiency Competition, 2018
3rd Prize, 14th the Hope Cup National Composition Contest, 2017
Champion, Junior High Girls Group, Qingdao Xinxing Cup Badminton Team Competition, 2016

YUTING HE

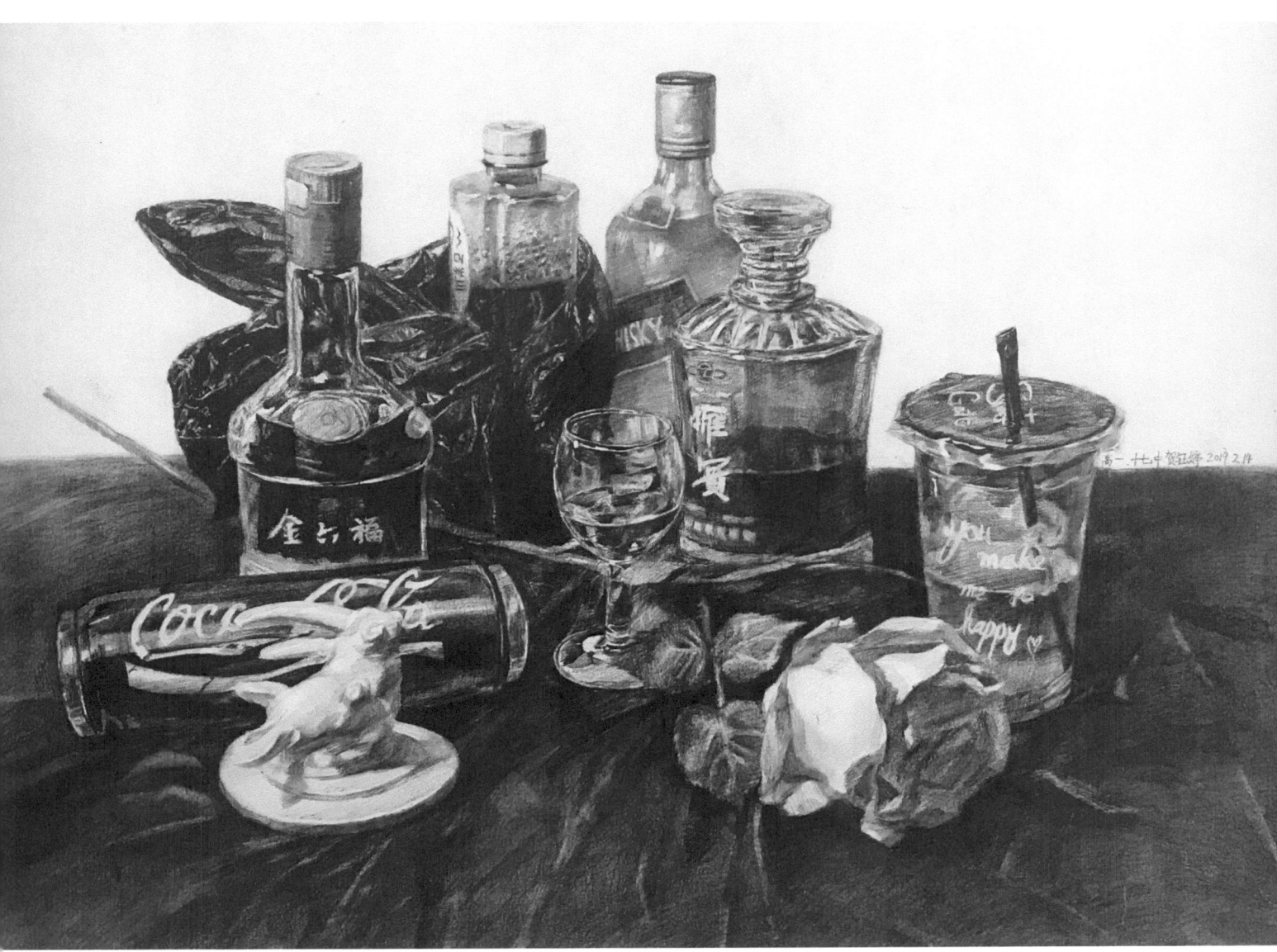

Still Life, pencil on paper, 2019

YUTING HE

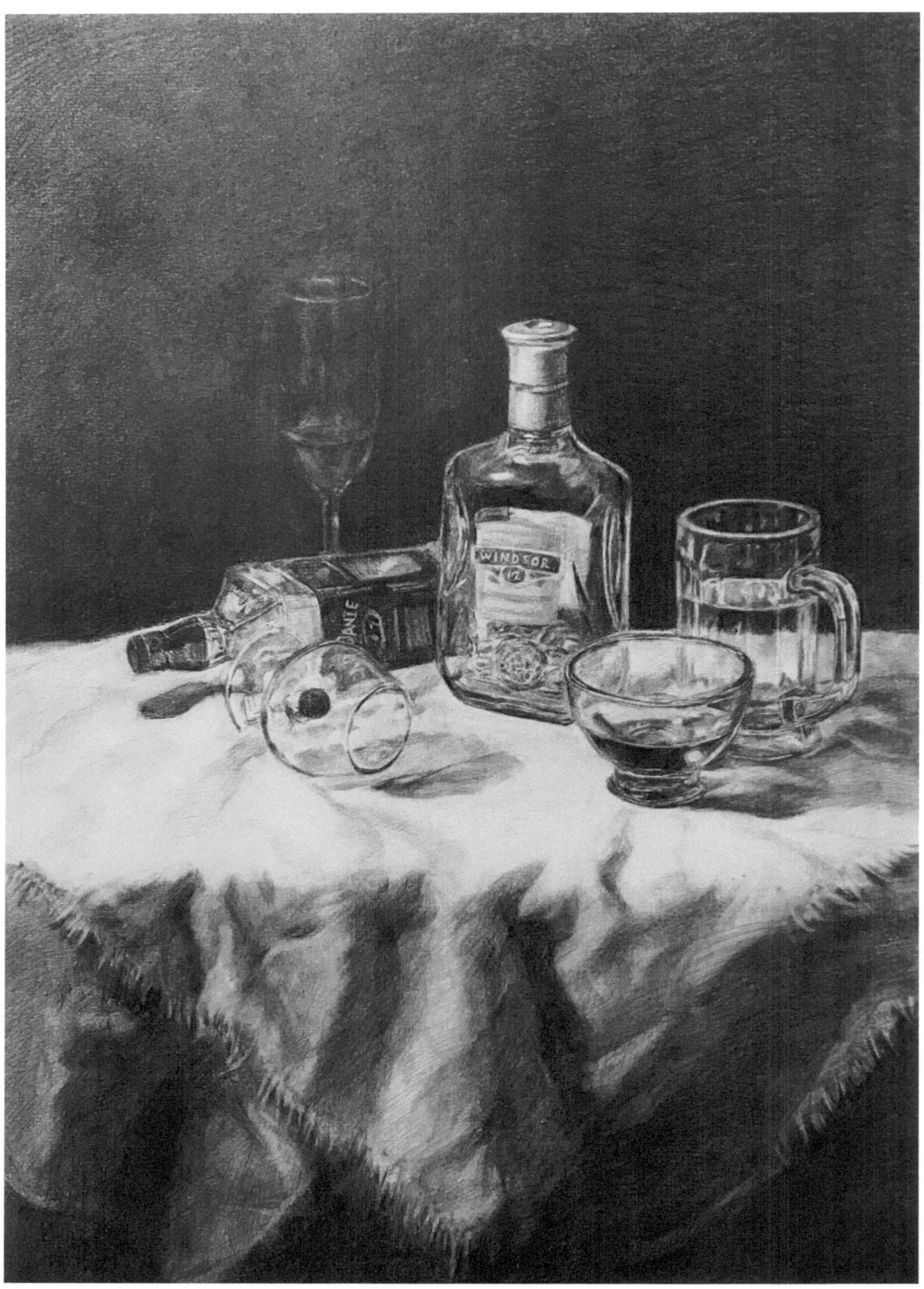

Still Life, pencil on paper, 2019

YUTING HE

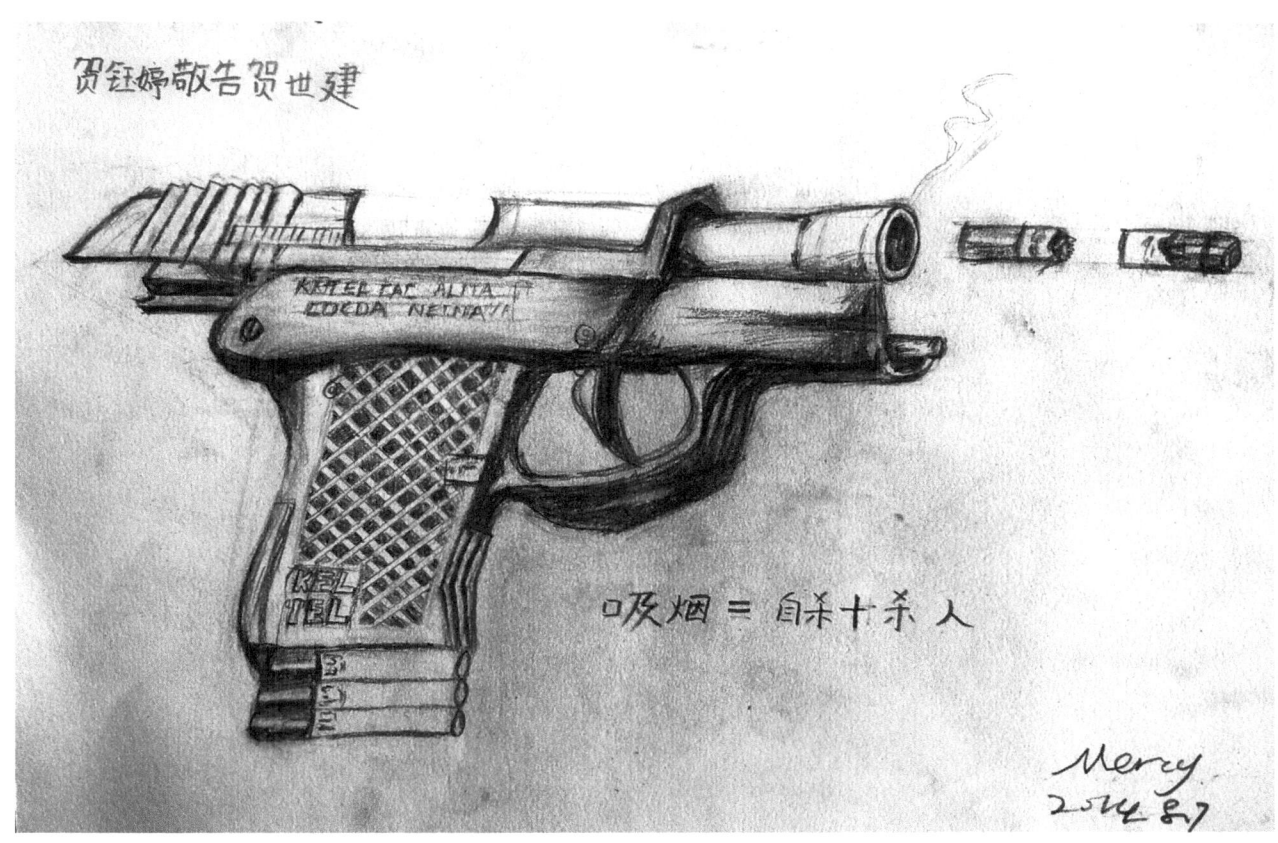

To Mr. He, pencil on paper, 2014

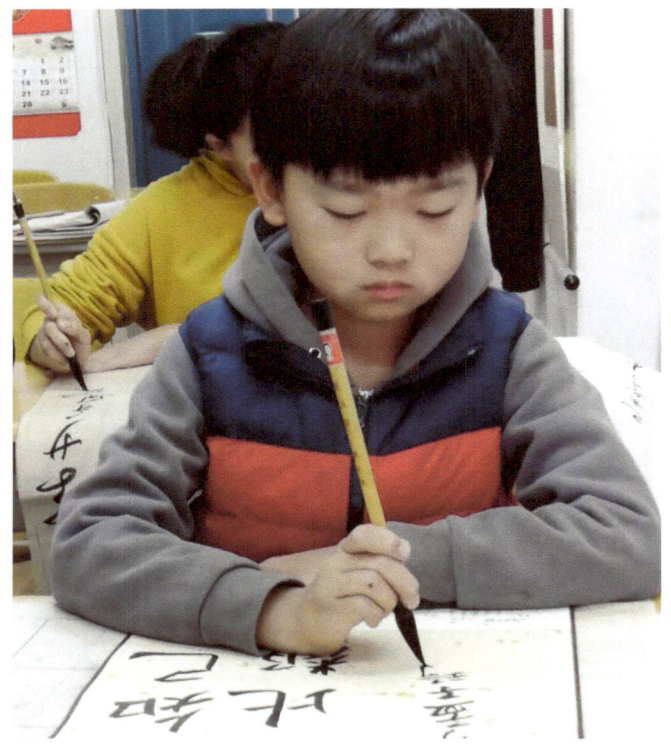

ZIQI MENG
Qingdao Baishan School, China

Bronze Award for Art, 2nd Liberty Awards, International Society of Young Artists, 2019
Rising Star Award, 1st Liberty Awards, International Society of Young Artists, 2018

ZIQI MENG

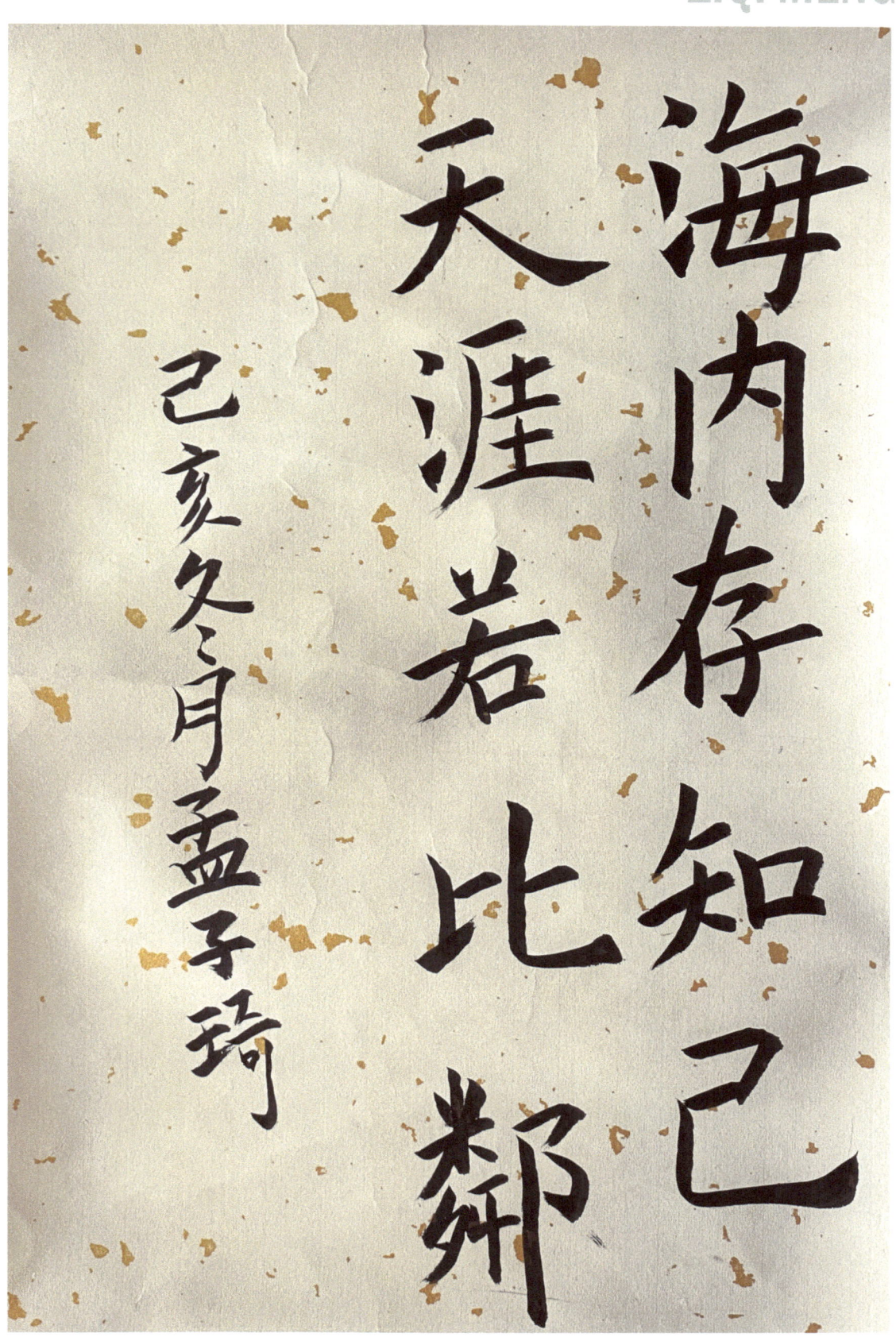

The Calligraphy-1, ink on rice paper, 2019

ZIQI MENG

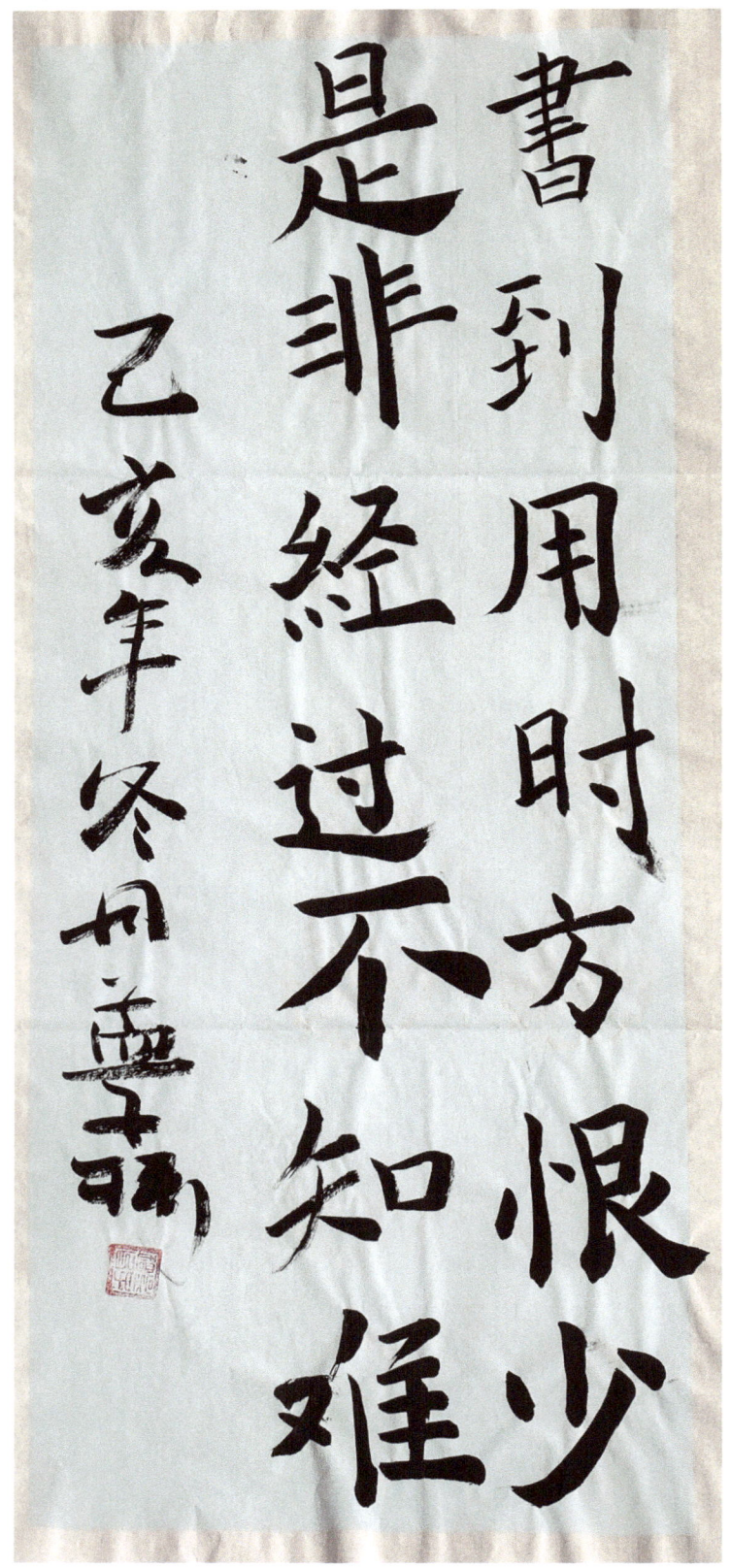

The Calligraphy-2, ink on rice paper, 2019

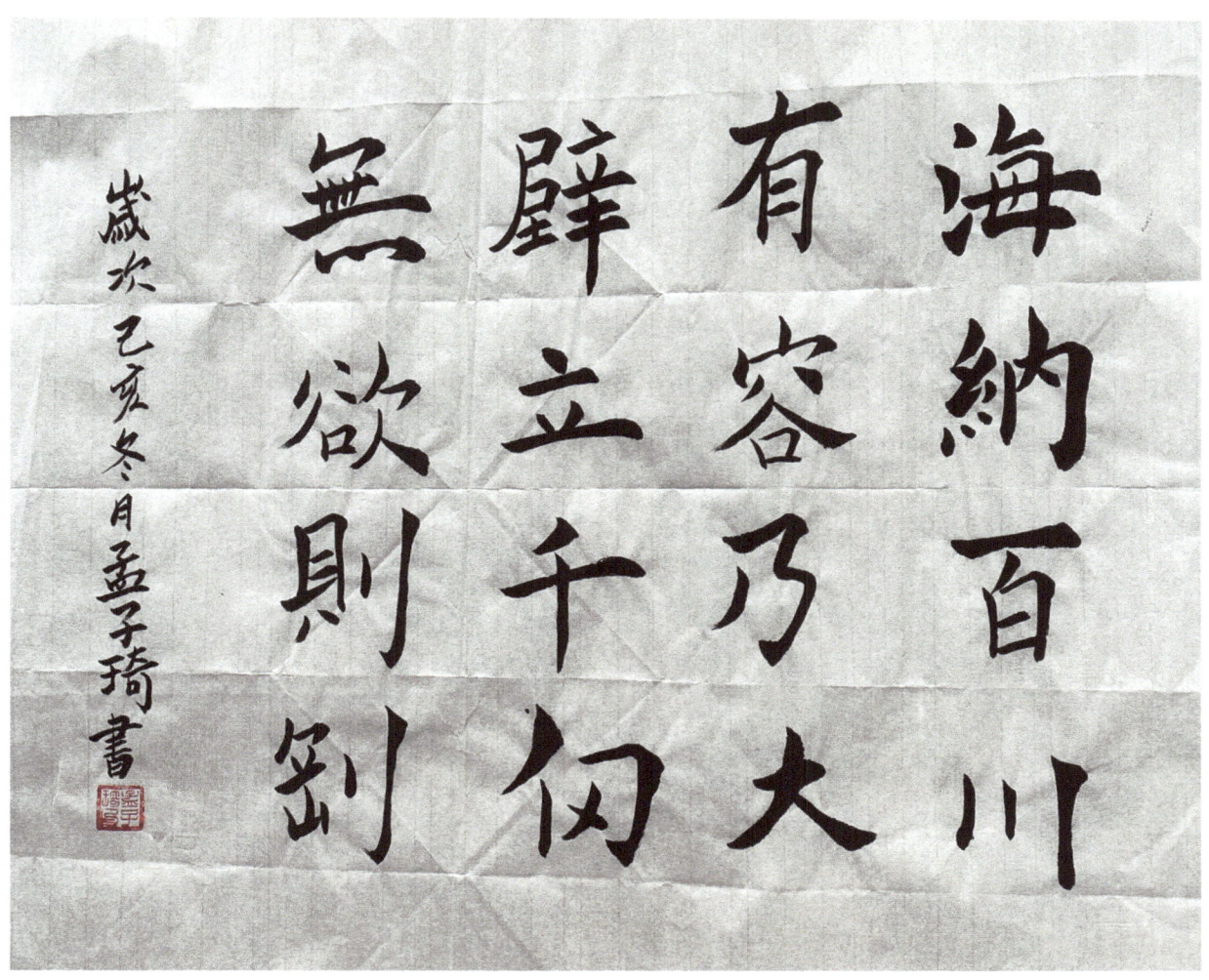

The Calligraphy-3, ink on rice paper, 2019

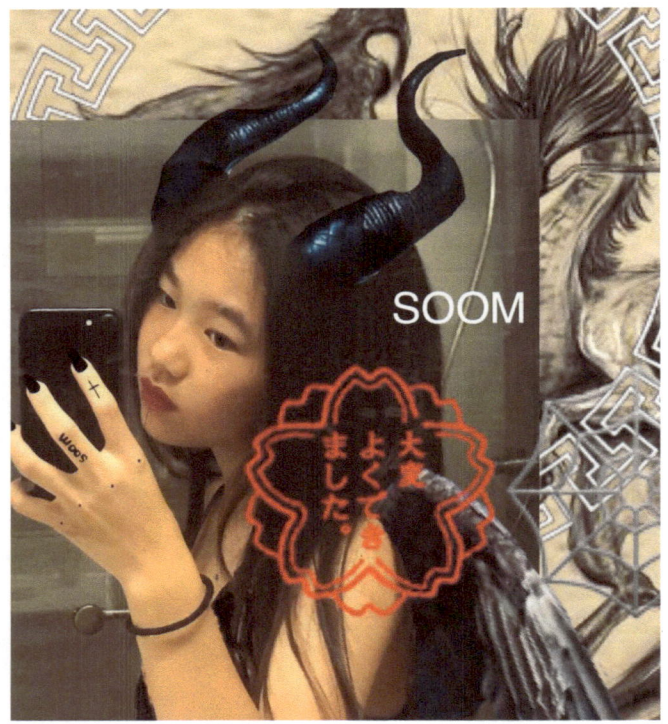

ZIYAN CHEN
Robert O Townsend Junior High, USA

Gold Award for Art, 2nd Liberty Awards, International Society of Young Artists, 2019

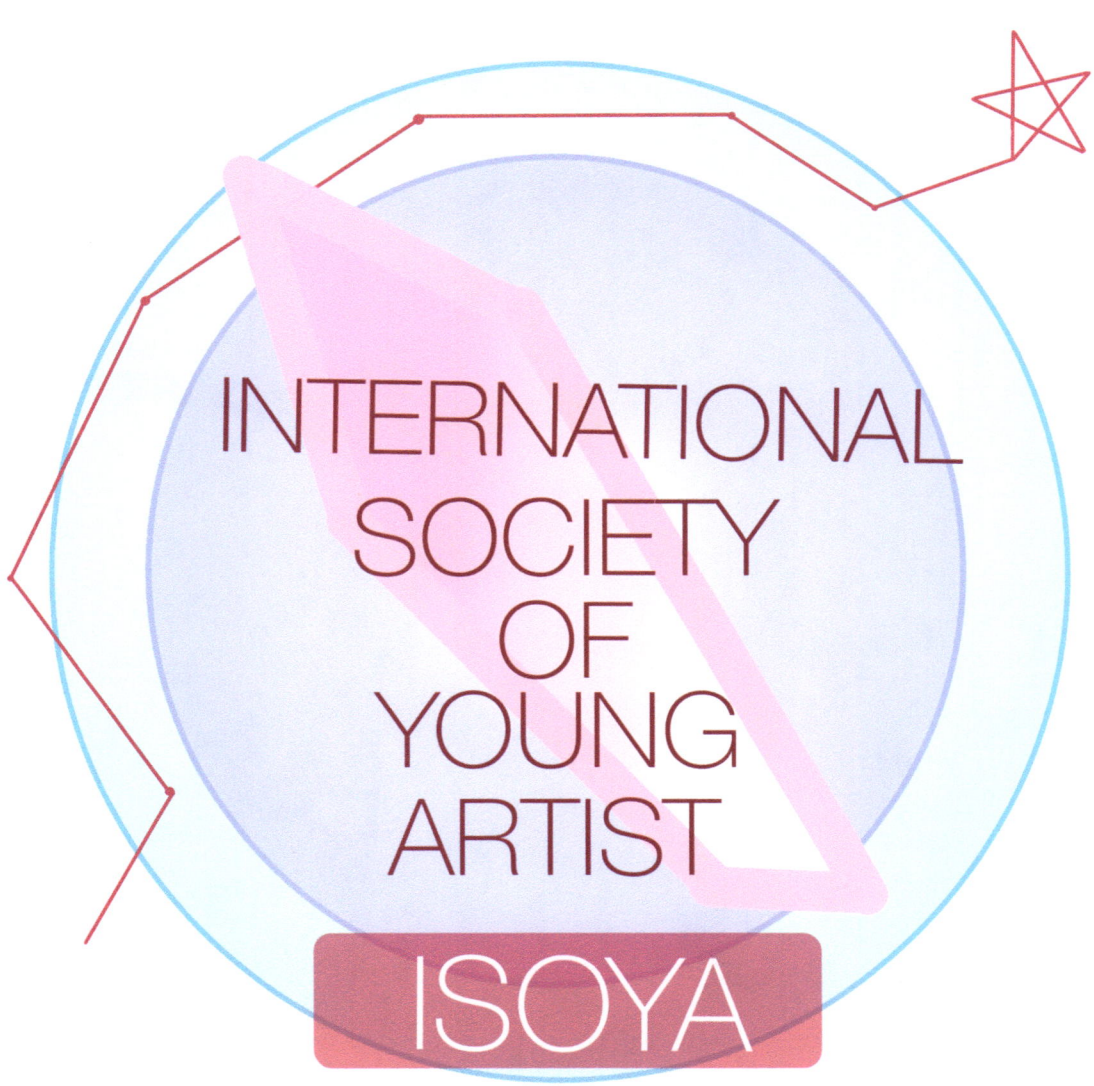

The Logo of International Society of Young Artist, digital, 2019

ZIYAN CHEN

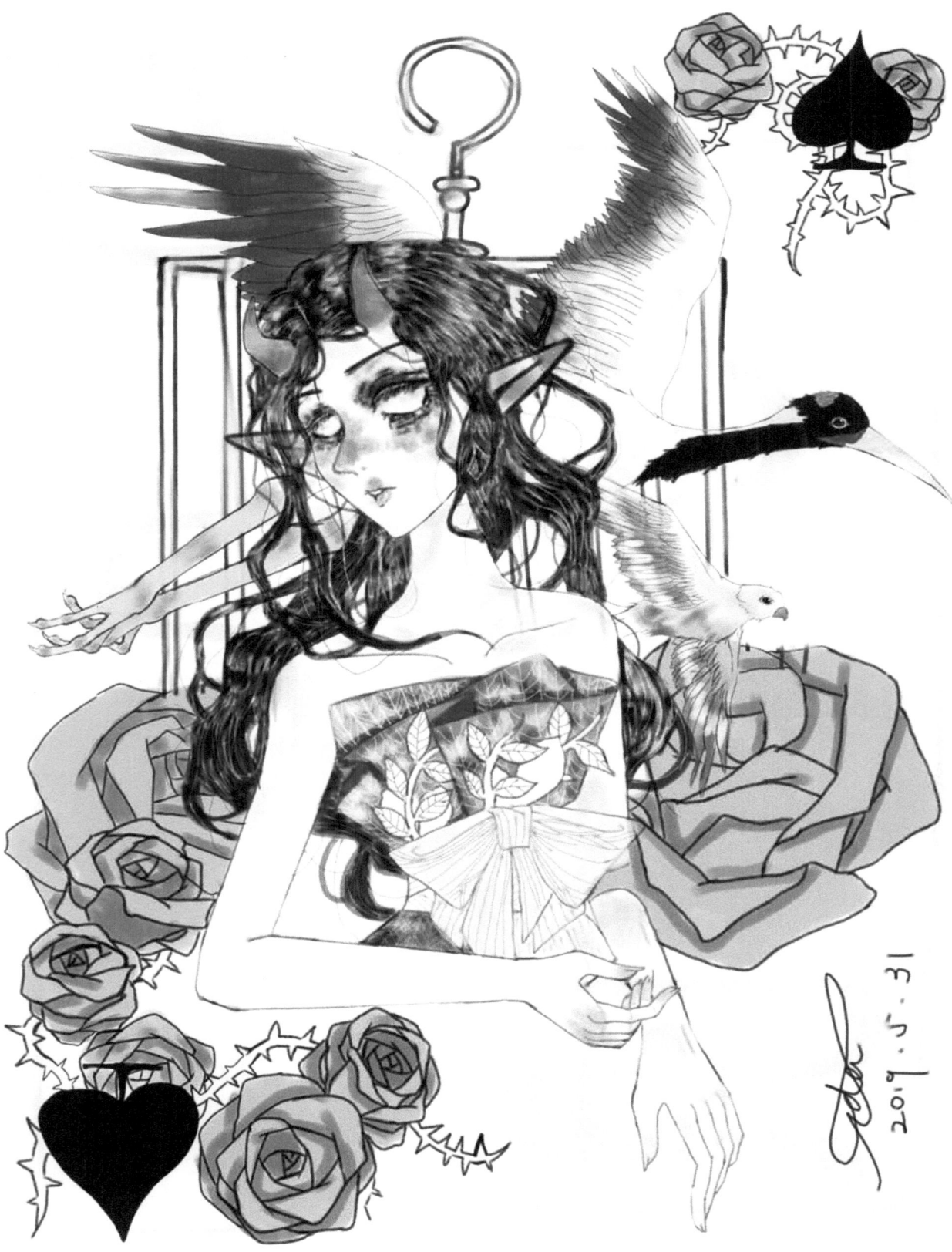

Trapped, digital, 2019

ZIYAN CHEN

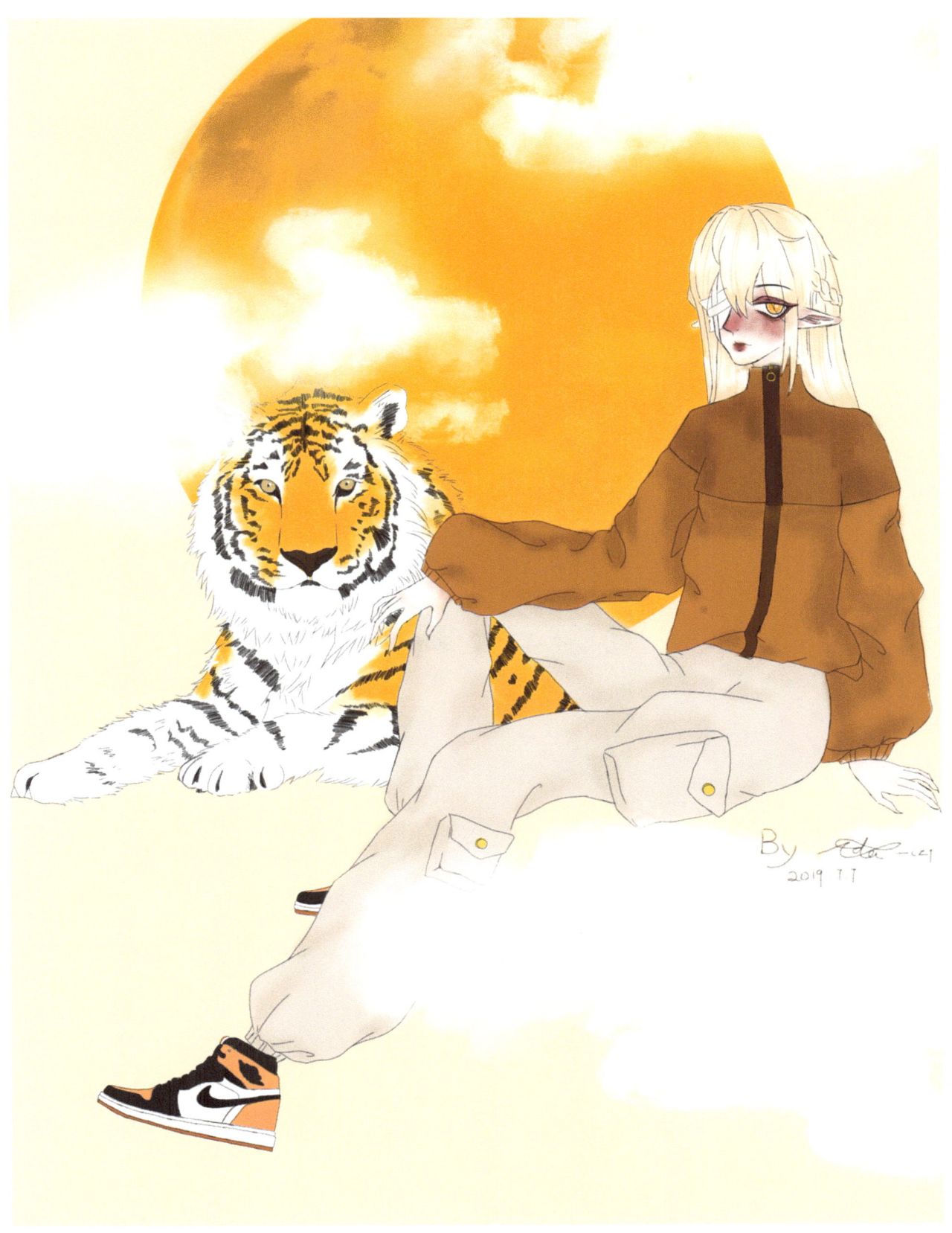

Tiger, digital, 2019

ZIYAN CHEN

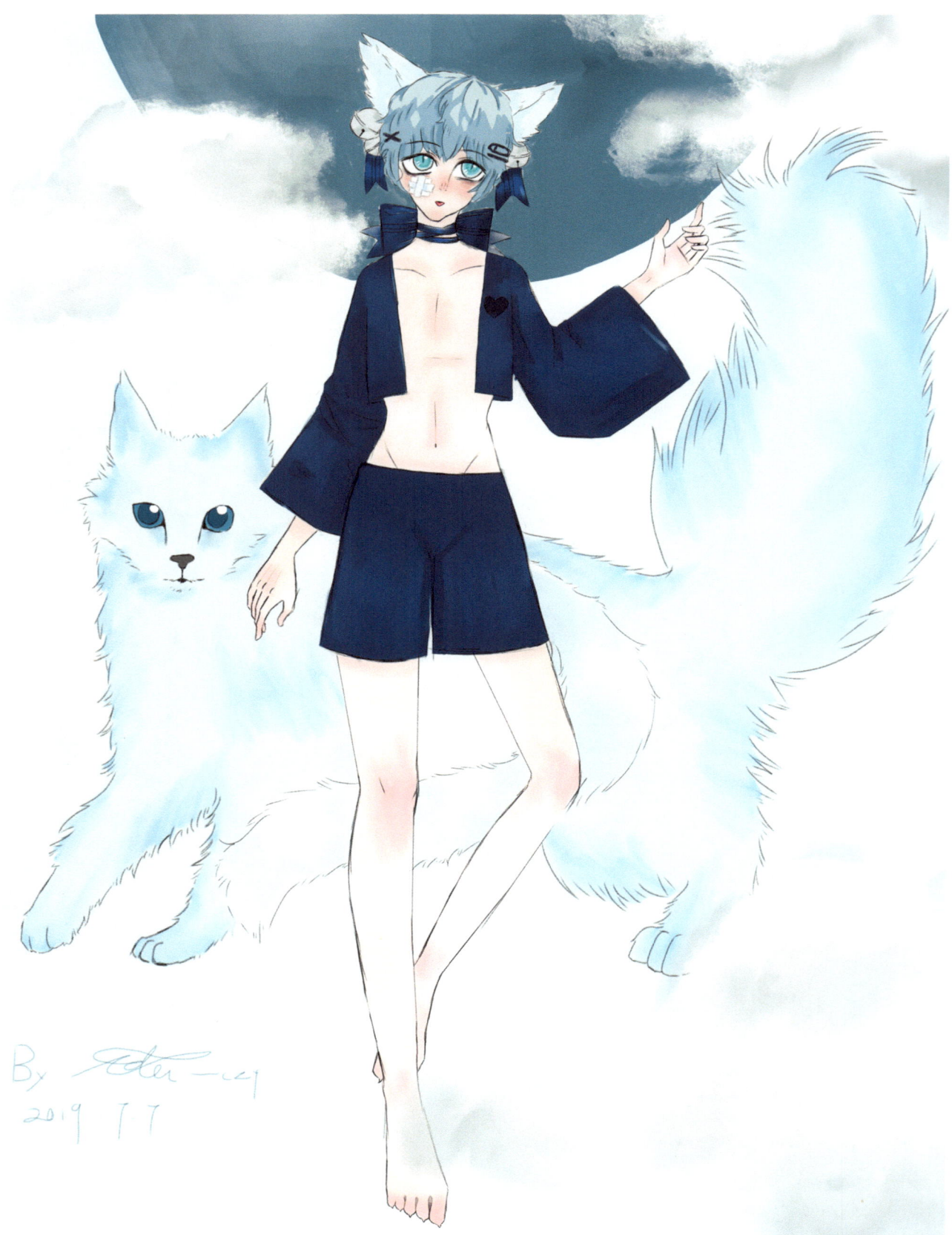

Cat, digital, 2019

ZIYAN CHEN

The Geniuses in the Morning

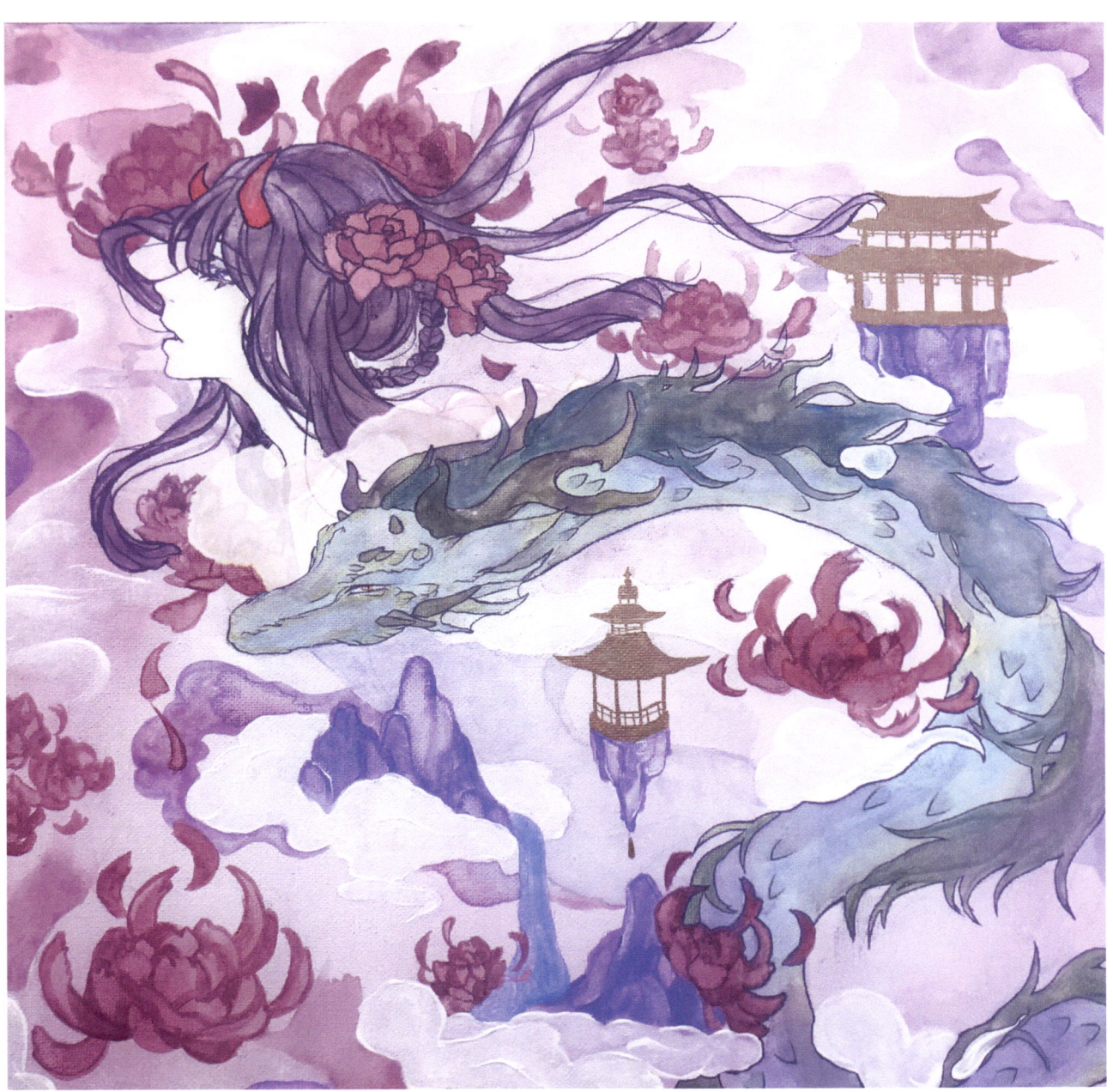

Dragon, acrylic on canvas, 2019

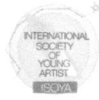

The publication of this book is part of a benevolent program - "The Vibrant Future" International Education Project for Young Artists, sponsored by the International Society of Young Artists. All of the earnings from the publication of this book will be donated to improve education for young artists.

LOSGET

Copyright © 2020 by Losget Press
All rights reserved.
Published in the United States by Losget Press, Los Angeles
Originally published in Paperback in the United States by Losget Press, in 2020
Title: The Geniuses in the Morning: International Youth Artist Artwork Series -1
Description: First Edition. | Los Angeles: Losget Press, 2020.
Identifiers: ISBN-13: 978-1-951364-05-2 | ISBN-10: 1-951364-05-8
www.losget.com
E-mail: contact@losget.com
Book design by Tiger Hupo
First Printing. 2020.

www.ingramcontent.com/pod-product-compliance
Lightning Source LLC
Chambersburg PA
CBHW051146220526
45473CB00003B/677